AROUND THE WORLD
IN 575 SONGS

AROUND THE WORLD IN 575 SONGS

TRADITIONAL MUSIC FROM ALL THE WORLD'S COUNTRIES

VOL 4: AMERICAS

NICK WALL

ISBN 978 1999631 468

British Library Cataloguing in Publication Data.
A catalogue record for this book is available from the British Library.

Printed and bound in Great Britain by 4edge Limited
Typeset in 11pt Minion Pro by Troubador Publishing Ltd, Leicester, UK

MUSIC IS POWER. MUSIC IS A LANGUAGE. MAYBE FOR ME, THE FIRST LANGUAGE. WE CAN USE IT TO DEVELOP LOT OF JUSTICE AROUND THE WORLD.

YOUSSOU N'DOUR

CONTENTS

NORTH AND CENTRAL AMERICA

SOUTH AMERICA

SERIES
INTRODUCTION

In 2013 I set myself the task of collecting songs from every country in the world. It's taken up five years of my life, but the results of my labours can now be heard on this website –
https://aroundtheworldin575songs.com/
and can be seen in the four volumes of this book. The book is your guide to the song list. In its volumes I will introduce all the selected songs, tell you stories about many of the artists, and give you some insight into the cultures that they represent. Please browse the website, listen to some of the streamed songs, and above all be adventurous! If I can lead people to discover new music and take inspiration from it, then this book will have served a purpose.

I'm going to be straight with you: this isn't quite the book that I had sketched out in my mind when I began this project. In fact, it's become a lot bigger. So what happened?

This is a project that began with a love of global rhythms and a desire to share some of this music with as many people as possible. To make the list more accessible and interesting I wanted to write about all the songs that I'd be selecting. The idea of a book immediately suggested itself, but the book I intended to write was something closer to a guide to the songs themselves. It's hard to say exactly when this changed. Was it when I first heard from Xavier Fethal about how rising sea levels are threatening to destroy his people's way of life on their Pacific island home? Or when Mariem Hassan told me of a life spent in refugee camps and in exile, dreaming of the day when Saharawi people would be able to live in peace in their homeland? To do justice to Xavier Fethal and Mariem Hassan, as well as telling their stories I would have to write something about their people and their culture.

What had begun as a search for culturally distinctive music from 200 countries had taken on new dimensions. We live in a world that's becoming less culturally diverse, more homogenised. The Eurovision Song Contest is a prime example: it's anything but a celebration of diversity. The songs are mostly pop-oriented, produced in ways designed to appeal to an international audience; and in 2017 no less than 35 of the 42 songs in the final were sung entirely in English. In this world it can sometimes take courage to stand up and say what is most valuable in our culture is what makes us unique. So it's been very interesting to look at artists who've adopted that standpoint, to see what motivates them and what they've been able to achieve.

As well as new insights, the expanding project raised certain questions in my mind. Why do we see so many struggles to establish a national or ethnic identity in every part of every continent in the 21st century? The world has changed so much in the last 100 years; you might say that in many ways it's moved on: is it still meaningful even to talk about unitary national identities? What, if any, are the benefits to humanity of reconnecting with our cultural roots? What's music's role in all this? Should it be left to musicians themselves to rekindle the flame of their cultural heritage, or should the state be supporting them to a lesser or greater extent?

But let's take a step back. I guess the first question that I need to answer is how did I ever end up doing this?

BEGINNINGS

I love compiling music lists. It's a bit of a hobby, but what makes it more rewarding than ever before is that there are so many more ways of sharing music now that billions of people have access to the internet.

In the spring of 2013 I put out this message:

Calling all folk music enthusiasts!

I'd like your help please in compiling a list of the most loved folk songs. What I need you to do is to decide on your 25 favourite folk songs (or a smaller number if you prefer), and send these to me by email.

I'll leave the question of what is a folk song essentially up to you. The songs may be in any language, or instrumentals, and they can be old or new.

I want the artist name and song title. If the song's been recorded by different artists, just choose your favourite version.

I didn't get as many responses as I hoped for, but some of the ones I got were very interesting. Fingal Folk Club polled their members and sent in a combined list (so they only got one vote!). The bulk of the songs nominated were Irish, but about a third were American standards. There may well be a few Americans living in the west of Ireland, but I had a notion that this was more to do with the influence of American music. I saw the same thing with some of the other lists. So even Colin MacDonald, who works for the Glasgow-based Celtic Music Radio, devoted 40% of his list to American singers.

There was something else too. The songs being chosen, whether traditional or modern, were nearly all in the English language, and in the main performed by white artists, though a few blues numbers by the likes of Leadbelly and Mississippi John Hurt did make the final list. There were no mentions for Chile's Violeta Parra, or for Zimbabwe's Thomas Mapfumo. This was not unexpected: after all, I'd been soliciting responses mainly from among people who'd attended folk clubs; this demographic is overwhelmingly white and English speaking; and most of the folk songs that they know and sing in the clubs are from the British, Irish and American traditions.

Such reflections kindled in me the desire to delve into the stock of fabulous music from around the world which I'd been quietly accumulating. In the late 1980s I was an occasional listener to Andy Kershaw on BBC Radio 1 and Charlie Gillett on Capital Radio, and riffling through my old vinyl collection I'm surprised to find quite how much African music I was buying at that time, though my interests were by no means limited to African music: Le Mystère des Voix Bulgares was often on my turntable, and one of my most memorable concerts was seeing Nusrat Fateh Ali Khan at the Hackney Empire. Twenty-odd years later, I now had a healthy collection (or so I thought) of world music on iTunes, and an urge to share some of it.

The time was ripe for a new project.

And then one morning when I was in the shower the idea grabbed me to collect songs from every country in the world. Straightaway I knew that this was a challenge that I couldn't turn down.

HOW THE SONGS WERE SELECTED

One trouble with a list that covers 200 countries is that it risks upsetting people from 200 countries.

So let me be clear what this list is not. It is not intended to be a reflection of what music is most popular in any particular country. And it's not a comprehensive guide. I am limited on numbers. I can't represent each and every region, or ethnic group, and I certainly can't represent every artist of importance. What I'm offering you is a small sampler of each country's music, it's a personal selection, and while I'm interested to know what you would have chosen, I hope that you won't be too hard on me for what I've left out.

THE COUNTRIES

There are currently 193 member states of the United Nations. I have included these 193, plus two 'observer states' (Vatican City and Palestine) and five others: Kosovo, Kurdistan, Puerto Rico, Saharawi and Taiwan. By including these five, and not others, I'm not trying to make any case for which countries are most deserving of recognition as nation states. I hope that it's clear from the narratives that I am supportive of the rights of self-determination of all geographical entities and self-defined populations. In my song choices I seek to represent not only the countries, but also, when I can, a few of the main population groups and cultures within those countries, so while there is no separate chapter on Scotland for example, Scottish music is represented and discussed in the book. Of these five countries Taiwan and Kosovo are recognised by most of the world as independent nation states, while Kurdistan, Saharawi and Puerto Rico all have compelling stories to tell about establishing a sense of identity which seemed deserving of separate chapters.

NUMBER OF SONGS PER COUNTRY

Fifty-nine countries have one song, 47 have two, 29 have three, 20 have four, 20 have five, 21 have six, three have seven (USA, UK and France) and one has eight (India).

There was no fixed formula. The only way to eliminate all argument would be to have one song per country, but in my view a list which gave the same space to France as to Monaco and to Spain as to Andorra would be of limited value. The decision whether to select one or six songs, or somewhere in between, was based on the amount of music available, and the minimum number of songs that I felt I needed to properly represent that country's music and to do justice to all the cultures and musical genres in which I had an interest.

The subjective element made planning the book more difficult as, while I had a set of targets for numbers of songs to include, these would often have to be modified upwards or downwards as I researched each country in turn and found that some surpassed my expectations while others fell short.

WHO QUALIFIES? – ISSUES OF NATIONALITY

There's probably no question that you can think of which I haven't had to answer when compiling this list. Let's take Iraq. Who qualifies as an Iraqi artist? Do they have to have been born in Iraq? Or hold an Iraqi passport? Or identify as being Iraqi? Many Iraqi musicians have been forced into exile at one time or another as a result of political repression and war. Should I be giving precedence to music recorded locally, or music recorded in Europe on international labels where the headline artist will often be backed by a band put together of musicians from several countries?

Saleh and Daoud Al-Kuwaity were Jewish brothers born in Kuwait to an Iraqi father, who spent the best part of their lives and careers in Iraq before packing their bags and going to live in exile in Israel. Which country would you place them in, if you had to pick one?

Rahim AlHaj, who was born in Baghdad, fled Iraq in 1991, when he was a young man. He's lived for many years now in New Mexico and is a US citizen. He aims through his music to bridge the gap between western audiences and Arab musical tradition, describing it as "a conversation between East and West". How confident would you be that the music he plays typifies Iraqi culture?

I never laid down hard and fast rules. However, there were plenty of artists who I decided to exclude because they were born in another country, or lived in another country, or because their work was defined by collaborations with musicians from different countries and traditions. To fully appreciate the reasons for this, you have to understand the nature of the project. I wasn't interested in music that happened to have been made by Iraqi artists but could equally have been made in any Arab country. I wanted to find that music which spoke to me most eloquently of the particularity of a musical heritage over 1,000 years old.

Living permanently in another country has a tendency to affect the music that you make. I have observed this on so many occasions that I believe it to be a fact. You're suddenly exposed to a wide range of new musical influences; perhaps you have opportunities to work with musicians from other cultures. You're performing in front of audiences who have completely different expectations from audiences in your home country, who may not even understand the language in which you sing. All these influences and pressures may change your musical direction. That's not a crime, it's through interaction such as this that music continually renews itself and new genres and traditions are born. Salsa music is a case in point: a musical genre created in New

York, predominantly by Puerto Rican immigrants, which was exported to Latin America where in a number of countries it's become part of the cultural fabric. Just because you live abroad doesn't mean that you can't contribute to the way in which people in your home country make music and add a new strand to their sense of national identity. Sivan Perwer had an immense influence on Kurdish music in Turkey despite spending most of his adult life in exile in Europe. So I am by no means excluding musicians who live in exile, but unless I can see that their music has a continued influence and relevance in their home country it's unlikely to be selected.

What type of music?

I have preconceived ideas. I want to find music that's rooted in a country's past heritage and culture, music that employs traditional instruments. I prefer to steer clear of songs that employ electronic instruments and I'm not interested at all in beat-heavy pop, R&B, hip hop and reggae: the globalised culture in which past traditions become meaningless.

I want to give a sense of cultures at their best and most vibrant. In some cases that will lead me to write about the music of the 1970s, '60s, '50s, or even earlier. I also want to give a sense of how those cultures are faring today, what current artists we should be paying attention to and what the future holds. Where there is a lot of current music that's of interest, I will focus on that rather than on the stars of the past.

There's no guaranteeing where all of this will take me. With each country that I look at, the journey that I take is different. In some cases, the direction of travel is fairly obvious. So it would be inconceivable to write about Mongolia without discussing throat singing, or Georgia without celebrating its tradition of polyphonic song. But what of South Africa? In the 1980s whenever you went to an anti-apartheid rally you could rely on hearing beautiful singing, and there were many great artists whose names will be forever associated with the movement. It would have been easy to use up the whole chapter just writing about Hugh Masakela, Miriam Makeba, Johnny Clegg, Ladysmith Black Mambazo, Mahlatini, etc. But there's another story here, and it's one that needs to be told: about how in post-apartheid South Africa the synthesiser has largely replaced traditional instruments, about how the youth of today no longer listen much to the music of these past giants which they see as a little dated, and about those traditionalists like Dr Thomas who are trying to fight against the tide.

I talk a lot in this book about traditional music. Probably more than I should, because it's one of these terms that mean different things to different people. The term is useful in that it can be applied to any pre-existing culture, while terms like 'folk music' and 'volksmusik' are more culture-specific. Is the term still meaningful though if applied to a song that wasn't passed on by oral tradition, and which the singer performs in their own manner, without reference to how it would originally have been performed? If 'traditional' is used in its general popular sense of something that is rooted in past tradition then we can, but we may feel that we need to make further distinctions, for instance between 'recovered tradition' which tries to reconstruct how music was originally performed, and 'reinvented tradition' – newly composed music that evokes past tradition without trying to imitate it.

An important reason for using the term 'traditional music' is to distinguish these songs from 'world music'. While there is some crossover there is a difference which may be explained in this way: 'world music' is aimed at a global audience, while 'traditional music' is primarily aimed at people from a specific region or ethnic group. World music glories in multiculturalism, and celebrates successful cross-cultural collaborations and fusions of beats and genres from diverse origins. Traditional music, on the other hand, is focused on a particular culture and suggests an unbroken relationship with the past.

WHICH SONGS?

The secret to compiling a good song list is very simple. The more candidate songs that you discard and don't use, the more confidence you can have that the finalised list is as good as it can possibly be.

With every artist on the list, I've had to consider which song to pick and from which of their albums. The choices were mine, though I've tried to accommodate any record companies, managers and agents who wanted me to promote a particular song. The one non-negotiable criterion for inclusion is that it has to be a song that I genuinely like and would be happy to own on iTunes. I'm not a linguist; where I can I've done some research into non-English-language songs to find out what they're about and this has helped guide me in my choice of songs. Where I'm unable to translate the lyrics or decipher a song's meaning I judge it on how it sounds to the ear, also taking account of the instruments used.

HOW TO LISTEN

This is a celebration of difference, an affirmation of the fact that in the globalised world that we live in, where kids in Mombasa and Mumbai can keep up with the latest musical craze in New York City, real music, the music of the people, still exists in thousands of different forms, and in every country there are people who recognise this and care passionately about holding on to what they can of the diversity of past musical tradition.

There will be pieces of music here which are unlike anything that you've ever heard before. You might find something that changes your life. You may equally hear things that leave you grabbing for the mouse so you can skip to the next track – songs that grate on your ear.

Much of this music is traditional in origin. Reflect on what that means. The earliest commercial jazz recordings only date back 100 years. Before that, music performance was limited to certain contexts: you had the elite culture such as western classical music and opera; folk music as would be played in communities, places of work and places of leisure; and music associated with religious rituals and ceremonies. For much of human history forms of unaccompanied singing were far more important than they are now. Musical instruments were not mass-produced, and examples of regional variants of a particular instrument are rife. Folk dancing was integral to many cultures, and entire musical genres and sub-genres were originally associated with particular types of dance. Genuinely traditional music is music that once had a reason for existing.

Besides this, be open to the strange and the new. Listen out for all the differences just in music that originates from the same country – such as Senegal, home to Youssou N'Dour's band and its soulful music, father to Malick Pathe Sow and Bao Sissoko with their gentle, intricate duets, yet also capable of producing the raw and raucous sound of Aby Ngana Diop. Above all, if you find something that you like, follow the links, check out the artist and buy their music.

MUSIC AND THE SEARCH FOR IDENTITY

Written music has existed since ancient times, but prior to the 20th century its use was the preserve of a privileged educated few. As for folk musicians, village singers, travelling players, gypsies, klezmorim, bards, griots, Bauls – none of them had ever learned to read music. Oral tradition was the means by which they gained their knowledge of music and passed it on to the next generation. It wasn't a pure science. Every time that a song was passed on a line or two would get changed here and there, and perhaps the young would stamp their own character on the song. So even a song like The Parting Glass which has survived remarkably well for over 400 years has undergone innumerable changes, has been known under many different titles, and so on.

Oral tradition extends beyond music. It underpins the transmission of culture – through language, sayings, storytelling, and the construction of myth and legend. By the late 19th century it was already becoming obvious to many observers that oral tradition was dying. This was happening not just in one country but all over the world, and everywhere the causes were the same: rapid urbanisation, large-scale migration, industrialisation and increasing literacy. In the 20th century the process of social change accelerated, while at the same time the emergence of modern mass media such as radio, television and the internet had a very damaging effect on traditional culture, effectively killing off oral tradition altogether except in a tiny number of isolated pockets.

This matters, fundamentally, to all of us. We are all a product of our past: not just our immediate ancestors, but the communities in which they lived, the cultures in which they grew up. We can choose to discard that past and take on new identities. But for many people, that's not an option. Language, religion, culture and tradition are the only things that are truly theirs, that establish who they are. Mass media can never replace this. So if you're someone who's been ripped away from your roots, you feel no special sense of kinship with the people living in your neighbourhood, you have a nagging sadness that part of you has been lost, what do you do, where do you turn?

Musicians have not been the only ones trying to provide

answers. Political and religious movements have done so too. And the linkage of traditional music with nationalist politics or organised religion takes us into sensitive territory. Earlier on I wrote glowingly about the close relationship of South African musicians with the anti-apartheid struggle back in the 1980s. During the same period though – unbeknownst to me at the time – in Croatia, Franjo Tudjman was evoking folk music as a means of stirring up support for his reactionary and dangerous brand of nationalism. Not every folk group joined Zlatni Dukati in performing at Tudjman's election rallies. Nonetheless, this was more than just a piece of opportunism by Tudjman. Half a century earlier, a whole folklore movement had been built up in Croatia linked to the centre-right Croatian Peasant Party which based itself on a sanitised, romanticised version of traditional peasant culture.

Some of my friends on the left view attempts to revive traditional music with suspicion, or even hostility. Their creed is internationalism, workers' unity; multiculturalism is their idea of what the world should look like. So music that looks back to the past, that is tied to a specific culture/ethnic group and that can be harnessed by nationalist movements, spells danger.

I'm all for multiculturalism, but denigrating certain music for not being multiculturalist enough is generally not a good idea. There's nothing reactionary in itself about studying, and celebrating, past history. Let's take the case of Croatia. Croatia has many traditional dances, and traditional costumes, which are associated with particular regions. Why so? Well, it probably has much to do with the area's complex history which has seen empires rise and fall, waves of immigration, battles over areas of land. Across the border, Serbia has its own complex mix of regional culture. But look at what's been taking off in Serbian music: Balkan brass band music, played by Roma musicians. This too is rooted in history. The brass band tradition goes back to the time when Serbia was part of the Ottoman Empire, over 200 years ago. Brass band music gave rise to the Cocek dance, and the music and dance was largely kept alive by Roma people who passed it on from one generation to the next. This is by no means untypical. Studying past tradition doesn't negate multiculturalism, but rather reinforces it, by revealing to us the varied mix of cultural influences which contribute to the making of a particular musical style.

Yugoslavia was a multi-ethnic state built on the aspiration that the constituent ethnic groups would move toward a unified Yugoslavian national culture. From our knowledge of the violent way in which Yugoslavia was ripped apart and ethnic rivalries asserted themselves, one might easily conclude that this was a utopian aspiration. I don't subscribe to this: the goal was perfectly reasonable, the problems stemmed from the method of getting there.

No one is born a patriot. Nations are political entities where people of different origins coexist. So every nationalism is a created narrative, a story that people are invited to buy into. It's also just one route to dealing with questions of identity. The past offers up many narratives; the challenge is to come up with a narrative that resonates with people's lived experience. Tito and the founders of the Yugoslav state failed this test when they assumed that ethnic rivalries would wither away. During World War II many thousands of Croats had fought with the Ustaše who sided with the Germans against Tito's Partisans. What proportion of the population they represented is unclear, but atrocities were committed; there was no reconciliation, leaving a toxic legacy of hatred and distrust.

The divisions that civil wars leave behind are the hardest to heal. Such divisions demand a response that goes beyond simple nationalism or anti-nationalism – the development of a different kind of narrative that celebrates diversity while also recognising and celebrating the specificity of individual cultures. Music, which is always connecting people across cultural divides, is integral to this whole idea. Yugoslavia's communists didn't see the progressive potential in traditional culture, understandably so perhaps, given the extent to which it had become identified with the political right in much of the country. Culture though is never completely static and unchanging. All cultures are fluid, they can change when people are influenced by new ideas, and at particular times in history this process can be accelerated. The state has to trust musicians and artists to navigate the process, and respect their artistic choices: the consequence of crude state intervention is likely to be that more and more artistic activity is driven underground. What the Communist state could have done though is what other states around the world have done, often to their benefit, which was to facilitate the study and practice of traditional culture, effectively opening the field up to greater numbers of young people who support the multicultural state.

The search for cultural identity in the 21st century is a reclaiming of lost values: like pride in one's region (the idea that 'local is beautiful') and in the language of one's ancestors. There's very often a political dimension to this. The growing reach of supra-national institutions such as the EU and NAFTA makes many people feel disempowered and disenfranchised. They see such institutions as bureaucratic and serving the interests of others, not their own. On both sides of the political spectrum you can find people who've reacted against this by embracing the politics of localism. Localism typically focuses on such things as regional promotion and investment, and greater local democracy. What it's not is a charter for secession. Secessionist movements gain critical mass for different kinds of reasons – because of wars, because of extreme economic disparities between regions, because the rights of one or more population group have been denied.

What makes music and dance so important to so many groups in their search for identity? It's a living link to the past. Being at a festival, a concert, dancing and applauding, you're bringing traditional culture into your life. It's very accessible. Learning to play an instrument to a basic level of competence is easier and, dare I say, more fun than learning a language. And that's the third point: music can be taught, can be passed on. This is vital to any culture that wants to renew itself.

THE TORCHBEARERS

There are many heroes in this book, but pride of place has to go to the torchbearers. It wasn't planned that way, I'm not a fanatical traditionalist by any means. But this project has really taught me to appreciate how vital a lot of the work done by folklorists of one kind and another can actually be – this is work that can change history, can affect the cultural life of a whole nation.

Torchbearers are those who pass on knowledge of traditional music to future generations. Traditionally, as we've seen, this would have been done by oral tradition – father to son, mother to daughter, and so forth. Oral tradition was part of a way of life that has largely disappeared. Today's musicians are very unlikely to be part of a community where cultural practices have continued over many generations. More likely it is that they'll see old languages being forgotten, they'll see young people growing up ignorant of their own musical roots and unfamiliar with traditional instruments. It's an existential threat, one that's prompted a good many musicians to look for bigger and bolder responses. And it's been inspiring to see some of the things that they've done.

For some, the starting point has been the realisation that there can still be found authentic tradition bearers, people who remember the time when there was a village community life, who remember the songs that family members used to sing. So they did what John and Alan Lomax and other folklorists have done before them: they travelled with their recording equipment, sought out those who had knowledge of old music coursing through their veins and invited them to sing. In every case this was a labour of love – an activity funded where possible by universities or grants from heritage organisations, with little or no hope of commercial reward. Some activists set up their own record labels, taking the view that this was the only way of getting this supposedly non-commercial music recorded and released to the widest possible audience. Ketebul Music in Kenya, Tao Music in the Philippines, Asasi Records in the Maldives, Amarrass Records in India, Wantok Musik in Oceania and Stonetree Records in Belize all have one thing in common: a mission to preserve traditional indigenous music. Then there are whole projects dedicated to making field recordings and publishing them online: Vincent Moon with his Collection Petites Planètes; Laurent Jeanneau (Kink Gong); the Singing Wells project of which Ketebul Music is a co-sponsor; the UK-based Song Collectors Collective. Sam Lee, who founded the Song Collectors Collective, is also very much a working musician who's won great acclaim for his reinterpretations of traditional songs. Other musicians who've wrestled with the question of how best to perform songs learned from field recordings include Russia's Sergei Starostin, Serbia's Svetlana Spajic and the Belarus ensemble Rada. They all want to honour the original recordings, but in each case the decision on how much to rework it comes down to an individual artistic decision.

Just as important as preventing the loss of old singing traditions is saving musical instruments from extinction. Nothing gives more character to a country's music than its native instruments and homegrown variants of instruments seen in other countries. And as the number of instrument makers becomes fewer and fewer, and instruments are being lost to the world because nobody plays them anymore, we are losing some of the precious diversity that once existed in our music. There are many examples of instruments being revived following a lengthy period of declining popularity, but the most striking stories are those where only the singlemindedness of individuals has rescued instruments from extinction. In Iceland we will meet Bára Grímsdóttir and Chris Foster: no one had played the fiðla for so many years that no recordings of the instrument existed, so having had one made they then had to figure out ways of playing it, relying on nothing more than their musical experience and instincts. Alan Stivell was a nine-year-old boy when he picked up the clarsach made by his father and tried to play it. He had tuition, but there were some things that could not easily be taught: no one really knew then what a Breton harp playing Breton music should sound like. Stivell not only mastered the instrument, but later through his recordings revived the fortunes of the Celtic harp, helping it along from virtual extinction to the icon that it is today.

In many of the world's poorest countries the state has very little money to spend on culture of any kind. They have other priorities, it's understandable. And yet these are often the countries where music education could have the greatest social benefit. It can give kids a skill, a purpose to their lives, a sense of being part of a wider community, thus helping to create the fabric of future society. The organisation Musicians Without Borders was established to "use the power of music to bridge divides, connect communities and heal the wounds of war" – they've been running successful programmes in places like Rwanda, El Salvador, Palestine and Northern Ireland.

Beyond this, formal education may be the only way to keep knowledge of certain traditional instruments and musical forms alive.

So it's very good to see the work that the Aga Khan Development Network is doing in Central Asia, setting up music schools, training teachers and mentoring of talented musicians. In Bhutan the singer Jigme Drukpa has set up the country's first private music school, while in Gambia Sona Jobarteh has opened the country's music school dedicated to traditional music. While the Bhutan school gets enough money from student fees to cover its costs, the Gambian school seeks to offer scholarships to students from poor backgrounds, and needs grants and donations to cover this.

Such initiatives are normally small-scale, but Ahmad Sarmast had a big vision: to improve the state of music education in Afghanistan. Very impressively, he was able to secure funds from the international community and support from the beleaguered Afghan government, and in 2010 the Afghanistan National Institute of Music came into being. There is still much to do to realise Ahmad Sarmast's vision, but in the chapter on Afghanistan you can read about some of the work that they've been doing.

These are the forgotten heroes. It's become like a mantra of music writers that we're always quick to praise the innovators, the creators: those who take music in new directions or successfully combine different musical forms. The assumption is that we should be looking to the future, not to the past. But as a great man once said, "in this bright future you can't forget your past". Identity matters, because who we are is also about our beliefs, our values, what we hold dear. Who we are can shape who we can become, adding purpose to our future.

RESEARCH METHODS

The information in this book has been largely obtained from research done on the internet. As a rule I have tried not to rely on a single source, but to verify facts from an independent source or sources. It's inevitable in a book of this scope that there will be some factual errors, and I take full responsibility for these.

I have had to access foreign language websites throughout the last four years, and I am much indebted to Google Translate, without which the book would have been the poorer. Needless to say though, the responsibility for any poor translations, or misunderstandings arising from clumsy translations, is entirely mine.

With names and words in languages such as Arabic which have their own alphabet, there are often alternative spellings. I won't bore you with the difficulties that this causes trying to google Arabic names, but suffice to say that where choices were available I have opted to use what appears to be the most commonly accepted spelling.

Artist interviews are quoted frequently throughout this book. I'm enormously grateful to those who took time to speak to me and write to me, despite the language barriers that sometimes presented themselves. Interview snippets have also been taken from newspaper and magazine articles, TV shows and documentaries, etc. As well as being a valuable source of information about the artists and their music, these interviews also document from time to time the views of the artists on wider cultural and social questions to do with their countries. These voices are at the heart of the book; because they are speaking of things that have touched their lives their insight and perspective is that much more penetrating. At times what they have to say may be combative, may get under the skin of some people. These words have not been chosen out of any lack of respect for the country or its peoples – quite the reverse. I could have just told you that Aaron Bebe Sukura plays a wooden xylophone called a gyil, and that would have been true, but it wouldn't have given you a full picture of what's happening with traditional music in Ghana. Aaron Bebe's sharp words about the lack of government support for traditional music come from the passion that he has about his culture, and I would be doing him a disservice if I failed to address the issue.

You may or may not recognise your own country in these pages. Each chapter is just a series of snapshots, and there are innumerable other stories that could equally be told. I hope that at least I have portrayed the artists accurately and fairly, and that the range of artists featured gives some sense of the uniqueness and diversity of a country's music. Among them are many brave and inspiring people, and great musicians, and while there may be some who feel that I've not represented their country as they would wish, one point I would make is that for me what makes a country is the people who reside there. Throughout this book, I avoid referring to national stereotypes, because I believe that countries thrive out of the diversity of their people, cultures and human experiences. So I invite you to celebrate not only the countries, but the artists and their music, which can be heard on the website that accompanies this book. Prepare yourself to be enthralled!

II INTRODUCTION TO VOLUME 4

When researching these chapters I had no agenda, other than to go where the music took me. Like anyone else, I guess, I had many deep-rooted preconceptions about the music of particular countries. But as I went, I asked questions about where the music came from, and how it had been evolving and changing. The answers were often fascinating, and forced me to admit that a good few of my preconceptions were wide of the mark.

I wasn't expecting, for instance, to find that black musicians had so much influence on early country music. And not having lived in places such as Hill Country Mississippi or Cape Breton Island it was startling to discover the strength of regional traditions in the USA and Canada even today.

The film Buena Vista Social Club draws you into the musicians' world, but the Cuba that it portrays is a romanticised version. The vast majority of black musicians in pre-revolutionary Cuba suffered from segregation and low pay.

Cuba was no exception. Across Central and South America, black and indigenous communities had to contend with poverty and discrimination: a legacy of slavery, of colonial pasts, and of institutional racism. What they had was a history and culture of their own. And, as they struggled to assert their identity and to secure their rights, again and again it was to culture and to music that they turned. The most striking example of this is the Caribbean carnival tradition. Canboulay in Trinidad and jab in Grenada are graphic representations of slave culture that have become integral to carnival, but in every carnival there are myriad ways in which black history and its connection to slavery is commemorated. The black Creole enclave of Bluefields, Nicaragua, has its very own carnival tradition, originally an amalgam of British and African traditions.

Many Latin American musical genres have multiple origins. Sometimes European and indigenous instruments are used together; sometimes African drums are added to the mix. But for a time at least there was a perception that these elements could produce a music that was truly national in character, spanning all racial divides. Joropo in Venezuela and pasillo in Ecuador are examples: one might also speak of the importance of the charango in Peruvian culture. In each of these countries, however, old certainties have been eroded as black and indigenous people have fought for greater recognition. In Venezuela, the election of Hugo Chavez brought about a new constitution, with indigenous rights enshrined and a redrawing of the political map. Ecuador and Peru also came to see indigenous rights being written into legislation. Musicians and cultural figures, by raising their voices and reclaiming their identity, had helped to prepare the ground for these political changes, and it's been a great privilege to be able to tell the stories of Peru's Susana Baca, Bolivia's Luzmila Carpio and Ecuador's Mishqui Chullumbu.

The theme of people trying to recover their heritage repeats itself in many parts of Central and South America. Stonetree Records was created by Ivan Duran not as a commercial proposition but as a means of preserving Garifuna culture. Brazil's Dona Onete and Mexico's Alejandra Robles aren't just singers; they're cultural activists whose careers are dedicated to the black music traditions of their home regions.

Music was becoming more commercialised: soca music, which became the driving force of carnival, had none of the charm and the wit of old-time calypso. At least soca was an authentic Caribbean invention. Up and down the continent the music of the United States was an inescapable part of life, an ever-present influence. The pressures to modernise and Americanise are hugely important, yet they're only parts of the story. In the chapter on Venezuela I explore how salsa music was first given birth in New York clubs by Spanish-speaking immigrant musicians, from where it was exported to the barrios of Caracas. From Belem to Caracas to Mexico City, bands playing Latin music are still a vital part of city life, but the music has changed enormously in the space of a couple of generations. Now the music crosses borders much more freely and salsa, cumbia and merengue can be heard nearly everywhere. This is all music with a strong rhythm and a significant African influence, and that tells you something about how much society has changed.

NORTH
AND CENTRAL
AMERICA

ANTIGUA AND BARBUDA

In 1945, workers making the long voyage home from the oil refineries of Curacao stopped ashore in Trinidad, where they heard for the first time a startling new sound. For some time the poorer classes of Port of Spain had been picking up discarded metal objects and trying to make music out of them. This led during the war years to the invention of a new instrument that would take the Caribbean by storm: the steel pan.

Back home in Antigua, the more adventurous of them took possession of some used oil drums and tried to replicate what they had seen and heard. They learned how to cut the drums to the required size, then hammer the top of the drums to make numerous indentations, rapidly heat and cool the drums to temper the steel, and carry out a lengthy tuning process by tapping the surfaces with hammers. The first steel band was formed, and by the late '40s competition between steel bands was already under way.

At this time Antigua was part of the British Leeward Islands, and the governor was the Eton-educated Oliver Baldwin, son of the former British prime minister, Stanley Baldwin. On Stanley's death in 1947, Oliver was made a lord. He had to give up his seat in the Commons, and in compensation (or perhaps to remove him from the scene) he was offered the Leeward Islands. He travelled there with his male lover, John Boyle, though the relationship was not public at the time. The maverick politician quickly developed a liking for steel pans, much to the horror of the local aristocracy, who petitioned him to outlaw the lower-class steel bands. He dismissed the petitions with the comment that: "if you can stop your dogs from barking all night long, then your requests may be considered." [1] To add insult to injury, the governor invited Hell's Gate, the leading steel band of the day, to play at various functions at Government House.

In 1955, Smithsonian Folkways recorded three Antiguan steel bands: Brute Force, Hell's Gate and Big Shell. I can't resist quoting part of the liner notes:

> *"Here then, in the warm and pleasant tropical evening, men of the Brute Force congregate by the house of Mr. and Mrs. F. V. D. Griffith, near St. Johns. Griffith, retired harbourmaster of Antigua is also bandmaster of the police band, and for a lifetime has been a musical force in the B. W. I. Under the steps leading up to the veranda a musically astute cricket keeps time with the Brute Force as they play*

and sing, Mrs. Griffith entertains graciously as the concert goes along; friends, tourists, neighbors and strangers drop in, attracted by music in the night, and all are welcome.

Farther down along the beach is a club where visitors may enjoy a quiet evening swim and the excellent native rum. Here in the shadow of the tropical palms, the Big Shell Band plays, and in the interval following La Paloma a la bolero, the quick restless surf rhythms of Antigua's northern coast are heard as the microphone volume is increased.

So from Antigua, an obscure island in the British West Indies, where we find one man who uses an 1837 gravestone for his coffee table, where the parakeets scream in a French patois, comes – steel band." [2]

It's not just the crickets: the music itself has an organic, natural feel. There's such a beautiful flow on the featured song **SATURDAY NIGHT**. This is Antiguan pan music at its purest.

Calypso music – in its early form – was all about the lyrics. It was the music of the streets, the 'poor man's newspaper'. Wit, humour and razor-sharp social commentary were its lifeblood. In Antigua, before calypso proper arrived on the scene its essential qualities could be heard in the songs of the itinerant pedlar John Thomas, better known as Quarkoo. As far as I know he was never recorded, but apparently he composed songs on the spot about topical issues of the day and sold printed songs in the streets of St John's. Some of these were so scandalous that they even got him arrested.

Antigua's greatest calypsonian, McClean Emanuel, was born in 1942, the youngest of nine children. At the age of 20 he entered his first calypso competition. Soon enough, under the name of King Short Shirt, he was winning them. Shelly Tobitt, a life-long friend, wrote many of his lyrics and together they were an irresistible combination. It wasn't just great dance music: the lyrics were becoming increasingly radical, full of social and political commentary. He was a tribune of the people.

In the mid-1970s, now at the height of his powers, Short Shirt released the album, Ghetto Vibes. It contains probably his finest political song – Nobody Go Run Me, a heartfelt cry of defiance. Many of the songs are clearly written with carnival in mind, but they lose none of their lyrical sharpness. In Hands off Harmonites he comments on the history of the carnival. Vivian Richards was a timely tribute to the greatest cricketer that the Caribbean has ever produced. And then there was TOURIST LEGGO. With gentle humour the lyrics satirise the foreign tourist getting into the carnival fun. The song's infectious chorus made it a sure-fire carnival hit. Decades later, many Antiguans still bemoan the fact that the song failed to win the 1976 Road March in Trinidad. (Its success was reputedly responsible for a ban on foreign entrants to the competition.)

King Short Shirt went on to win the Calypso King title of Antigua 15 times before retiring from competition, becoming a born-again Christian and taking up gospel singing. Will Antigua see his like again? One of his contemporaries, King Obstinate, when interviewed in 2007, was not optimistic:

"*Right now, to me, calypso in Antigua is a dying art. We don't have the support... The young people are more into hip hop and soca, not the real hard calypso, and people are not going to the tents; they have to be sponsored to survive... I'm telling you, this is 50 years of Carnival, and you're still interviewing King Obstinate, you still have to go interview Short Shirt, and Swallow. You still hearing the same names. The other guys are there, but they're not generating the interest. Right now, you sing a song and it's a Carnival song. After Carnival, the songs die. I hope I don't sound too negative, but it is what I am seeing. I could be wrong.*" [3]

NOTES

1. http://whensteeltalks.ning.com/photo/1949-gov-baldwin-hells-gate
2. http://media.smithsonianfolkways.org/liner_notes/cook/COOK01042.pdf
3. http://www.antigua.gov.ag/pdf/ict_magazine/
   CommemorativeMag07_40-79.pdf

BAHAMAS

Blake Alphonso Higgs (1915–86) was born at Matthew Town in the Bahamas island of Great Inagua. A precocious kid who learned to play a wide variety of stringed instruments with remarkable ease, he went blind at the age of 16 (hence the moniker Blind Blake – not to be confused with the American blues singer of the same name). According to one source, this came about as a result of staring at the sun for extended periods. [1] Undeterred, he was soon performing for money round the bars and taverns of Nassau. In 1933, he was given a job at Nassau's Royal Victoria Hotel, where he was to remain entertaining tourists for the next 30 years.

In 1935, Higgs had his first hit called Love, Love Alone, it was a very topical calypso about the love affair between King Edward VIII and Wallis Simpson. He took calypso-flavoured island music and added character and light humour and banjo playing. This mellow Bahamian style was called goombay music, after the goatskin covered drum that provided its percussive beat. Higgs's name and reputation preceded him, and his songs were covered by The Kingston Trio, Pete Seeger, Harry Belafonte, Acker Bilk, Pat Boone, Johnny Cash and many others.

Then in 1966, something extraordinary happened. A cover of one of Higgs's songs appeared on what was to become one of

the most influential albums in the history of popular music – Pet
Sounds by The Beach Boys.

JOHN B. SAIL, or, as Brian Wilson named it, Sloop John B, was
an old and much-loved Bahamian folk song. Its enduring appeal
isn't hard to fathom: as well as a strong chorus, it's funny, and
its sea-weary cynicism is easy to relate to. The oldest published
version appeared in an article by Richard Le Gallienne in Harper's
magazine in 1916. A few years later, Carl Sandburg, poet, writer
and folklorist, wrote:

> "John T. McCutcheon, cartoonist and kindly philosopher, and
> his wife Evelyn Shaw McCutcheon, mother and poet, learned
> to sing this on their Treasure Island in the West Indies. They
> tell of it, 'Time and usage have given this song almost the
> dignity of a national anthem around Nassau. The weathered
> ribs of the historic craft lie imbedded in the sand at Governor's
> Harbor, whence an expedition, especially sent up for the
> purpose in 1926, extracted a knee of horseflesh and a ring-bolt.
> These relics are now preserved and built into the Watch Tower,
> designed by Mr. Howard Shaw and built on our southern
> coast a couple of points east by north of the star Canopus.'" [2]

Higgs's John B. Sail doesn't differ markedly from the earlier texts, or from the 1935 recording made by Alan Lomax while visiting Nassau. The most notable feature is his gentle banjo playing. But this was surely the point at which the song began to travel, making its way to The Kingston Trio, to Lonnie Donegan, to Jimmie Rodgers, to The Ian Campbell Folk Group – and eventually to The Beach Boys.

By 1966, the decline of goombay music had already well set in. Ed Moxey (1933–2014), a young musician who was elected to parliament in 1967, was among those trying to keep the culture alive. Rake 'n' scrape replaced goombay as the general term for black Bahamian music. Closely related in style to goombay, rake 'n' scrape's defining feature was an ordinary saw that the musician would place on his lap, bend, and scrape with an old nail or any such implement that came to hand. Other improvised instruments were also used. Moxey was instrumental in founding Jumbey Village – a cultural centre – and was pushing ahead with plans for a Jumbey Festival when the government pulled the plug on him, effectively consigning the Village to its fate. Rake 'n' scrape has survived in some form, as witness the fact that there is a rake 'n' scrape festival that takes place every year on Cat Island. But I understand that true rake 'n' scrape players who play in the old style are few and far between. As the system of passing on knowledge through oral tradition no longer exists, recordings are an increasingly valuable asset. This leads me to mention an excellent compilation released in 2017 that features several leading figures from the Golden Age of Bahamian music: GOOMBAY! Music from the Bahamas 1951-59.

NOTES

1. http://bahamasentertainers.com/Artist/BlindBlake/blake_bio.html
2. Carl Sandburg, American Songbag.

BARBADOS

The year was 2012. The scene was a formal dinner ceremony at the giant Hilton Hotel, which bestraddles Bridgetown's beachfront. Barbados's minister of culture, Stephen Lashley, was delivering a speech paying homage to the guest of honour, Anthony Carter, who'd been awarded a doctorate by the university for his contribution to national culture. What makes this scene so interesting, even remarkable, is that Dr Anthony Carter is better known as The Mighty Gabby, a calypsonian whose songs have made him, on many occasions, a real thorn in the establishment's side.

Born in 1948, Gabby grew up in the Bridgetown suburb of Emmerton. "Calypso touched my life when I was seven years old," he remembers. "Miss Walcott had the first gramophone in our village. We used to hear merengue, calypso – Lion and Atilla, Houdini, Growling Tiger, all on those 78 records." [1] It's no accident that all four of the artists he names here were Trinidadian. Before the country gained independence in 1966, and for some time after, its music scene made it very much Trinidad's poor relation. It hadn't produced any outstanding calypsonians who could compete with the stars from Trinidad. Barbados at the time had no equivalent of Trinidad's great carnival: calypso singers struggled to make a living and in a country with a complex system of social divisions they were regarded as low-status. So most of the music played on the radio those days would have come from Trinidad.

Gabby's mother didn't want him to become another no-hoper calypsonian, so she pushed him to do well at school. But in 1965, instead of sitting his final exams, he went to a calypso competition instead – without telling his mother. Somehow he knew he had to find a way of earning a living as a singer. In 1967 he landed a job on a cruise ship. Singing regularly for tourists proved a great way of building up his experience and confidence. He was writing more and more of his own material: one humorous song called Heart Transplant won him the title of Calypso Monarch in 1968. To prove it was no fluke he won the competition again the following year with another topical song on the controversial subject of family planning.

There was no competition in 1970, or in the following years. It seemed that Barbados still didn't regard its calypso singers that seriously. For a few years, spouge was all the rage: a fusion of ska and calypso. But Barbados's first entirely home-grown musical genre didn't leave a lasting legacy. The simple beats of the songs would soon sound outdated as West Indian music developed rapidly in the 1970s and '80s, while the lyrics lacked the punch of calypso or reggae.

Meanwhile, Gabby was in New York City. He'd hopped on a plane in 1971 – "I just wanted to see what the US looked like. And I had a girlfriend whose mother had sent for her and she was up there and I missed her a lot." [2] He stayed, got a job in a factory, and got his first acting job. By the time he returned to Barbados the country finally had its own carnival.

The English brought sugar cane to Barbados, and from the 1640s onwards sugar was to completely dominate the small island's economy. For 200 years African slaves worked in the sugar plantations (although the British abolished the slave trade in 1807, they didn't get round to abolishing slavery in the British Empire until 1834). The annual Crop Over celebration had long been a feature of plantation life, and it continued after slavery, with adaptations. The burning of Mr Harding (who was represented by a stuffed effigy) became a central part of the festival and symbolised the hope of the labourers that the winter months, when work was scarce and wages low, would not bring too great hardship.

Since being revived in 1974, Crop Over has grown and grown into an event lasting several weeks, attracting thousands of tourists and exiled Barbadians such as the singer Rihanna, and generating millions of dollars in revenue. It's become a vital part of Bajan identity, a link with their colonial past, while also being a source of great pride and recognised as one of the great Caribbean carnivals. It hardly seems necessary to say that music is at the heart of it, with calypso tents and hotly contested competitions. As well as the Calypso Monarch, another that the big stars vie for is the Tune of the Crop, or Road March Song, which was won in its inaugural year (1979) by Gabby with Burn Mr Harding.

Gabby was now one of the biggest stars in a growing scene, but his songs had an awkward tendency of getting banned by the radio, and he was struggling to get a recording contract. Then in 1982 he met Eddy Grant. This was the beginning of a relationship that was to transform his career. Grant was a Guyanan-born artist and producer who'd lived most of his life in London. Just as his solo career was taking off in the UK, Grant took himself off and decided to make a home, not in his native Guyana, but in Barbados. He bought up a run-down plantation on the east coast of the island and built new recording studios. The Blue Wave Studios became the centre of operations for his Ice Records label. Ice Records have gradually acquired the rights to a lot of classic early calypso – mainly from Trinidadians such as Mighty Sparrow, Lord Kitchener and Roaring Lion. But they've also put Bajan (Barbadian) music on the map by making high quality recordings of top artists such as Mighty Gabby, Mighty Grynner and Square One. And Grant never seems to have had any doubt that Gabby was the cream of the crop. He loved him as an artist and as a person.

The hits flowed, one after the other. A word about these hits: though described as calypso music, the sound is more akin to soca than to the acoustic calypso of earlier decades. The emphasis on the lyrics, and the punchy subject matter, are among the things that make it calypso rather than soca. But Gabby isn't just a calypso artist; he's also an award-winning folk singer. I do recommend listening to Gabby the folk singer alone with his guitar playing more reflective songs. But for this we have to turn to live videos on YouTube, because this side of his work is missing from the highly produced Ice Records releases.

BOOTS is a protest against militarism. Here's Gabby's account of how it came to be written: "There was no particular national crisis at the time so we were amazed when we came upon these soldiers with back packs marching through the streets. To me it's a waste of tax payers money. I was angry. When I got home I kept hearing in my head 'left, right, left, right the government boots.' This stayed with me for a couple of days and about three weeks later, the Grenada Invasion took place." [3] The song that emerged was Gabby's finest moment. It's an uncompromising attack on the prime minister of the day, Tom Adams, which doesn't shy away from asking the hard questions. At the same time it works as a dance number, drawing people in with its memorable hook.

In The List, Gabby is equally fearless in his choice of subject. By the late 1980s, Aids was spreading fast across the Caribbean, and the stigma that it carried was such that authorities were afraid to launch any serious sexual education campaign. What concerned Gabby was that: "The way people were dealing with the problem was by spreading rumors about one another. I was at a friend's home and overheard these women talking about all who they heard had AIDS. It was all he say and dem say. I decided there and then that I would write a song because I wanted to stop people from spreading rumours." [4] The song he wrote was one long send-up, consisting of a list of scandalous rumours sung without comment. It's all intended to make people think, and to stimulate debate.

As the 21st century dawned you might have expected that by now Gabby, who was the wrong side of 50, would be basking in his status as a popular hero and enjoying a comfortable semi-retirement. Instead we find him winning yet another Calypso Monarch title, and doing so with a song that was just as committed as anything that had gone before. In The Wuk Up Song, Gabby avoids any ambiguity by declaring at the start that he's angry – i.e. this is a protest song. He's unhappy with the Crop Over Festival's direction of travel; what he says he wants is to put Africa back into it. Africa, in the song, signifies authentic Barbadian culture whose roots can be traced back to the days of the slave trade. Gabby's passion for preserving home-grown elements of the national culture was something that didn't go unnoticed. In 2003, the former school dropout was appointed as Barbados's first cultural ambassador, a role that he's filled with distinction.

NOTES

1. http://caribbean-beat.com/issue-7/no-eclipse-mighty-gabby#axzz3DTj5ISWx
2. Ibid.
3. http://www.icerecords.com/artists/artists-gabby.html
4. http://www.icerecords.com/artists/artists-gabby.html

BELIZE

In 1635, two Spanish ships were wrecked close to the Caribbean island of St Vincent. The African slaves who were being transported escaped and made it to the island, where they took refuge among its Carib population. Over time the two populations assimilated through intermarriage, so creating the Garifuna. The next significant date for the Garifuna is 1796. After several years fighting against English colonisation, they were finally defeated. Many Garifuna were expelled by the English to the small Honduran island of Roatan. It was a long and terrible voyage and over half the prisoners died before they reached their destination. During the 19th century many Garifuna migrated from Roatan to mainland Central America, and communities grew up, mostly in Honduras and Belize.

Garifuna identity is rooted in a shared history, a common language derived from Arawak, an African-inspired culture, and experiences of discrimination and oppression. Its culture is noted for its storytelling, its fund of proverbs, its traditional dances and its unique cuisine. It's a legacy that's long been under threat from cultural assimilation and mass migration of Garifuna to the United States, but there has also been recognition of the need to preserve this minority culture. In the 1940s, 19th November

HATTIE

The Garifuna Women's Project

SEREMEI BUGUYA

The Garifuna Collective

was first declared a holiday by certain districts, and since 1977, Garifuna Settlement Day has been a national public holiday, marked by church services, parades, street music and dance.

Since the mid-1990s there's been a huge increase in global awareness of Garifuna culture. This is thanks to music, and to two men in particular: Ivan Duran and Andy Palacio.

When they began collaborating I don't think either Ivan or Andy foresaw where this would end up. What brought them together was a sense that Garifuna music had lost its way, a desire to create something more authentic. Punta rock had become the music of the youth, it dominated the airwaves. It still had an African character, but, for Ivan, the electric guitars and synths detracted from this: "Much of Garifuna music had become just about the beat, keeping one rhythm going for hours." [1] He loved the mellow paranda style, with its slower tempo and Spanish-sounding guitars.

Andy had actually made his name as a punta rock musician, but he had become passionate about Garifuna culture and was keen to incorporate roots elements into his music. So Ivan agreed to produce him, and the album Keimuon was recorded. For Andy, this was the moment when he began to connect with fans and critics around the world through his music and his advocacy of Garifuna culture. For Ivan, this was the album that launched Stonetree Records.

Stonetree is Belize's first and only record label, and what Ivan Duran has achieved there is nothing short of amazing. There were no recording studios anywhere, so a studio was built. He had no interest in chasing record sales. Instead, he looked for reasons why recordings deserved to be made: in particular, he wanted to record albums that showcased the best of Garifuna tradition. In this, he followed his own instincts, and they rarely let him down. There was the ageing Paul Nabor, still capable of blowing the competition away when he sang paranda. There was the Honduran, Aurelio Martinez, the new soul voice of paranda. There was Creole accordionist Wilfred Peters, one of the few remaining masters of brukdown music. There was Leroy Young, a dub poet who styles himself The Grandmaster. These were no single-take recordings: each album was treated as a project. Ivan wanted to make music that spoke to people today. Much time and care was invested in deciding what instruments to play on each track, choosing between different mixes, and so on.

The Garifuna Women's Project album, Umalili, is a good example of the kind of work that went in. Ivan had already spent some years listening to Garifuna women and recording the traditional songs that they sang. In the course of this he identified a number of talented singers. He couldn't bring them all to the studio, so he brought the studio to them:

"Duran set up a recording studio in a small, thatch-roofed hut that rests on stilts just steps from the Caribbean Sea... The songs, many of which were composed by the women who sang them, included moving ballads, upbeat anthems of celebration and religious chants. It wasn't always easy getting the women he wanted into the studio because they were so busy with their daily chores and jobs. But the

women knew they were part of something exceptional, a project that would link them to their Garifuna brethren in other areas and one that would present their voices to the outside world." [2]

He then spent another five years adding to and remixing the songs until he had a product that he was completely satisfied with. The Garifuna Collective, a group of musicians put together by Ivan and Andy, added instrumental parts. The most difficult decision was which of the dozens of singers recorded to leave out of the final cut.

The mixes are good. But what really sets the album apart is that it's so real and personal. Every track had a reason for existence, each woman a true tradition-bearer with things to say or stories to tell. Sofia Blanco sings of the pain of childbirth, Bernadine Flores about getting a job to provide for her sons. HATTIE, in the song by Sarita Martinez and Desirée Diego, is Hurricane Hattie, which struck in 1961, one of many large hurricanes to hit this corner of the Caribbean. I'll let Ivan tell the story of the song:

"While working in Hopkins, I kept trying to arrange for a local woman named Sarita to come by the studio and record her aunt's song "Hattie"... Finally, Sarita made it to the studio one afternoon, where she promptly sang the song and prepared to leave, not realizing that she would have to sing it several times in order to get the best take. The song is a typical paranda but Sarita had never recorded with musical instruments and she also had to get used to the studio environment. Years later, we added the voice of Desere singing in unison with Sarita's track..." [3]

The album followed in the wake of the huge international success of Wátina (2007). Billed as an Andy Palacio and the Garifuna Collective release, in fact Andy only sang on half the tracks, other vocalists used included Paul Nabor and Aurelio. Andy though was definitely the star attraction. The album represented the culmination of his musical journey, what he himself describes as a "180 degree turn". [4] It's an acoustic album, it stays true to the old Garifuna rhythms, not embellishing them too much, and it's sung in the Garifuna tongue. Once again, the songs are direct and powerful.

Within a year, Andy Palacio suffered a stroke and heart attack and died. He was only 47. He was honoured with an official state funeral and several days of mourning, interspersed with song.

It takes more than a death to subdue the Garifuna people.

In 2013, the Garifuna Collective was back again, with the album Ayó. This time there was no lead singer. "We don't want anyone to come in and be Andy Palacio," Ivan explained. "We are going back to the core values of the project, which is to present Garifuna music to the world, not in a traditional way, not in a museum, but as a living musical form. When you listen to the record you feel that spirit of being in the village with everybody singing along, everybody being a part of a song, not following a single singer or star." [5] Traditional Garifuna instruments, drums and maracas, are used along with a big rhythm section of guitar, bass and cuatro. The songs cover a range of subjects, some echoing traditional lifestyles, some telling stories of infidelity, some reflecting on issues such as poverty and inequality.

Like other Stonetree releases, it balances between revering the past and looking to the future. Ayó means 'goodbye', and there is a sense of leave-saying on the album, but it's also very much about continuing Andy's work. On the closing track, SEREMEI BUGUYA, Justo Miranda joins voices with Aurelio Martinez and Lloyd Augustine; they're hoping that they could get such a great send-off as Andy when they die. The easy rhythm and the uplifting chorus makes it anything but a sorrowful song. Tragically, a few months later, Justo Miranda died of a heart attack under a tree in Honduras, and it wasn't till many weeks after his death that the news reached his band mates in Belize.

It takes more than a death to subdue the Garifuna people.

NOTES

1. http://www.folkradio.co.uk/2014/10/landini-interview-with-aurelio-and-ivan-duran
2. Liner notes by Jacob Edgar – http://www.cumbancha.com/files/artist_pdfs_general/umalali_liner_notes__lyrics.pdf
3. Liner notes http://www.cumbancha.com/files/artist_pdfs_general/umalali_liner_notes__lyrics.pdf
4. http://archive.rockpaperscissors.biz/index.cfm/fuseaction/current.press_release/project_id/295.cfm
5. http://www.cumbancha.com/the-garifuna-collective-biography-eng

CANADA

If you speak the English language, chances are that you'll have a favourite Canadian singer. Mine is Joni Mitchell. Her remarkable life, replete with so much beautiful art, passion and tragedy, seems to be coming to an agonising end. She survived a brain aneurysm in March 2015, but the rare condition Morgellons Syndrome continues to play havoc with her physical health.

What does it mean to be a Canadian singer or musician? Most Canadian music seems interchangeable with that of the USA: the genres are the same, the influences are the same. American artists are inspired by Canadians and vice versa. Joni is a case in point: she left for the USA in 1965, before her career had taken off, and her magical early albums are inseparable from her experience of the Laurel Canyon counterculture in late 1960s, early '70s California. One of the most popular Canadian singers in the world today, the crooner, Michael Bublé, has made a career of covering American standards.

Canada is a diverse, multiracial country. It has a unique racial mix, one that reflects its rich, many-sided history. To drive this point home, allow me to share a few facts with you. Canada has two official languages: 67% of the population speak English at home, and 22% speak French. (In the province of Quebec, French

CONFÉDÉRATION	*Le Vent du Nord*
McCORMACK'S BREAKDOWN	*Aaron Collis and Emilia Bartellas*
DONALD & GORDON'S	*Kenneth & Angus MacKenzie*
BRING YOUR CLOTHES BACK HOME	*April Verch*
FAREWELL NELLIE	*Annie Lou*
DAMP ANIMAL SPIRITS	*Tanya Tagaq*

is the sole official language.) In the 2011 census, Canadians could identify as being of one or more ethnicities. Only 32.2% picked Canadian as their ethnic origin, as compared to 19.8% English, 15.4% French, 14.3% Scottish, 13.8% Irish and 9.7% German. Around 15% (5 million) are of Asian origin; 767,000 are African; 628,000 are Caribbean. 1,370,000 call themselves First Nations (North American Indian), 448,000 Métis and 73,000 Inuit.

What those stats don't tell us is how much importance Canadians place on their ethnic origins. Past surveys have reported that most Canadians feel a stronger attachment to their national identity than to any ethnic identity. The main caveat to this is that French speakers in Quebec are more likely to identify as Québécois than as Canadians. And Quebec is by no means the only province with a distinctive culture and sense of identity. It's in traditional folk music, more than any other type of music, that regional cultural differences are expressed and so, in the limited space allotted, what I decided to do was to make a whistle-stop musical tour of Canada by province.

Quebec has a strong tradition of instrumental music,

performed on the fiddle and/or the accordion and drawing heavily on Irish and Scottish dance tunes. One of the most comprehensive collections (though not the easiest to come by) is 100 Ans de Musique Traditionnelle Quebecoise, a series of four double albums on Transit Records compiled by the ethnomusicologist Gabriel Labbé. The music is divided chronologically:

> "Disc one is divided almost evenly between fiddlers and accordionists, with the fiddlers winning out in the '20s, the squeezeboxes picking up speed in the '30s. Some of these musicians were self-taught lumberjacks, others classically trained violinists, all of them skilled and respected in their day. Accordionists appearing on the first disc include Alfred Montmarquette, probably the greatest accordion player of his era. His Babies' Waltz is a highlight, accompanied by piano and bones. Clog Waltz presents Joseph Latour who after learning the instrument as a child, worked 36 different professions before devoting himself to music at age 40." [1]

Appearing on a couple of the later CDs is Jean Carignan (1916–88), a home-taught fiddler of exceptional skill. Born in Levis, a town on the St Lawrence river, he began learning to play the violin from his father at the age of four. When he was seven his father lost his job and he began busking in the streets. "People started hiring him for church meetings, country fairs and dances, and even for political rallies, and by the time he was eight, he was making as much as $10 a day." [2] Despite his abilities, music would not always provide a reliable source of income in his adult life. Folksinger, Alan Mills, reports that when he recorded for Folkways in 1960 he was working every day as a taxi driver on the streets of Montreal, in addition to his musical engagements. He adds that, "although I've heard Johnny play many times, I've always found something new in his playing that seems to make each time I hear him more exciting than the last, and I've watched a number of classical violinists and other musicians wonder at his bowing skill and the marvellous sounds he makes." [3]

1976 was a momentous year for Quebec. The Montreal Olympics that summer gave the province a chance to advertise itself to the world, and its music and culture were briefly exposed to the international spotlight. Then, just weeks later, the separatist Parti Québécois swept to power in regional elections. Finally, in hindsight, 1976 was also the year when a band was formed who would revolutionise the music of the province: La Bottine Souriante. There was a rapid growth of interest at the time in Québécois identity and French language culture, and La Bottine Souriante were able to ride on the crest of it. They stood out from traditional groups because they were a large band who played many instruments and sang in French. In 1980, a referendum on secession was lost, which was a massive setback to the movement, but as audiences dwindled in Quebec the band were given a chance to tour the USA. "It's very unusual to travel in the States and sing only in French," reflects band leader Yves Lambert, "but we've done about 15 tours in the United States without ever singing a song in English." [4]

La Bottine Souriante are still going – but without any of the group's founding members, all of whom have departed at one time or another. The band's music evolved away from a more traditional Celtic-influenced style towards a freewheeling fusion. However, as Quebec embarked on a second roots music revival, the band's status as father figures of Quebec music remained secure, and many of the new generation of musicians would take inspiration from them. The trio, De Temps Antan, was formed when fiddler André Brunet left La Bottine: their brand of high-energy dance music is reasonably representative of the current scene, in which a number of bands draw on both traditional and modern influences. Montreal's Bon Débarras do an engaging take on traditional dance music using guitars, banjo, upright bass, accordion, washboard and harmonicas.

Currently the most successful champions of traditional Quebec music are Le Vent Du Nord, who released their 8th album, Têtu, in 2015. Each of the four band members are singers and multi-instrumentalists, and the instruments range from accordion and fiddle to hurdy-gurdy and Jew's harp. On the album, traditional tunes are turned into high-energy footstompers, and of the self-written songs perhaps the most interesting is **CONFÉDÉRATION**. I'll let hurdy-gurdy player Nicolas Boulerice introduce it:

"I owe the premise for this song to S. Harper [prime minister of Canada], who announced that he would hold grand celebrations in 2017 for the 150th anniversary of Canada, the Confederation having been signed in 1867. What a strange idea! My ancestors' Canada is over 400 years old! And my Native great-grandmother probably would have added a few thousand years to that count... 'Confédération' is about our collective selective memory." [5]

The band have also added a catchy accordion-led melody.

According to a recent survey by Statistics Canada, the part of Canada where people report the strongest sense of belonging to their province is interestingly not Quebec but Newfoundland and Labrador. [6] It's not so surprising perhaps: here's a settled community, with its own unique time zone, mainly living on islands, bonded for generations to the sea and to the fishing trade and to the unpredictable Atlantic weather.

The music of Newfoundland reflects people's sense of attachment to this way of life. The sea and seafaring provide the dominant theme, while Irish music is very popular. "It's one of the few places in the world," according to Jim Payne, "where the Irish and the English settled side by side and got along with each other." Until quite recently, songs were sung unaccompanied: "people just love to sing in Newfoundland, a lot of people couldn't read or write", so the songs became a source of oral history. People also loved to dance: "it was mostly in people's kitchens, where they didn't have much room to move. So the music just clipped along, and the footwork was kept close to the floor." [7]

These elements were all very much present in the music of Figgy Duff, formed in 1976 by Noel Dinn, who became key players in the folk revival. Lead singer Pamela Morgan recalls that: "Noel was a visionary and a strong-willed person. He wanted to take Newfoundland music out of the rut it was in. He rediscovered the older ballads, beautiful laments and unique dance tunes and presented them in a rock format in order to attract a wider audience." [8] Elsewhere, she vividly captures the impact that the band had on the community:

> "In the very early years we traveled what seemed like every square inch of Newfoundland, seeking songs and music from people. We played community halls, clubs, festivals, kitchens, full houses, empty houses, to audiences indifferent, hostile, enraptured. In St. John's we were eyed with suspicion by the folklore set... We favored velvet and lace, and were vegetarians who smelled strongly of garlic and had a taste of poetry and copious amounts of fine wine. I remember a maze of dinner parties with songs, music, laughter, and discussions far into the night of Blake & Yeats and Newfoundland nationalism... Some of the folk purists were downright outraged that their precious folk music was being tampered with by long haired 'urban intellectuals' using drums and amps." [9]

With the benefit of hindsight, as the popularity of young bands like Figgy Duff grew so too did the audience for more traditional folk music. Old-time fiddlers Émile Benoit, Rufus Guinchard and the accordion player Minnie White were all over the age of 60 when they started out on their professional music careers in the wake of the folk revival. And then there were the songs and ballads: what joy it must have been for this new generation to encounter songs from Newfoundland written with a delightful humour to match anything from Ireland – Johnny Burke's Cod Liver Oil, Arthur Scammell's Squid Jiggin' Ground and, more recently, Tom Cahill's Thank God We're Surrounded by Water (recorded by the Newfoundland singer Joan Morrissey in 1973).

Newfoundland remains proud of its traditional folklore, and its enduring popularity is testified in festivals, pubs and concert halls – anywhere that music or dance is performed. The music has become much more diverse, while still retaining some of its original character. The line-up of the 2014 Newfoundland and Labrador Folk Festival gives a flavour. Local artists performing included Jim Payne's group, A Crowd of Bold Sharemen, a band with a great knowledge of traditional songs and dances (mostly with a nautical theme), and they've also written a few themselves. The Irish Descendants, and Connemara, are traditional Celtic music bands. Matthew Byrne (who's also vocalist for The Dardanelles) sings old songs and ballads. And Aaron Collis and Emilia Bartellas, also taking a break from The Dardanelles, are a fiddle and accordion duo.

The daughter of a Cypriot father, Emilia Bartellas was brought up in the Battery, a neighbourhood by the harbour in St John's where the houses cling to rocky cliffs. When she left to study classical violin at the University of Toronto she wised up to the uniqueness of the Newfoundland fiddle music that she'd grown up with. The self-titled Aaron Collis and Emilia Bartellas album came out in 2013: Emilia was now in her mid-20s and playing with a joy and an energy that was helping to turn a lot of people on to the music. Though the album's instrumental, the music is never dull: "Even just in Newfoundland dance tunes, within that there are reels, there are jigs, there are types of tunes called singles and doubles and even triples, there are waltzes. In the dance halls there'd be just an accordion player or just a fiddle player, so the majority of the album is just that, and then we have some accompaniment on some of the tracks." [10] **MCCORMACK'S BREAKDOWN** is a reel that lifts the spirits and makes you want to dance.

Across the Gulf of St Lawrence from Newfoundland is Cape Breton Island, the easternmost point of Nova Scotia province. And those approaching the island from the Atlantic may catch a glimpse of the Big Fiddle: a landmark 60-foot statue of a fiddle and bow, designed and constructed in solid steel by local artist and welder Cyril Hearn, which has stood on the Sydney waterfront since 2005. Today, Cape Breton fiddle players are famed throughout the world: great names include Natalie MacMaster, Ashley MacIsaac, Wendy MacIsaac, Brenda Stubbert, Andrea Beaton, and Chrissy Crowley and Rachel Davis of the group Còig – and that's just the current generation. Cape Breton is well endowed with musical families where the torch is passed on from one generation to the next: the Rankin family, the Barra MacNeils. Natalie MacMaster is the niece of the celebrated fiddler Buddy MacMaster, who died in 2014 just short of his 90th birthday.

The future was not always so bright. In 1972, a TV documentary was broadcast entitled The Vanishing Cape Breton Fiddler, which voiced fears that young people were tuning in to modern music and the island's fiddle heritage was under threat. The documentary touched a nerve and stirred people into action. A few men met up and came up with the idea of getting 100 fiddlers performing together. Various obstacles had to be overcome, but finally Cape Breton got its fiddlers' festival in July 1973. The organisers had no idea what to expect. It was an event the like of which Cape Breton had never seen before: 130 island fiddlers participated over the weekend, and 102 were squeezed on stage for the Sunday finale. The Scotia Sun reported a "feeling of universal friendliness and co-operation". [11] There was also a huge sense of pride and achievement. But in many ways this was only the beginning. The new organising body became the Cape Breton Fiddlers' Association, who have continued the work of preserving and promoting traditional Cape Breton fiddle music ever since. The Cape Breton Fiddle Festival quickly became an annual event. And fiddlers, recognising the need to reach out more to young people, started up new classes and workshops. In the late 1990s, a group of enthusiasts formed a Celtic Music Interpretive Centre Society. They soon realised that to host a rapidly expanding audio and visual archive, and to host events, they would need a much bigger space than the one they had. So they began fundraising. The community raised $300,000, and with the addition of $350,000 from the province and $1.45 million from the federal government the Celtic Music Interpretive Centre opened in 2006 in Buddy MacMaster's home village of Judique. It's a research and archive centre, with an interactive exhibit room for more casual visitors; its Sunday ceilidhs are the highlight of its programme of live events and it hosts Gaelic language classes and workshops in fiddle, piano and dance.

When you play the next track, Kenneth and Angus MacKenzie's **DONALD & GORDON'S**, the first thing you'll hear is the sound of the bagpipe. Wait a minute, I hear you ask, what's this got to do with Cape Breton culture? The answer, it turns out, is rather a lot. In the early part of the 19th century thousands of Highland Scots emigrated to Cape Breton, and their influence on the life and culture of the island has been vast. It's present in much of the fiddle music, and in the step dances. And the Scots also brought bagpipes. "For most of the 19th and early 20th centuries pipe music was nurtured in the home, in a largely Gaelic environment and in several instances by women of the house, or extended family… Sadly, by the end of the 20th century there were only a handful of these musicians still alive." [12]

The quote is from Barry Shears, a Cape Breton native long since forced to retire from competitive piping due to a shoulder injury, but who has continued to devote years of research to the subject, authoring the book Dance to the Piper: The Highland Bagpipe in Nova Scotia.

Kenneth and Angus MacKenzie belong to another of these musical families: they're brothers, and a third brother, Calum, plays piano on the album. "My father," says Kenneth,

"moved here from South Uist... and my mother was a Rankin born and raised here in Mabou, having roots that go back to the Lochaber area of Scotland... Our parents raised my siblings and I speaking Gaelic and immersed us in the local Gaelic music, song and dance tradition of rural Mabou and area." [13]

Kenneth and Angus learned the pipes and fiddle at the Gaelic College in St Ann's, Nova Scotia. They now live an ocean apart: Angus is based on the west coast of Scotland, where he helped to found the high-profile Gaelic group Daimh. They still love playing together though, and Piob is Fidheall is a lovely piece of work, a blend of power and tenderness. Kenneth plays fiddle on the album, while Angus is on Highland and Border pipes and whistles. Donald & Gordon's is all about the wail of the pipes, but a blend of other instruments creates a nice contrast.

An obsession with the fiddle is not confined to the maritime provinces. While researching Ontario, I came across one annual fiddle and step dancing competition, and then another. Hoping to get some sort of overview, I eventually searched for a list and was amazed to find details of fiddle and step dancing contests taking place in towns all across the province. There had to be a story behind this, and the story that emerged was that Irish immigration had been key to the development of Ontario in the 19th century. The Rideau Canal was constructed between 1826 and 1832 by the British military, and the labour force included thousands of Irish. They worked in appalling conditions, and a thousand died of malaria and other diseases. A settlement was formed where the canal met the Ottawa River, named Bytown after the British officer in charge of the construction. In 1855, the town was renamed Ottawa, and in 1857 it was appointed by Queen Victoria to become the capital of Canada, which it has remained ever since.

After 1832, most Irish immigrants would end up in the logging industry. The great white pine forests of the Ottawa Valley were a prized source of timber, and as industrial activity took off new settlements sprang up along the Ottawa River. April Verch described to me how the lumberjacks would create their own entertainment:

"The lumberjacks spent the cold, dark winters working hard all day long. In the evenings they retired to the shanty house, unwinding and entertaining themselves with fiddle and accordion music. Those without an instrument would often use their feet to accompany the music, with nails driven into the heels of their shoes, and that is how this special form of dance originated. Over the years it continued to evolve, picking up influences from other types of dance as well. It is not tap dancing, Irish hard-shoe dancing, clogging or flat footing, yet the Ottawa Valley form of dance has some similarities to all of these styles. It is a genre of dance that is generally fast-paced, energetic and extremely percussive. The Ottawa Valley style of dance is known for larger and higher movement in the legs and dancers have free (not choreographed) arm movements. It is social, fun and most of all, memorable to everyone who gets a chance to experience it!" [14]

The dancing would be very informal: a floor would be cleared and people would tap their feet to the melody. That was until Donnie Gilchrist came along. Donnie Gilchrist (1925–84) had a lumberman father and an Irish mother. He began dancing almost as soon as he could walk, and in 1931 his parents invested in a pair of dancing shoes. In the mid-30s the family moved to Ottawa and Donnie would earn his crust by dancing in bars. After the war Donnie performed all over the province and in many other countries, introducing people to the dancing customs of the Ottawa Valley lumberjacks. He gave lessons to many aspiring dancers in his own unstructured style, and his skill and passion became the inspiration for all the thousands of dancers who've carried on the tradition to this day.

One such who learned his first steps from Donnie Gilchrist was Buster Brown (1950–2014). "Donnie danced from his heart," remembers Buster. "He'd move his feet the way the music told him to and I'd watch his flying feet and practise the moves until I could do them." [15] By the age of 10, he was making up to $50 dancing in bars on a Saturday night. At 12, he took on his first students: because he was so young he had to hire a driver to take him to their houses. He became a champion dancer and a father figure, whose rigorous teaching and theory have helped Canadian step dancing to become the highly choreographed art form that it is today.

The fiddle scene was also changing. The 1950s was the era of the dance band: a successful dance band such as Mac Beattie and the Ottawa Valley Melodiers would have about six men, would do regular live radio broadcasts, and would be geared up to do a range of material from dances with a caller to country ballads. With the demise of the dance band came new opportunities for fiddlers to play at concert venues, to receive lead billing and to become the focus of attention. The days of the logging camps, when fiddlers were just musicians who accompanied a dance, are long gone: now they are stars in their own right, each asserting their right to follow their own personal creative path.

Fiddle stars don't come any bigger than April Verch, born and raised just outside Pembroke in a small place called Rankin. Many of her earliest memories are rooted in music and dance: her parents loved the old-time music; it was always music, concerts, festivals. April began step dancing at age three and got her first fiddle at age six. When she was 12 she bought her first full-size fiddle – made by Robert Glier in 1890, it remains one of her most treasured possessions. While at school she entered competition after competition, winning many trophies. By the age of 20 she'd added to her CV a first place in the Canadian Grand Masters Fiddling Championship and the solo open class in the Canadian Open Old Time Fiddle Championship, besides releasing a couple of albums.

April confirmed my impressions of the strength of the Ontario music scene. "I am able to apply for grants & funding from both the provincial and national government for various projects and tours, and have been grateful to receive support from both. There is great support for the arts, and for our traditional music. In certain counties in Ontario there are fiddle and stepdance programs in our schools." Traditional culture isn't as strongly embedded as it was a couple of generations ago, when "there were house parties and square dances every single weekend". But its future seems very secure, with many young people learning to dance and play fiddle and taking part in all the jamborees and contests.

On 7th April, 2015 (her 37th birthday), April released her 10th album, The Newpart. The title speaks of the importance to April of her connection to her musical past. The Newpart was the name of a room in the family house – "It's the place we gather to jam, to practice songs for family baptisms, funerals, and weddings. It's where I practiced countless hours and wrote many tunes, including the songs on this album... It's the most special place in the house, the scene of my most cherished memories." [16] "We did a lot of research and listening to material from a few different sources," she told me, "especially from a couple of collections released by Dust to Digital," though they don't include any old-time Ottawa Valley songs. They do include a number called Gilchrist (a tribute to Donnie), which is just the sound of April tapping. Speaking to the Ottawa Citizen about her dancing, she told them, "It feels good, it's a joyous thing, it's like playing an instrument. It's expressing something I can't always do with words." [17] **BRING YOUR CLOTHES BACK HOME** is notable as being the first time in her career that she's sung, danced and played fiddle all at the same time – an achievement that you can only begin to appreciate when you've seen her performing live, as I did in Cardiff in 2013. It's also just a delightful song with its folksy imagery. The song was written by John Hartford, an American bluegrass composer who April admires, but April and producer Casey Driessen have reworked it, bringing in the upright bass, and in the pared back arrangement the bass line adds to the light-hearted mood.

Canada's roots music scene extends far beyond the communities so far discussed. Its strong, healthy state is the result of many factors. Most Canadians didn't grow up in fiddle-playing communities. They didn't grow up with that sense of continuity with a past going back many generations. Instead, they listened to music from many genres and made personal choices along the way. Certainly not all the musicians playing varieties of old-time, stringband and bluegrass grew up with the music. What brought musicians to it was a yearning for something that felt authentic. Here's Sam Parton from the group Be Good Tanyas:

"I knew what I needed to hear in a song for it to resonate with me. It needed to be grounded in history in some way. I felt there was blood and soil in that music, and coming out of treeplanting, it felt natural. I don't know what it is in me and in Frazey and in Trish that needs the sense of continuity... it's a feeling of belonging to a lineage of music and harmonies where you can hear what's come before. For me, harmonies are the most important thing in music. And, where do you hear more beautiful harmonies than in roots music?" [18]

People mostly looked to American music because American music had that incredibly rich history, being the birthplace of country music and blues music and jazz, and an endless stream of sub-genres. And roots-influenced music has always had a resonance, particularly in rural areas. Sam Parton cites the Carter Family as an influence. Amanda Blied of The Sweet Lowdown, a roots trio based on Vancouver Island, "fell in love with old time music in 2000 upon hearing the recordings of Doc Watson and Clarence Ashley", according to the group's website. And the list goes on. Pharis and Jason Romero are now living the rural dream, running a banjo-making business from the tiny village of Horsefly, BC, and recording superb mountain music. But for them too this represents the end of a long journey. Jason took up the banjo at the age of 20 when he was living in California, and spent years listening to some of the banjo greats. Then one day he met Pharis at an old-time jam in Victoria (Vancouver Island) and they figured out that they made a pretty good duo.

How much do these groups – Be Good Tanyas, The Sweet Lowdown, Pharis and Jason Romero – have in common? They're all based in British Columbia, but they're not trying to follow in the footsteps of their own forebears. They acknowledge that a lot of their inspiration comes from south of the border. And if we analyse their music we'll find significant differences in style and approach from one artist to the next. What unites them is something more fundamental than this: a common philosophy and a kindred spirit. They have a deep understanding and respect for old-time American music, and this informs their musical direction, the instruments that they play, and so on. The strength of the movement brings people together, causing new networks and new communities to form. In the town of Victoria you can join a Folk Music Society, a Storytellers Guild or a Bluegrass Association, and Vancouver Island is host to folk music festivals and bluegrass festivals.

Anne Louise Genest (Annie Lou) never played any instrument

as a kid; in fact, she only began learning the guitar at age 30. And that was because a couple of musician friends would come and jam round the kitchen table, and she thought she could join in too. At first she was happy to play the guitar and sing, then she began to write songs. She was falling in love with bluegrass and old-time mountain music (she lists as influences Hazel Dickens, Ola Belle Reed, Coon Creek Girls and Roscoe Holcomb: all musicians from south of the border). This influenced her songwriting and inspired her to learn banjo, fiddle and mandolin as well. All this time she was living in the Yukon, far away from any big cities or cultural hubs. But working with a few like-minded musicians she released a couple of albums. Then Annie Lou and her husband moved south as a lifestyle change, ending up in Parksville on Vancouver Island. It was a lucky accident – "from a musical perspective I have quite a bit more access to resources and colleagues than I did in Whitehorse. And although I really appreciated the wilderness of the Yukon, there is plenty here." [19]

End Zone (2018) has many nods to America's musical past: Farewell Nellie is an AP Carter composition, Fire in the Hole is by Hazel Dickens, and You'll Be an Angel (Sail Away Ladies) is a traditional song made immortal by Uncle Dave Macon and the Fruit Jar Drinkers in 1927. For the casual listener it's often hard to distinguish which tracks are old and which are self-written, but this album does come with an extra personal edge – the songs were written while Annie Lou's mother was dying, and the title track is directly drawn from this harrowing experience. The pace and mood of the album is never constant, but I was drawn to the slow sorrowful FAREWELL NELLIE with its gentle melody and the wail of the steel guitar. Although it's a romantic love song, it's also a song about parting, which dovetails with the album's theme.

Tanya Tagaq's music is challenging. It's experimental. On the face of it, it's not representative of any culture that ever existed. For these reasons some may question its inclusion here, but I have to go with my instincts on this.

Tanya was born and brought up hundreds of miles from the nearest Walmart in the Inuit community of Cambridge Bay. This is the real frozen north, more Arctic than Canada, an area where many European sailors once died trying to discover the Northwest Passage. There's nothing romantic about it: life there is tough and sometimes hellish, and the suicide rate is alarmingly high.

She went to art school in Halifax, NS. Then one day: "Tagaq's mother sent her a cassette tape of traditional throat singing. Although she was already familiar with the practice, she had never considered herself musical; then in her early twenties, emotionally unmoored and far from home, the songs affected her profoundly. She began imitating the sounds on her own, singing in the shower or lying on the floor, developing throat singing's rapid inhale-exhale technique. Sometimes, she wept as she did so." [20]

Learning about throat singing was also a step in Tanya's political education. Her eyes were opening to the fact that the reason Inuit culture was invisible, was that past Canadian governments had suppressed it, and the decline of the self-sustaining Inuit way of life was partly attributable to the forced relocations carried out by Canadian governments in the 1950s. As her career developed Tanya would speak out more and more on Inuit issues, making herself known as a fiercely committed champion of her people.

So began an extraordinary journey. Although the traditional throat singing helped her discover her own mode of expression, she uses her own techniques; in fact, almost nothing in a Tanya Tagaq performance is traditional. Her live shows are almost entirely improvised and are an intense emotional experience for all who've witnessed them. When, in 2014, Tanya won Canada's prestigious Polaris Music Prize for her album Animism (the other nominees included multi-million selling artists Drake and Arcade Fire), she was introduced on stage by the musician Geoff Berner:

"You can hear the living land, and the land under assault. You can hear children being born and conceived. You can hear the torture of the innocent, and the glory of the tenacious, unstoppable force of life. If you listen you can actually hear the sound of a people defying genocide to rise, wounded but alive, strong, and ready to fight." [21]

Undaunted, she delivered a remarkable set that blew away the distinguished music industry audience.

From the Animism album, **DAMP ANIMAL SPIRITS** is an experience as much as it is a song: the musical elements are overlaid with guttural growling and breathless gasping. For five or six minutes it moves towards a climax as the drumbeats get stronger and the vocal effects more intense. Then suddenly the background music dies away and the song enters a new phase: we hear a sequence of gasps and groans that sound like they've been ripped from the core of Tanya's being.

NOTES

1. http://www.greenmanreview.com/cd/cd_va_100ansQuebecoise.html, retrieved July, 2015
2. Alan Mills, liner notes to Old Time Fiddle Tunes Played by Jean Carignan (Folkways 1960), http://media.smithsonianfolkways.org/liner_notes/folkways/FW03531.pdf
3. Ibid.
4. http://www.stevewinick.com/bottine
5. https://www.popmatters.com/192008-le-vent-du-nord-confederation-audio-premiere-2495544373.html
6. http://news.nationalpost.com/news/canada/canadian-first-strongest-ties-are-to-country-respondents-tell-survey-on-belonging
7. http://www.rambles.net/payne_interview03.html
8. http://www.folkworld.de/32/e/morgan.html
9. http://citizenfreak.com/artists/95023-figgy-duff
10. http://www.thetelegram.com/News/Local/2013-12-02/article-3526170/Emilia-Bartellas-and-Aaron-Collis-of-The-Dardanelles-release-CD-as-a-duo/1, retrieved July, 2015

11. Quoted by Marie Thompson in The Myth of the Vanishing Cape Breton Fiddler, https://journals.lib.unb.ca/index.php/Acadiensis/article/view/10596/11209

12. Barry Shears – As I See It: Pipe Music in Cape Breton, http://theotherpipers.org/index/?p=4098

13. https://celticlife.com/kenneth-mackenzie/

14. Email 19/7/15.

15. *Ottawa Citizen*, 14th January 1985, https://news.google.com/newspapers?nid=2194&dat=19850114&id=ibwyAAAAIBAJ&sjid=We8FAAAAIBAJ&pg=3229,1960596&hl=en

16. http://www.billscorzari.com/heartstrings-magazine/blog/heartstrings-exclusive-old-meets-the-newpart-an-interview-with-april-verch

17. *Ottawa Citizen*, 13th April 2015, http://www.pressreader.com/canada/ottawa-citizen/20150413/281904476701925/TextView

18. http://nodepression.com/interview/%E2%80%98not-done-yet%E2%80%99-new-interview-sam-parton-part-ii

19. http://www.thefreelancewriter.ca/samples/music/Annie_Lou-Interview-EyesOnBC-Mar_2013.pdf

20. http://thewalrus.ca/howl

21. http://polarismusicprize.ca/blog/geoff-berners-introduction-speech-for-tanya-tagaq

COSTA RICA

I don't think I'm saying anything too controversial if I say that Costa Rican music has never really set the world alight: it does, however, have a few surprises in store. One of these is Manuel Obregón, who served as minister of culture and youth in Laura Chinchilla's government (2010–14). Obregón is not your average government minister. One, he's a professional musician: I'm looking at a photo on his website of him sat at a piano and clad in a white suit, with long, flowing white hair. Two, his creative work has led him into other disciplines such as dance, theatre and cinema. And three, his many past projects include lugging his piano deep inside the rainforest and recording an entire album there, so that he could capture the natural sounds of the jungle and weave these into the music.

Obregón is a visionary, a dreamer. He brought together 14 musicians from different Central American countries to form one ensemble: Orquesta de la Papaya. He wanted to create a band that would go back to its roots but be forward-thinking, and which could bring the musical traditions of Central America to the world. Well, it was a start. A seed had been planted, and it wasn't long before the first shoots began appearing:

ANORANZAS   *Pilar Rodríguez*

"I got calls from a number of places asking if it would be possible to create other orchestras of regional integration using the same format. So I began by visiting the Jesuit missions, which cover the territory that is now Brazil, Argentina, Paraguay and Bolivia, where the musical culture is immense... Orquesta de las Misiones grew out of this and evolved into Orquesta del Río Infinito." [1]

The Orquesta del Río Infinito was a group of musicians who travelled down the region's rivers, spending a few days in each community, not just performing but listening to local artists as well, having conversations about environmental issues and filming as they went along. "People say we're rescuing culture, but I think it's the other way around," says Obregón. "It's culture that will end up rescuing society. It's important to point out everything we still have to learn from these cultures and the natural environment." [2]

Obregón formed his own record label – Papaya Music – as a vehicle for his own projects and for other Central American musicians who shared the same kind of vision. It's worth taking a quick look at a couple of Papaya albums. A Todo Swing is a compilation of Costa Rican dance tunes that gives a sense of the range of Latin music genres that the people there love to listen to, from salsa to bolero and swing criollo. The album features some of the country's best dance orchestras, including Los Brillanticos, La Solucion, Calle 8 and Son de Tikizia. By contrast, Babylon was an album of very traditional acoustic calypso songs by an unassuming master of the genre, Walter Ferguson.

Walter Ferguson was born in Panama but since he was a toddler has lived in Cahuita, a small town on Costa Rica's Caribbean coast with a mainly Afro-Caribbean population. He learned to play music on borrowed instruments and his knowledge of calypso came from listening to many of the original calypso greats perform. He seems to have been a bit of a latecomer to songwriting, but once he'd started writing calypsos he couldn't stop: his songs are beautifully simple, rooted in the life he knew in Cahuita. He would probably be a forgotten figure today had not Obregón persuaded him, in his 80s, to record an album. Ferguson had only one condition: he didn't want to travel to San Jose to record, so Obregón rigged up a studio in his Cahuita home, covering the walls with mattresses to shut out the noises of the street. The result was so successful that Obregón later returned to Cahuita to make a second album.

In July 2016, musical groups from across the region with a shared love of calypso music descended on Cahuita for the 4th edition of the Festival Internacional de Calipso Walter Ferguson. Ferguson himself, now 97 and losing his eyesight, played no part in the weekend's events, but I understand that more than a few veteran calypsonians knocked on the door of his modest home and paid their respects.

I liked Walter Ferguson's story, but I wanted to listen to Costa Roca's national instrument, the marimba, and to its Spanish-influenced dances such as the tambito, the pasilla and the parrandera. The best place for these kinds of music, I learn, is Guanacaste province, on the northern reaches of Costa Rica's

Pacific coast. At this point, however, I start to run into difficulties. There are no big stars popularising the music, and there's none of the compilations that are often indicators of a high level of activity. One group of note are Los de la Bajura from Santa Cruz, who've released over 20 albums of marimba-led music since the early 1990s, but after a time-consuming search I have to concede defeat: I've not found any sites where I can purchase any of these albums, either digitally or in CD format. For a time the group organised a festival of music from Guanacaste, called Guanafest, but this doesn't appear to be still going.

The core issue is that most Costa Ricans don't claim the music as their own: it doesn't reinforce their sense of identity. Marimbas are large, expensive instruments predominantly played by old men; tambito and parrandera aren't part of any national myth; they're descriptors of rhythms that will very often be used as part of a wider repertoire that includes other Latin musical styles.

There are other dreamers though, like Manuel Obregón, who believe that Costa Rica can reclaim its musical heritage. One of these is Abel Guadamuz, a founder member of Los de la Bajura, who has devoted much effort into giving classes in Santa Cruz where young people can learn to play the marimba and how the traditional rhythms should be performed. Another is Randy Juarez, who's been giving training in the skilled art of marimba construction in the hope of replenishing the small and dwindling number of marimba makers. [3]

Guanacaste en Voz de Mujer (Guanacaste in women's voice) is a project by Karol Cabalceta, a young Guanacaste musician who works at the Ministry of Public Education. She's put together a compilation of original songs by seven female composer/singers of the province. The songs were mostly written some time ago, but all seven women are still alive and through the project have been given an opportunity to tell something of their own stories. It's a low-key project, but somehow it reassures me that there is some vitality in Guanacaste music yet. Here are women, most of whom have had limited musical training, yet what comes across in their singing is a genuine love and feeling for these Spanish inspired rhythms.

Pilar Rodriguez's **ANORANZAS** is a song about lost traditions: it won her first place at el Grano de Oro Festival in 1989. The marimba and the easy flowing rhythm place it within rural Costa Rican tradition, but there is also a confidence and a smoothness of execution here that broaden the song's appeal. Pilar, we're told, grew up in a family of musicians: her father, grandparents and uncles were once part of the Banda Nacional de Guanacaste, and most were marimba players. Now a music teacher and a multi-instrumentalist, she herself is a preserver of lost traditions, a specialist in Guanacaste music and song from the 1920s. [4]

NOTES

1. http://panorama2go.com/Contenido/web/articulo/EN/530
2. Ibid.
3. http://www.nacion.com/archivo/Zumba-zumba-marimba_0_1149285149.html
4. http://www.vozdeguanacaste.com/es/articulos/2016/07/15/las-cantoras-de-guanacaste

CUBA

The story of Buena Vista Social Club is too well known to repeat here. How the American guitarist Ry Cooder and the British producer Nick Gold went to Cuba for one project and ended up working on another project entirely: gathering together a few veteran musicians to record an album of son music. The album, and the film of its making, both went on to become unlikely smash hits around the globe. More important than all the millions of units sold and all the awards collected, Buena Vista Social Club found an enduring place in people's hearts, transforming perceptions of Cuban music and culture and helping Cuba become a favourite destination for the culture-savvy traveller.

Almost the only place that greeted Buena Vista Social Club with less than unbridled enthusiasm was Cuba itself. The project didn't receive a lot of exposure in Cuba, and only slowly and over a period of some time did most Cubans gradually become aware of the kind of success that the film had had internationally. Even then, the reaction was mixed. While some were delighted to see Cuban culture getting the attention that it deserved, others had reservations. The name Buena Vista Social Club had once belonged to an actual club in Havana, which closed down in the 1940s – before the revolution. And here were a group of ageing

QUE BUENO BAILA USTED	Benny Moré
NO ME VAYAS A ENGANAR	Omara Portuondo
MADURO, PERO SABROSO	Septeto Santiaguero
TA' JULIAN	Muñequitos de Matanzas
FEY OH DI NOU	The Creole Choir of Cuba
MADRES	Daymé Arocena

musicians, at least some of whom had started their careers before Castro came to power, playing a style of music that had long since gone out of fashion in revolutionary Cuba. Now this was being packaged and sold to American audiences as 'authentic' Cuban music, but was it really so authentic?

The idea that the 1940s and '50s were a golden age in Cuban music is not one that you're likely to hear repeated very often inside Cuba. Stories are still told of how Havana had become a playground for wealthy Americans, how gambling and prostitution had become rife, how racial segregation was enforced in some of the popular nightspots frequented by the Americans. Fidel Castro changed all this, closing down the casinos and nightclubs and banning segregation in public places. For some, this was a threat to the lifestyle to which they'd become accustomed. Celia Cruz had grown up in poverty, but had spent the last decade performing with one of the most popular ensembles of the day, La Sonora Matancera. The entire group fled Cuba after Castro came to power. And there were other major figures who went into exile around the same time, men such as Bebo Valdés and

Cachao. Outside of the real high-end nightspots from which they were generally excluded, Afro-Cuban musicians earned modest levels of pay. So, when Castro offered all working musicians a guaranteed salary, most were happy to take it. There were serious downsides: performing in the USA or even selling records in the huge US market was impossible as long as they remained in Cuba; access to radio and television and the opportunity to perform abroad was all dependent on the state; and so forth. On the other hand, the stability that the state provided elongated many careers. And some of these careers were quite remarkable. When his father, Bebo Valdés, fled Cuba, Chucho Valdés was a mere 18 years old, but he chose to remain. In 1967, he was a founder member of Orquesta Cubana de Música Moderna, a big band that employed many of the country's finest singers and musicians. A few years later he formed the pioneering group Irakere, who mixed jazz and a range of other styles with wild abandon. It was the start of a journey that would win him worldwide acclaim and five Grammy awards.

So before Buena Vista Social Club came along, although the only Cuban music that most Americans had been exposed to was the music of exiles such as Celia Cruz and Gloria Estefan, Cuba was far from being a cultural desert. In fact, in Cuba, the music of the exiles was banned from the airwaves and so was rarely heard, so people's pride was reserved for home-based artists. With all this in mind, I want to go back in the next few paragraphs to the music of the 1940s and '50s and to ask the question: what made it so great?

By 1940 the seeds of change were germinating. More young people were getting an education, and there was a growing consciousness among the underprivileged Afro-Cuban community, which had begun to express itself through literature and the arts. Arsenio Rodriguez, who had been blind since childhood when he was kicked in the head by a horse, was one of many young black musicians then trying to get a foothold in an industry in which discrimination had long been rife. (Even white musicians played a part in this. In 1932, some Afro-Cuban musicians formed their own union because the established musicians' union barred those who couldn't read music, which included most black musicians at the time.)

When Arsenio arrived on the scene American-style jazz music was all the rage. Son, which had flourished briefly in the 1920s, seemed destined to become a footnote to history. Arsenio changed all that by transforming the son band (conjunto), and hence also giving the music a complete makeover.

> *"Rodriguez improved [the sound] by using two or three trumpets instead of one, and introduced a piano, and later a conguero (conga drummer)... [he] also added a new repertoire and a variety of rhythms and harmonic concepts to enrich the son, the bolero, the guaracha and some fusions, such as the bolero-mambo and the bolero-son... The overall 'feel' of the Rodriguez conjunto was more African than other Cuban conjuntos." [1]*

Yet another element was the campana (a large cowbell), which also added to the African flavour. This was a new type of big band dance music, and it caught on like wildfire. Conjuntos were springing up everywhere. The hand-played conga drum, which not so long ago had been sneered at as jungle music, was now very much in demand. White jazz bands still pulled the crowds at the most prestigious venues, but they too loved the music and infectious rhythms of the conjuntos. Mambo, popularised by Perez Prado in the early 1950s, borrowed from Afro-Cuban rhythms.

Beny Moré was used to living on the edge: the oldest of 18 kids, he'd never had any money to speak of. He would only have been 16 or 17 when he first headed into Havana, spending six months selling fruit and vegetables in the street with his uncle before returning home and hooking up with his brother, the two of them finding work cutting cane. He got himself a new guitar, but with no musical training at all his prospects didn't look good. Within a few years, though, he was back in Havana, street selling by day and wandering from bar to bar at night playing to anyone who'd listen for a few coins. He won a radio contest and things picked up a little from there, but his real break came after Ciro Rodríguez of Conjunto Matamoros heard him singing in a bar. One day the group's singer was unwell and Moré was invited to stand in. He must have impressed, because the group adopted him soon after as their new lead singer.

Moré travelled to Mexico with the Conjunto Matamoros. They were a successful band, and he must have learned a huge amount through performing all the popular song styles, but after a time he got itchy feet: there was more that he wanted to do, and felt capable of. After parting company with the band, he remained in Mexico, where he found work recording with leading orchestras and appearing in films. Most notably he joined Perez Prado's orchestra for a period in the late '40s when the 'King of Mambo' was at the height of his powers.

Now famous across the Caribbean, he came back to conquer Cuba. In 1953, he formed the band he'd been dreaming of for years which he called Banda Gigante (giant band). So now this country boy who still couldn't read a note of music was directing a large orchestra with some of the country's finest musicians. "He created all the arrangements for his orchestra by humming the different parts of each instrument to the musician playing it. He directed his band with a cane and his body movements." [2] The band played many styles of music and, as a singer, Moré was equally adept with slow, sentimental boleros, picking up the rhythm of a quick mambo, or firing out the hard-hitting lyrics of a guaracha. QUE BUENO BAILA USTED is a son; the drumming and clacking rhythm could only have come from an Afro-Cuban band, but what I like about it is that the horns, the strings and percussion are all in perfect balance; there's a natural harmony to the piece, which was composed by Beny Moré himself.

Success came at a price: Moré lived to excess and became an alcoholic. By 1959, his health was fast deteriorating. He remained in Cuba after the revolution, where he must have driven his doctors to despair by refusing to rest, performing around the country and fulfilling numerous engagements, and staying on the booze. In 1963, at the age of just 43, he died from cirrhosis of the liver. We're told that 100,000 people attended his funeral.

Buena Vista Social Club looked back to pre-revolutionary Cuba, but in a very specific way. The original Buena Vista Social Club was one of many clubs for blacks that flourished in Havana in the 1950s, a place where Afro-Cuban son music was regularly played. And the Buena Vista album was a celebration of son music, which has become such an integral part of Cuban culture. So the ensemble included Rubén González, who'd played in Arsenio Rodríguez's band, and it included Pio Leyva, who'd sang back-up for Beny Moré and written one of his hits, and Francisco Guayabal. He also sang with Bebo Valdez.

In October 2015, a small group of Buena Vista musicians led by Omara Portuondo and Eliades Ochoa played at the White House, becoming the first Cuban-based musicians (as opposed to émigrés) to play there in over half a century. Obama told them that he'd bought the Buena Vista CD when it came out in 1998.

Omara Portuondo was then approaching her 85th birthday. Back when she was still a sprightly 77, Mondomix magazine asked her if she had any regrets. "Regrets? There are those that all people know, such as no longer having my parents. Luckily, I have a son and a granddaughter. If I stumble, I get up. It's my nature and my strength. As far as music is concerned, I have none. All was so positive! I shared the stage with amazing artists from Nat King Cole to Maurice Chevalier taking in Ibrahim Ferrer... the list is long." [3] On the Buena Vista film, she and Ibrahim Ferrer duetted on the achingly beautiful Silencio. As the song finished she couldn't restrain the tears, and Ibrahim reached over to dab her face.

What else could Omara be but a lover of romance? Her own mother was a woman from a rich Spanish family who married for love, to a tall, black Cuban baseball player, at a time when mixed race marriages were almost unheard of and highly scandalous. No surprise either that Omara loves to mix cultures in her music, and a feature of her long recording career has been that she's never stood still, she's also welcomed in different musical influences. Nonetheless, I can't help feeling that since joining up with the Buena Vista musicians she's found her true musical home. In 2000, a Buena Vista follow-up CD was released, Buena Vista Social Club presents... Omara Portuondo. A collection of 11 songs in the familiar styles of son, guajira and bolero played by the Buena Vista ensemble, it places Omara's vocals at the centre of every track. From the first notes on Rubén González's piano you know that NO ME VAYAS A ENGAÑAR is going to have a timeless, classic quality. The arrangement is perfect, leaving you hanging on every word that Omara sings. All achieved, as Omara reminds us, without formal musical training: "None of the band who acted in the Buena Vista Social Club had conservatory training, but we were born with the need to sing and to play." [4]

Although Buena Vista's success surprised everyone, Cuba's traditional music had never gone away; it was always there if you looked for it. The previous decade had been a very harsh time for anyone living in Cuba, a deep economic crisis brought on by the collapse of the Soviet Union. There was very little fuel for cars, energy was in short supply, basic goods were scarce and food was rationed. The state record company Egrem lost its government subsidies. So of course it had been a difficult decade for musicians. Despite this, many of the Buena Vista musicians were still performing; indeed some of them including Rubén González, Ibrahim Ferrer, Pío Leyva and Cachaíto had already recorded an album with Nick Gold a couple of years earlier under the name Afro-Cuban All Stars. And, entirely separate from this, in 1995, a traditional son group was formed in Santiago de Cuba calling itself the Septeto Santiaguero.

In two decades the group has never wavered in its commitment to the traditional forms of dance music, and for this we can thank one man, Fernando Dewar, who founded the group and has directed it ever since through countless line-up changes. The personnel may have changed but the group are still a septet, with three singers, guitar, bass, trumpet and drums, creating a full and exciting sound. Their 2010 album, Oye Mi Son Santiaguero, was released through a Spanish label because the Cuban economy was once again going through a crisis. "It includes songs in our usual genres – son, bolero-son, la guaracha – that we've been playing for some time, but have never recorded," says Dewar, "but it also goes further back to the roots of Cuban music with genres such as nengón and changui. The last two are similar: they're country rhythms from Eastern Cuba, from Granma and Guantanamo, and towns such as Bayamo and Manzanillo." [5]

The Septeto do south-eastern Cuba proud. MADURO, PERO SABROSO grabs you with its explosive horn sound and won't let you go: it's fast, frantic and fun. After years of hard graft the band are now enjoying some recognition and success, in which I include their two Grammy nominations. Dewar may now be able to pay the rent, but his goals are much the same: to continue exploring the roots of Cuban music and to inspire others to revisit the old musical styles.

In recognising Dewar's achievement, it must also be recognised that he has been swimming against the tide. In the 1990s the dominant musical style in Cuba was timba, an urban folk genre that used son rhythms and created a dense sound by adding modern instruments such as keyboards, and brushing against other genres such as rock, jazz and hip hop. Among the pioneers of the new style were NG La Banda, a group put together by flautist José Luis Cortés after he was dropped from Chucho Valdés's Irakere. According to Professor of Ethnomusicology

Robin Moore, "timba is performed primarily by black Cubans", and consciously references Afro-Cuban culture. [6] "Timba," he says, "is written in the direct parlance of the street... often including slang words and phrases from poorer black neighbourhoods. Lyrical themes are often ironic, humorous, bawdy and irreverent. Many songs deprecate women, describing them as shallow, vain and mercenary in their use of sexuality." [7] Born at a time of poverty and deprivation, it's a music of the slums, and by the 21st century another form of street music was flourishing in Cuba's slums: hip hop.

Since the mid-1990s the Cuban music scene has mushroomed. There's a proliferation of new groups and a proliferation of musical styles. A lot of this is rhythm-based dance music. I understand the sentiments of those who look nostalgically back to the past, and to the brilliant musicianship and the charm of those 1950s combos. But what we're seeing now is a freedom and a space for self-expression that Cuban music hasn't enjoyed for many years, and this makes for exciting possibilities for roots and acoustic musicians who want to connect with new audiences. What follows is just a small sample of some of the interesting directions that musicians are taking.

Hearing **TA' JULIAN** comes as a shock: this sounds more like West African music than Caribbean music. The band chant in harmony while pounding on congo drums and cajon box drums: it's a powerful physical sound probably best appreciated live, when you also get to see the superb dancers who are attached to the group. A strong melody also makes the song very accessible. The album is from 2009, but Los Muñequitos de Matanzas were formed in 1952 by a group of dockworkers in the port city of Matanzas. Their music is derived from the customs of Santeria, a Caribbean belief system that developed out of mythologies brought to the New World by Yoruba slaves. Many band members belong to abakua, Afro-Cuban male fraternities that have their own rituals and ceremonies.

In the run-up to their 50th anniversary celebrations, the band played for the first time in Miami and Bárbaro Ramos Aldazabal gave an interview to an American magazine. We learn that Bárbaro's grandfather danced with the group in its early days, and that his father is director of the group. All but one of the founder members of the group had already passed away, but, in Bárbaro's words, "we stay very close to the vision of the founders of the group." [8] Some of their songs honour the Orisha spirits, and some are traditional rumbas: a potent reminder that all Afro-Cuban music can trace its ancestry to the culture of African slaves.

Rumba has always been outside of the mainstream, never officially recognised. Much of its history isn't recorded; it lives in people's memories. The En Clave de Rumba project is trying to preserve this heritage, seeking out people in every region who can tell them something of the history, and collecting information and testimonies. "Many prejudices remain," says musicologist and activist Cary Diez, "but Cuba's cultural policies have been geared towards preserving the tradition. Rumba bands have recorded albums... but an immense number of other bands remain unknown. We've had spaces for rumba music, like Sabados de la Rumba, the Callejon de Hamel and the Peña del Ambia." [9] Cary Diez has also been working with a number of rumba bands.

The Creole Choir of Cuba make music that's totally their own. In Cuba they're called Desandann and I think I prefer that name, which carries with it a stronger sense of identity because Desandann (descendants) is exactly who they are. They all have Haitian blood in their veins. They're among hundreds of thousands of Cubans whose ancestors came over from Haiti at certain times in that country's turbulent history – after Spanish, Haitian Creole is the second most commonly spoken language in Cuba.

The Creole Choir are a choir: various instruments are used in their recordings, but the instruments seem a little superfluous. The vocal harmonies are so good that you wouldn't feel cheated if you had to listen to them without accompaniment. The group was formed by members of a professional choir in Camaguey, so they're all musically trained to a high level.

There is state support in Cuba for Haitian arts and culture, a few Haitian-Cuban cultural festivals have become regular events, and the Creole Choir have played their part in promoting these events, which have helped the community discover a sense of itself. The community has had no prouder or sadder moment than in January 2010. This was when the country of Haiti was laid to waste by a magnitude 7 earthquake, which killed tens of thousands of people. No country responded more quickly or more generously than Cuba. As part of the relief effort, Cuba sent a contingent of several hundred doctors and health workers, and the Creole Choir travelled with them. And they stayed in Haiti for weeks, singing in hospitals, orphanages and makeshift camps during the day and sleeping on mats at night in the hospital courtyard. They found that by singing in Creole they could break down barriers: "We went to an orphanage and the children had no idea what had happened to their parents because they were too young to understand... There was a very frightened child who wouldn't approach us, but after singing in his own language, totally changed and we helped him to recover." [10]

Following on from this, they've released two albums on Peter Gabriel's Real World label which have established them as one of the most admired acts on the world music scene. The first thing that strikes you about both albums is their diversity. As their manager, Kelso Riddell, explains it, "they sing in all different genres because Haiti has such a varied and rich, rich culture musically. There are songs which make you happy. There are songs which make you laugh. There are songs which make you cry. And there are songs which make you just get up and want to dance." [11] The songs deal with a range of subjects, including one that reflects on the earthquake. But their aim isn't to make a statement: they want to convey their love of Haiti and its culture, and you can't help but feel this love in **FEY OH DI NOU**, a song about traditional healing. Both lead and backing vocals are female and it's a very melodic soothing sound. There are several differences between the two albums, and one of these is that, while on the first the male vocals are quite prominent, the later release, Santiman, is a much more female album.

I can't let you leave Cuba without inviting you to listen to some Cuban jazz music. Since the 1940s, Cuban musicians have been breaking with American jazz and developing their own grooves. One name that often crops up is that of Dizzy Gillespie, who spent quite a bit of time working with Afro-Cuban musicians. Over the years Cuba has produced many, many important and original jazz musicians. Many of them are featured in the Jazzcuba series on Rumor Records, which runs into at least 20 CDs. It's a retrospective compilation, focusing on music recorded between the 1950s and the 1980s, but it certainly seems like a useful introduction. Since the 1980s the Havana International Jazz Festival has been attracting people to Cuba from far and wide. Among the Cuban artists who've often graced its stage are Chucho Valdés and Bobby Carcassés.

Daymé Arocena is a young jazz singer at the start of her career. **MADRES**, the standout track from her debut album, is full of little joys and surprises. Daymé belongs to the Santeria faith, and Madres is a prayer song to her two spirit mothers Yemaya and Ochun. The song evokes the hushed mood of an Afro-Cuban prayer ritual; you're almost seduced into thinking that it was recorded in some natural setting, but there's a lot more going on than this: sound effects and samples are being built up using modern production techniques, there are layered vocals in Yoruba and Spanish.

Is this the face of modern Cuba? Daymé learned about Santeria culture from her grandmother and sang Santeria songs at school; she studied Western classical music at the Conservatory and developed an interest in choral music before deciding to turn her hand to jazz; she also has a love of American soul music, which comes over strongly on her album. "Cuban musicians," she says, "are always trying to learn from everywhere and showing us around the world... Every day you can discover a new rhythm or a really good young player doing something really fresh and deep. Cuba is a paradise to discover... even more than all the old traditions that the people know." [12]

And though the rest of the album doesn't quite fulfil the promise of Madres, Daymé carries with her a rare vitality, and I feel sure that there's a lot more to come. It will be fascinating to see how she marries her Afro-Cuban heritage with her other musical passions in the future.

NOTES

1. http://www.thecubanhistory.com/2015/05/arsenio-rodriguez-cubas-marvellous-music-blind-man-arsenio-rodriguez-el-ciego-maravilloso-de-la-musica-cubana
2. Viviana Carballo – Havana Salsa: Stories and Recipes (Atria Books, 2007), p182.
3. http://www.mondomix.com/news/omara-portuondo-comblee-par-la-vie, retrieved March, 2016
4. http://www.elconfidencial.com/cultura/2012-07-28/omara-portuondo-las-raices-musicales-nos-identifican-a-todos_502852
5. http://www.klavelatina.com/id134.html
6. Robin D. Moore – Music and Revolution: Cultural Change in Socialist Cuba (University of California Press, 2006), p125.
7. Ibid., p128.
8. http://www.salsapower.com/Interviews/munequitos-de-matanzas.html
9. http://www.havanatimes.org/?p=99883
10. http://www.bbc.com/mundo/america_latina/2010/05/100521_haiti_cuba_coro_consuelo_victimas_terremoto_refugiados_concierto_fp.shtml
11. http://www.npr.org/2011/10/24/141652174/creole-choir-boasts-roots-in-haiti-fame-in-cuba
12. http://revive-music.com/2015/06/09/okp-first-look-dayme-arocena-dont-unplug-my-body-video-interview/#.VuCyjak0HQl

DOMINICA

Dominica is a tiny Caribbean island (29 miles long by 16 miles wide) with a wealth of natural resources, notably the beautiful rainforest that covers the island. Its main export trade is in bananas, but world trade wars in bananas have hit Dominica hard. The number of banana farmers is a fraction of what it used to be, and without the support of Fairtrade it would be lower still.

One export that has seen some growth is eco-tourism. The rivers that run down from the mountains provide the island with a natural water supply and half of its electricity. Large parts of the island are designated as National Park and as eco-tourism sites. A former English backpacker, Jem Winston, created the 3 Rivers & Rosalie Forest Eco Lodge. Indian-born Hitesh Mehta, who's a big hitter in the eco-tourism industry, opened the Kwanari Ecolodge in December 2013. These places certainly sound very tempting…

For a population of 70,000 people, Dominica has also exported more than its share of music. Two men who can claim some credit for this are Gordon Henderson (born 1949) and Jeff Joseph (born 1953).

Henderson moved to Guadeloupe in 1970 to become the lead singer of the group Les Vikings. He recorded several songs with the band that became hits. But before long he was moving

PAS DANSEZ EN BAS COCO SEC   *Les Gramacks*

on again. In 1973, he formed his own group, Exile One, which included Dominican musicians as well as a Trinidadian and two Guadeloupeans. Over the years the group would retain its international character through many line-up changes. Exile One were original and adventurous in their music from day one. It wasn't long before they'd developed a new style, which they called Cadence-lypso. Cadence-lypso drew on the varied roots of Dominican culture. French and English settlers have both laid their mark on the island, as has the history of slavery in the Caribbean. English is the official language, but many speak a French-based patois called Kwéyòl. Cadence-lypso was a marriage between calypso (a music of the English-speaking Caribbean) and cadence rampa from francophone Haiti. Lyrics were often sung in Kwéyòl, which was a revolutionary step at the time.

One of the first bands to adopt the new cadence rhythms was Gramacks. The name was derived from the names of the two high schools that the band members had attended (Dominica Grammar and St Mary's Academy). Jeff Joe (Jeff Joseph) wasn't an original member but joined the band and became lead singer. In 1974, the band made the trip to Guadeloupe, where Exile One was based, and cut their first record. **PAS DANSEZ EN BAS COCO SEC** is a lively and entertaining song from their 1975 album. In 1976 they recorded their most famous song, Wooy Mi Debar (Look Trouble), which was inspired by a fight at one of their gigs. The song opened doors for them, and in 1977 they did a deal with the organisers of the Tour de France to follow the Tour and perform their songs.

Other Cadence-lypso bands of the 1970s were Midnight Groovers, Liquid Ice and Bill-O-Men. It was a time of national awakening: Dominica was granted independence by the UK in 1978. The music helped to strengthen a sense of national identity, partly through the traditional rhythms and use of Kwéyòl but also through the directness and frankness of the lyrics. Exile One's Twavay Pou Anyen dealt with the history of slavery, while Bill-O-Men had a song entitled Grève Général (General Strike). Other songs addressed everyday social realities.

For a few short years Cadence-lypso was popular in Dominica and across the Caribbean before going into a rapid decline from which it's never really recovered. In its place grew zouk music: a carnival music whose rhythms are a variant of Cadence-lypso.

Jeff Joseph died in November 2011, shortly after performing at the 15th World Creole Music Festival, an event that he played a big part in helping to promote. The country's prime minister, Roosevelt Skerrit, said, "Jeff Joe was no doubt synonymous with Dominica in the French countries from Paris to the French departments of Guadeloupe and Martinique, local Caledonia and French Guyana. He was no doubt a true ambassador of our country promoting our art form, promoting our country as a whole and really encouraging people to visit Dominica. I believe the entire country is in shock as a result of his death." [1]

Gordon Henderson lives these days in France. Previously, as international director of Dominica's World Creole Music Festival, he's played a pivotal role in bringing international stars to the island while also promoting Dominica and its music. His book

Zoukland, written in English and French, journeys through the history of Caribbean Creole music. He's currently pushing for the introduction of world Creole music awards.

NOTES

1. http://www.mnialive.com/caribbean/171-connect/1695-a-tribute-to-dominicas-cultural-ambassador-jeff-joe-v15-1695.html

DOMINICAN REPUBLIC

Merengue, the national music of the Dominican Republic, is traditionally played on three instruments: diatonic accordion, tambora and guira. The accordion, which replaced the guitar as the lead instrument a century or so ago, embodies the European influence on the music, while the two-headed tambora drum, and the metal scraper that is the guira, are of older origin.

To Dominicans, these instruments carry great significance. They're a link to the culture of their ancestors, a signifier of national identity. And on the eastern half of the island of Hispaniola people set a lot of stock in matters of identity. The country has been permanently separated from Haiti since the 1840s, but the chain of events that led to the division began decades earlier, when slaves successfully rose against their masters and took control of the island. Most of the former slaves were to remain in Haiti, thus entrenching a racial division. Haitians are nearly all black, while most Dominicans self-identify as blanco (white) or indios (Indian). They describe themselves as of Spanish or Taino origin, not acknowledging any African or Haitian blood. Former leader, Rafael Trujillo, used to have his skin whitened, a practice that keeps the local beauty industry lucrative to this day.

EL PROBLEMA DE RAMON   El Ciego De Nagua
EL BAJADERO   El Prodigio
MARIA ELENA   Joan Soriano

In recent decades the fortunes of the two countries have been in marked contrast. While the Dominican Republic (DR) has enjoyed political stability, an expanding economy and a booming tourist trade, Haiti, even before the devastating 2010 earthquake, was politically unstable, poor, debt-ridden and notoriously corrupt. Dominicans deny accusations of anti-Haitian racism: they say they're the good guys, they've taken in refugees and migrants, and they were the first to give help after the earthquake. However, the influx of refugees following the earthquake has clearly raised tensions. Since 2013, battles have been fought in the country's highest courts over whether the government have the right to expel tens of thousands of Dominican-born children of undocumented migrants. There is overwhelming popular support for the government's position.

Scientific studies tell us that today's Dominicans are of mixed ethnicity: most possess DNA of African origin, while only 15% have genes from the indigenous Taino people who greeted Columbus in 1492. [1] Within the country there are longstanding 'black' communities who practise recognisably African cultural traditions. One such, the Brotherhood of the Holy Spirit of the Congos of Villa Mella, was formally recognised by Unesco in 2001 for its cultural significance. Founded by African slaves in the 16th century, they worship the goddess Calunga, celebrate the festival of the Holy Spirit and dance to the pounding of drums at festivals and funeral rites. For many years until his death in 2008, Sixto Minier led the Brotherhood through poverty and hard times – "my job," he would say, "is not to let our tradition ever fade away." [2] The Ministry of Culture co-sponsored a CD of their music and a documentary DVD to mark Sixto's death.

And, yes, merengue also has African music in its DNA. Despite the claims that the guira is an indigenous instrument that was used by the Taino, little or no evidence exists of Taino musical practices, and Fradique Lizardo has argued more plausibly that the instrument was introduced in the New World by African slaves. The tambora drum originated too from West Africa.

It was in the DR, though, among the poorest sections of society, that the music (in the form known as merengue tipico), and the associated merengue dance were born. Among the first great accordionists was Nico Lora (1880–1971). From a young age he worked as a farm labourer with his father. He loved the merengue, but his father had no savings, so he ran extra chores himself to earn the extra cents he needed to help him buy his first accordion. When finally he owned an instrument, he had to teach himself to play it, as he'd no formal education or musical training. He went on to become a prolific composer, writing hundreds of merengues inspired by his love of the country and the world in which he lived. He was known as a brilliant improviser who could write songs on any subject at a moment's notice.

Few places can have produced more acordeonistas than the industrial coastal town of Nagua. Ramón Amézquita Díaz, known as Matoncito, moved to Nagua from Los Llanos de Altamira. Francisco Ulloa, no mean accordionist himself, said of him that, "what we, the musicians of today, do with two rows, Maton did with only one." [3] He never had much money, and left no recordings behind, but his legacy survives in the memories of those who heard him play and the musicians who studied under him.

One of these was Tatico Henriquez (1943–76). Tatico's father and his uncle were accordionists too, and they were his first instructors. I read that he was employed early on by his local baseball team, as all the baseball teams took a tipico trio with them to provide entertainment. At the end of his apprenticeship with Matoncito, he was recruited by one of the country's leading tipica trios, Trio Reynoso, to replace the recently deceased Pedro Reynoso. At the time, Nagua had no shortage of able accordionists, but Tatico outshone them all. He went on to form his own band, Tatico y sus Muchachos, and introduced new instruments to the traditional ensemble. His name is revered in Nagua to this day.

Pereira González "Bartolo" Alvarado (born 1947) was born blind, one of a family of 10 children. He started drumming when he was barely old enough to walk. After practising on the harmonica, he took up the accordion at the age of seven or eight and performed on a radio talent show when aged nine. He was from the border village of La Jaguita, but after he earned himself a weekly two-hour slot on Radio Nagua he was dubbed El Ciego de Nagua (the blind man of Nagua), and the name stuck. He had his own following and was even regarded as a competitor of Tatico Henriquez.

The track **EL PROBLEMA DE RAMON** is old-style merengue tipica. Without the addition of extra instruments it's got a light, easy feel. The accordionist seems to have more freedom to express himself: at any rate, the jaunty playing on the song matches the wicked fun in Bartolo's voice.

El Prodigio was not even born when El Ciego de Nagua laid down his song, but in **EL BAJADERO** he shows in splendid fashion that merengue tipica still has plenty of life left in it. Improvisation had always been a part of tipica: it's the prerogative of the accordionist, usually when they do their solo during the latter part of the song. El Prodigio takes this and runs with it, letting loose with his accordion from the very start of the track. It's fast, freewheeling and exhilarating. He's from Cabrera, which is just a few miles up the coast from Nagua, and he's a great admirer of El Ciego de Nagua. So, while he loves to experiment, he's also respectful of merengue tipica and is careful not to let go of its danceable melodies and sense of joy. After a long career in music, El Ciego must have been delighted to be invited by the young star to perform on album tracks and concerts, and in 2012 he was among the stars performing at his protégé's wedding, along with female accordionist, Fefita La Grande, and singer, Sergio Vargas.

Merengue tipico had travelled a long journey since Nico Lora first picked up the accordion. At that time, the elite classes regarded it as an inferior form of entertainment, probably for a combination of reasons: it was also referred to as perico ripiado, reputedly the name of a brothel; the lyrics were often suggestive; and the merengue dance in which couples danced together was seen as overly sexual. Its status changed after Rafael Trujillo, himself of modest origins, seized power in 1930 and actively promoted the music. Today, the music itself is transforming as a result of globalisation. Not only can American music be heard everywhere in the DR, but there are now a million immigrants from the DR living in the United States. As merengue competes within a crowded Latin music market, tipico bands are turning to electronic instruments, while 'pop merengue' artists fuse merengue with other styles such as disco and salsa. Juan Luis Guerra still lives in the DR, though he was educated at Berklee College of Music in Boston. He has two Grammys and 15 Latin Grammys to his name. His style can't be summed up in a single word or phrase, because he's always moving on, as he incorporates different rhythms in his music. But there's always an intelligence and a maturity to what he does: he's often sung about social issues, and his 440 Foundation has provided much-needed medical care to many Dominicans.

Another threat to merengue tipico comes from bachata music. Bachata is a guitar-led music that deals with subjects of romance and heartbreak, and is associated with the bachata dance, which is derived from the bolero. Not unlike merengue, for decades it was a marginalised rural form of music. According to Benjamin de Menil, "despite bachata's popularity, TV and radio stations in the Dominican Republic would not play it and neither would the upscale performance venues. That began to change in the late 1980s but there are still remnants of that attitude today." [4] Likewise, Joan Soriano (born 1972) recalls that: "I started listening to bachata when I was a kid. Back then there was only one radio station that played bachata in the DR, it was Radio Guarachita, which I used to listen to every day with my family. That was it. No one else played it because bachata wasn't popular then." [5]

From the 1990s, the popularity of the genre grew rapidly. But it did so, claims de Menil, by turning its back on its acoustic roots: "bachata went electric in the 1990s and along with that change the music adopted a pop ballad sound." For de Menil, coming into contact with old-style bachata musicians came as a revelation:

"I was taking New York's F train uptown. When the doors opened at the 14th street station I heard an incredible voice coming from the platform. It was a Dominican singer I would later work with for many years, Super Uba. I had just begun putting together a home studio at the time, so I invited him over. He arrived with Edilio Paredes, the legendary guitarist of the Bachata Roja Legends. I had never heard the old school bachata before and as soon as Edilio and Uba began playing I knew I had to do something to get this music out to a wider audience." [6]

That was in 2001. Within months he'd formed his own label, iASO Records, to record an album by Super Uba's band, but marketing it proved difficult. He found himself a job at the NYC-based world music label, Putamayo, then went to study at Harvard Business School. And then, having got his Harvard degree, he decided that what he really wanted to do was to promote bachata music. He began seeking out the best bachata musicians that he could find, and trying to get them to sign to his New York label.

Over the last decade, iASO has become a good model of what a small independent world music label should look like. It's focused on one genre. It has its own philosophy: that everything they release should be recorded live, with no overdubs. It has a first-class website, full of resources and information. And it's released some of the finest bachata albums around: albums by Super Uba, Joan Soriano, the veteran Puerto Plata, and supergroup The Bachata Legends.

In 2013, iASO teamed up with non-profit organisation the DREAM Project to open a music academy in a school built by DREAM in Cabarete. "We announced to the classes, 'We're offering music lessons in bachata. If you are interested, please come to the tryout,'" de Menil says. "Pretty much every student came. There were hundreds of them." [7] The only problem is that they just have capacity for 40 students, but maybe one of these days the funds will be found to open another Bachata Academy. The academy aims to plug the gap left by the declining rural community culture: "We're not teaching music at all in the way that it is usually taught in a formal setting. We're mimicking more how music is taught traditionally." Joan Soriano was one of the first instructors recruited by de Menil. He says that "I wish I could have gone to a music school like this one". [8]

In fact, Joan Soriano had little formal education of any kind. One of 15 children, he left school to carry out farming duties for his father. He made his first guitar out of an old oil can and a fishing line, and taught himself to play. Even on this, people could see that the kid had some talent, but his father couldn't afford to buy him a proper guitar. So, says Joan, "the neighbours took up a collection and gathered the necessary amount. At 12, I left home. I became fast man playing bachata everywhere." [9]

I was drawn to the song MARIA ELENA by its danceable rhythm

and Spanish-style guitar work. Joan was already an established artist when de Menil knocked on his door, but since recording for iASO his life has changed: he now gets invitations to perform round the world, and has money enough to build his own house. He remains, though, a simple man, deeply loyal to his family. On a second album for iASO several of his brothers and sisters were given starring guest roles. Sadly his father, Cande, who was his most passionate fan, passed away in January 2014.

NOTES

1. http://uctp.blogspot.co.uk/2010/06/15-of-dominicans-have-taino-dna.html
2. http://www.diariolibre.com/noticias/2004/10/01/i48561_sixto-minier-estampa-viva-del-adulto-mayor-dominicano.html
3. Sydney Hutchinson – Merengue Tipico in Transnational Dominican Communities: Gender, Geography, Migration and Memory in a Traditional Music (ProQuest, 2008), p229.
4. https://lucidculture.wordpress.com/2008/07/31/sixteen-questions-for-benjamin-de-menil-producer-of-the-bachata-roja-legends
5. http://latindancecommunity.com/interview-joan-soriano-el-duque-dela-bachata
6. https://lucidculture.wordpress.com/2008/07/31/sixteen-questions-for-benjamin-de-menil-producer-of-the-bachata-roja-legends
7. https://www.alumni.hbs.edu/stories/Pages/story-bulletin.aspx?num=4498
8. http://latindancecommunity.com/interview-joan-soriano-el-duque-dela-bachata/
9. http://www.aarp.org/espanol/entretenimiento/expertos/info-04-2012/el-duque-de-la-bachata.html

EL SALVADOR

Why does a country that's seen so much sadness produce such relentlessly happy music?

Perhaps it's just part of Caribbean culture to maintain a positive attitude through life's ups and downs. How else does one explain the fact that surveys consistently place El Salvador among the happiest countries in the world, even as thousands of its citizens leave the country every year in hope of a better life abroad?

Los Hermanos Flores, Salvador's answer to The Jacksons, were formed as an act of love. On 31st December 1960, in the city of San Vicente, Don Andrés Rodriguez was getting married to Dona Fidelina Flores. For a while he'd been running, with some of his older sons, a small marimba-led orchestra, and he wanted to try something new, replacing the marimba with the trumpet. Mindful that the trumpet lends itself very well to festival and dance, he prepared to put on a show for his own wedding day.

The new band, Los Hermanos Flores (Brothers Flores), was officially founded in 1962, and included five of the brothers: José Angel, Andrés, Arnoldo, Tito and Antonio. Fifty years later, though, Arnoldo ('Nono') still proudly recalls that the band's true debut was that New Year's Eve wedding gig.

ARRIBA EL SALVADOR   *Los Hermanos Flores*

During the half century that the band have been playing their trumpets the country has seen decades of military rule, a deepening crisis in civil society as left-wing guerrillas and paramilitary death squads have taken up arms, an army coup, the assassination of the humanitarian Archbishop Oscar Romero, a decade of civil war that took thousands of civilian lives and, in recent years, gang-related violence spiralling out of control, giving El Salvador one of the highest murder rates in the world.

Throughout this time, the orchestra has kept the competition at bay by a combination of musical excellence and an uncomplicated approach to music: they simply want their audiences to dance and have a good time. The younger siblings were raised from an early age to take a part in the orchestra – Nory started learning the sax at the age of 11 and first took to the stage when she was just 13. Today she is the focal point of the band, the most important lead singer, and the only remaining female member. (In all the photos and videos I've seen she's accompanied by around 15 men sharply dressed in matching suits.) She never planned on being a singer, she says, but she was talked into it by her father, who was keen to have a family member take the role. [1] It was a shrewd decision on his part: not only is Nory an accomplished vocalist and frontwoman; she also feels a very strong attachment to the orchestra. She reserves her harshest words for her brother, Tito, who left in 1984 to form the rival band Orquesta San Vicente. "One's the genuine article and the other's a copy," she says, "an immoral, disloyal copy. He's recorded our music and is always trying to take our members."

ARRIBA EL SALVADOR is Salvadoran cumbia music at its best, the huge brass section taking the lead and creating an irresistible dance rhythm. How's the band preparing itself for the challenges of the next 50 years? They've successfully integrated a few other Latin dance rhythms such as merengue into their repertoire; they need to do more of this, according to Nory, and to develop new talent through their youth orchestra.

To take a wider perspective, the one thing that can be safely predicted is that, whether or not the current high levels of migration continue, the diaspora – those living abroad who can claim Salvadoran ancestry – will have a big influence on the character of Salvadoran music as it develops over the next 10 or 20 years. In 2011, the Census Bureau estimated that there were two million people of Salvadoran origin living in the USA, 35% of them in California. This is probably an underestimate. Elsewhere I read that the El Salvador consulate in LA reckons that there are a million Salvadorans living in California alone. The bonds between this diaspora and El Salvador are strong. Californian Salvadorans send generous amounts of money to families in El Salvador, they vote in Salvadoran elections and they feel connected to Salvadoran culture. Every year Los Angeles celebrates a Dia del Salvadoreño (Salvadoran day), and judging by reports it's a big occasion:

> "Walking through the blocked streets were people proudly wearing white and blue shirts – reminiscent of the color of the El Salvadorian flag. There were people who even dressed up their dogs in a Salvadoran shirt. 'What part of El

Salvador are you from' and 'do you know this family from...'
were common conversations that could be overheard." [2]

Already changes are taking place: the LA connection helps to account for the growing popularity of hip hop and reggaeton. Since November 2015, reggaeton has been banned by the El Salvador legislature: the minister of culture optimistically predicted that this would help to improve educational achievement and reduce teenage pregnancy. Exposure to different cultural influences affects not only musicians who are part of the diaspora, but also those Salvadoran musicians who rely on the income generated by overseas touring and international record sales. This fast changing social landscape poses difficult questions for groups such as Los Hermanos Flores, whose music is rooted in the past.

NOTES

1. http://www.laprensagrafica.com/fama/espectaculos/40262-el-retiro-no-pasa-por-mi-mente retrieved, March, 2016
2. http://intersectionssouthla.org/story/15th-annual-salvadoran-day-celebrated-in-los-angeles

GRENADA

"The Jab-Jab is sort of like an expression of when slavery was abandoned. We express it with the chains that we carry – they're the ones that we choose to carry. We eat as much meat as we want, so you see some people playing mas in something like a cow head or a saltfish. It's basically saying that we can have our own meat to eat now and we can eat whatever we want when we want it. It's about freedom."

Shortpree [1]

Spice Mas is the main event in Grenada, a magnet for tourists coming to the Caribbean in mid-summer. And one of the big highlights of Spice Mas is J'Ouvert. In the hours before sunrise, masqueraders and revellers take to the streets, their bodies blackened with used motor oil, molasses or other greasy substances, plus generous lathers of brightly coloured paint, and wearing horned helmets. Some may be wearing chains or padlocks or have fish hanging from their mouths. It's an occasion for wild fun, where you can expect to be splattered with paint and oils yourself, before cleaning yourself up for the festivities due to take place during the day.

DISS MAS *Shortpree*

The essential aspects of this event were once a very striking part of slave culture. The slaves were excluded from the carnivals run by the plantation owners, even the act of organising their own celebrations was a kind of rebellion. Of the traditional mas characters, jab jab and jab molassie were the most openly rebellious: they were intended to shock. Later, when carnival became the commercial enterprise that it is today, there were some who felt that it would be better off without jab, and the prime minister of the day, Sir Eric Gairy, even tried to ban it, but he was defied by people who took to the street in great numbers anyway to reclaim the tradition.

Since the turn of the millennium a new brand of carnival music has taken root in Grenada, which draws inspiration from jab tradition. Jab jab music, or jab jab riddim, is an Africanised form of soca characterised by a heavy beat, conch shell blowing and chanting. What makes it so interesting to me is this: here's a modern musical genre with obvious appeal to the hip hop generation, which also places great store in its roots in centuries-old traditional culture.

The artist who put jab jab on the map is Tallpree (born 1973). Notable for his spiky haircut and very deep voice, he started out as a dance hall singer under the moniker, Mr Evilus, before moving to soca in his mid-20s. Since having his first smash hit in 1999, he's become a regular big hitter at Spice Mas while also doing his thing in many other countries. He doesn't just do jab music, but it's what he's most famous for.

Shortpree, from the island of Carriacou, is one of the upcoming stars inspired by Tallpree: his stage name, he says, was given him by Tallpree. DISS MAS is the riddim that won the prize of Groovy Monarch at Spice Mas in 2015. It's an anthem to jab jab: an upbeat celebratory song that relies on the classic ingredients of a sweet rhythm and a catchy hook. Groovy soca is a slower, more melodic form of soca, and Shortpree is a great believer in keeping the music 'real':

> "A lot of great Soca performers used to perform in Europe in front of big crowds who enjoyed the music – They loved the authentic old-time Soca/Calypso style. That's who I look at to sharpen up my skills, people like Mighty Sparrow and Arrow, to listen to what made them great and what it was that they did that made the people say they are the greatest. I try to emulate them to make sure my style represents Soca/Calypso to the fullest." [2]

There's an interesting debate rumbling on about the relative merits of soca and calypso. The sound of modern calypso is not dissimilar to soca; the crucial difference lies in the lyrics. And in my view Grenada's most impressive calypsonian is Scholar (born 1970). Unfortunately, despite his many carnival triumphs, very few of his recordings are available, but the songs can be listened to on YouTube. Although he obtained his stage name almost by accident, Scholar has more than lived up to it: in 2011, at the age of 41, he obtained a master's degree in human resource management from the University of Manchester in England. Here he is criticising modern soca artists:

"The majority of them make songs geared towards a soca monarch performance. Therefore they have a nice hook line in their chorus which is where they will give the crowd the opportunity to 'get on bad'. A song must have verses, however. So they make 'verses' but the main intention of the whole song is to get to the chorus as quickly as possible. As a result you do not find a well developed story line in the verses at all. It is worth noting though that Grenada especially has had a tradition of story telling soca. In fact that was one way of easily recognizing a Grenadian soca. Inspector, Squeezy, Ajamu and others came up with some wonderfully written stories to complement the nice hook lines in their choruses. Today we still see some of the guys in Grenada like Tallpree, Four Brass and General Pepe still having well written stories. But well written stories in soca are quickly becoming the exception rather than the rule." [3]

Scholar acknowledges the declining importance of calypso. My wish would be that younger calypsonians will take inspiration from his own example as a writer of songs that mean something and can also be sung to and danced to.

NOTES

1. http://carnevalenetwork.co.uk/index.php/latest-news-4/interviews/723-getting-groovy-in-grenada
2. Ibid
3. http://bigdrumnation.org/calypso/Scholarchats.pdf

GUATEMALA

uatemala is a country saddled with the consequences of a genocide that still burns in the memories of many of those alive today. With the country in the throes of a seemingly never-ending civil war, the army embarked on a programme of destruction of entire indigenous communities, which escalated in the early 1980s to terrifying levels of violence:

> "Each community was rounded up, or seized when gathered already for a celebration or a market day. The villagers, if they didn't escape to become hunted refugees, were then brutally murdered; others were forced to watch, and sometimes to take part. Buildings were vandalised and demolished, and a 'scorched earth' policy applied: the killers destroyed crops, slaughtered livestock, fouled water supplies, and violated sacred places and cultural symbols." [1]

Over 600 villages were destroyed in this way. The USA colluded in the genocide, providing the Guatemalan government with arms, equipment and military training.

The 1996 Peace Accords were intended to pave the way to a more democratic and inclusive society. However, there were problems from the start. It took legislators two years to hammer out a set of amendments to the constitution, and when these were finally put to a vote in a referendum, people voted against the reforms. A low turnout of only 19% was further evidence that national reconciliation wasn't high on people's wish list. Since 1996, violence and murder have been rife in Guatemala, while the indigenous peoples continue to suffer from racism, discrimination and poverty. There is a 13-year gap in life expectancy between indigenous and non-indigenous people, and the statistics for extreme poverty and illiteracy within the indigenous population are truly appalling.

I'm aware that I'm making the indigenous people sound like victims. It shouldn't have to be this way. One of the must-see places for visitors to Guatemala is a vast archaeological site deep in the heart of the jungle. Tikal was once one of the great cities of the ancient Maya civilisation, and the ruins of its temples and palaces are still mightily impressive. Guatemala also has a living Maya heritage. Today 21 totally distinct Mayan languages are in use. As well as preserving these languages, the millions of Guatemalans who claim Mayan ancestry are proud of their colourful costumes, their culture and their festivals.

Lisandro Guarcax was a young man with a dream – that Mayan arts and culture could flower once again. He founded Sotz'il, a Kaqchikel-speaking youth organisation that sought to research, rescue and recreate some of the culture of their ancestors in art, theatre and music. They did some amazing work, reconstructing ancient costumes and ancient instruments and learning dances and tunes whose roots were centuries old. He also wanted to establish a Mayan cultural centre, which would be the hub of a new artistic community.

On 25th August 2010, Lisandro was abducted. His body was found a couple of days later. He was only 32. This, according to his co-workers, was a targeted killing – "he was killed because he worked to preserve Mayan art and because he openly discussed painful moments in Mayan history." [2] His dream, though, did not die with him. Sotz'il regrouped under the leadership of Lisandro's younger brother Daniel. In 2013, they began workshops for children and youth, and, as demand for the workshops increased, in 2016 the centre that Lisandro had wanted, Centro Cultural Sotz'il Jay, finally opened its doors.

Sotz'il have made two albums, one with Lisandro and one without him. It's unusual music to say the least: ancient rhythms seen through a modern lens. On **CH'A'OJ** we hear low drumming and flute playing, and a range of other sound effects – some from obscure instruments, some sampled sounds of nature. I should stress that this is also an elaborately composed piece of music. The ancient Mayan peoples revered nature and believed that their gods existed in the natural world. They left no written records about their music, but archaeologists have found a multitude of instruments ranging from the simple to the very complex. There is much theorising about when and how these instruments would have been used. One of the main uses would certainly have been for ritual ceremonies, at which there would probably have been groups of men playing different instruments. The music would have served many purposes – it was a call to dance; it was a way of communicating with the gods.

Here's how Sotz'il describe their own instruments on their website:

> "*All the instruments were made with natural materials such as mud, cane, bamboo, wood, palm, wasp wax, tecomates, jícaras, rubber, pita of maguey, animal bones, shells, etc. Among the instruments are xul, xäq xul, tunkul, kök, tun, tzuy q'ojom, chïrchïr, ch'ab'itun, t'ot 'and roq'roq'. We believe that the musical instruments possess an energy (rajawal q'ij) because they sing, cry, shout, whistle, laugh, talk and remain silent.*" [3]

While impressive, this isn't quite as remarkable as you might think. Writer and blogger Elizabeth Rose claims that on the streets of Guatemalan cities "you'll often see small troupes playing traditional music using instruments that are not unlike the instruments of their ancestors." [4] Another Mayan group with an online presence, Música Maya Aj, have also been reconstructing old instruments and creating new music in similar vein. They have a professional-looking website and several videos on YouTube.

Most Guatemalans identify as either Ladino or Maya, but there are two other much smaller ethnic groups, Xinca and Garifuna. By far the most important outpost of Garifuna culture is Livingston, a small town on the Caribbean coast accessible only by boat. Isolation from the rest of the country has helped it to develop its own music, cuisine and customs. It's produced more than its share of good music over the years, but my recommendation is an album entitled, Ibimeni: Garifuna Traditional Music from Guatemala. Recorded in 1990 by ethnomusicologist Alfonso Arrivillaga Cortes, this is a real taste of Africa in Central America, with a lot of heavy percussion and call-and-response singing.

The marimba is Guatemala's national instrument, and is widely regarded as a symbol of Guatemalan national identity. So, one might ask, can it help to unify this divided country? It does have a place in both Ladino and Mayan culture. However, the two groups trade claims about the instrument's origins! From what I've learned, the case for an African origin seems much the stronger. The wooden-barred marimba is very much part of the same family as African xylophones (even the word 'marimba' is of African origin), while its connection to a primitive Quiché Mayan instrument called the gog is tenuous at best.

Ladinos can certainly take the credit though for the modern Guatemalan marimba:

> *"The composer and band conductor Julián Paniagua Martínez suggested to marimba builder and player Sebastián Hurtado that he add a second row of soundbars to the single-row, diatonic marimba, creating chromatic pitches that were the equivalent of the black keys of the piano."*

After a few attempts, Hurtado managed to produce an instrument that met the specifications.

> *"The chromatic instrument became extremely popular from 1901 forward, and it evolved into two complementary instruments, the marimba grande (large marimba), played by four musicians, and the marimba tenor (smaller, higher-pitched marimba), played by three musicians."* [5]

Although the single-row marimba would survive in a few rural areas, the chromatic marimba swept all before it, supplying the soundtrack to the lives of generations of Guatemalans. Having a chromatic scale opened up new possibilities for the instrument, and it began to be used to play more European styles of music.

I knew I had to choose some marimba music to represent Guatemala. But the more that I listened to, the more difficult I was finding it. Every album that I found, almost without exception, was purely instrumental. And they sounded a lot alike: light sentimental melodies, with the same tonal range, and with allowances for variations between dances, played at much the same pace. It felt like the instrument had a potential which wasn't being fully explored. So I continued to search for an artist that I could really believe in.

My search led me back in time. The Marimba Orquesta Gallito have worked under a few different band names. Originally, when they worked at the Excélsior nightclub, they were Marimba Excélsior, then they were hired by the nightclub El Gallito, where they worked "for thirteen consecutive years, every day, from nine in the evening to two in the morning, and often due to public demand, until three or four in the morning." [6] In 1952, they found time to visit a recording studio and cut a couple of tracks: these were an immediate success and in no time the group had a recording contract. These were some of the earliest commercial marimba recordings in the country: in years to come an entire industry would be built up around marimba music, and the Orquesta Gallito would be a big part of it. Mardoqueo Girón Castellanos (1927–2000), who directed the band during its glory days, was also an accomplished composer who wrote many of their songs.

What Orquesta Gallito give us on tunes like TABAQUERA is a playfulness, an exuberance. The other thing that sets it apart from the rest is that there's more going on. While the marimba is still the centrepiece, the percussion is heavier, saxophones and trumpets blare away, and yes we have vocals too. If Orquesta Gallito could achieve such success by expressing themselves in different ways, what's stopping bands today from doing the same?

NOTES

1.   http://www.ppu.org.uk/genocide/g_guatemala1.html

2. https://globalpressjournal.com/americas/guatemala/mayan-cultural-center-opens-guatemala-realizes-dream-activist-killed-2010
3. http://www.gruposotzil.org.gt/qojom-musica
4. https://travelwriter-liz.blogspot.co.uk/2013/07/tortoise-shells-and-gourds-guatemalan.html
5. Chapinlandia – Marimba Music of Guatemala (Folkways 2007), liner notes by Dieter Lehnhoff, http://media.smithsonianfolkways.org/liner_notes/smithsonian_folkways/SFW40542.pdf
6. http://marimbaorquestagallito.blogspot.co.uk/2010/04/marimba-orquesta-gallito-grabaciones.html

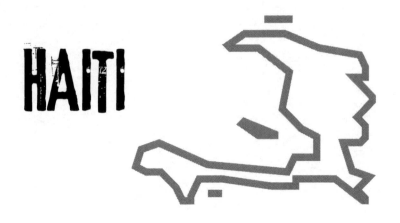

HAITI

"I was born a slave, but nature gave me a soul of a free man."

Toussaint L'Ouverture

It's an assault on your senses. The fast drumming, the insistent blaring of horns, voices chanting and wailing over it all. Listening to **RARA 2**, you may feel like you're in the middle of a large crowd with things happening all around you. If so, good: that's more or less how rara music is supposed to be heard. It's a street music, most often heard during Easter festivities. Rara troupes will make their way through the festivalgoers playing their instruments: vaksins (bamboo trumpets of varying lengths), konets (metal horns) and an array of drums and percussion instruments. Dancers follow them round, collecting money. For obvious reasons, recordings of rara music are thin on the ground, but the CD on Soul Jazz Records, Rara in Haiti: Street music of Haiti, recorded in Port-au-Prince, captures the spirit and energy of it admirably.

Another thing that may strike you is that rara sounds a lot more like African music than Caribbean music. Of course a great deal of Caribbean music does have African roots, but this

----

RARA 2   *Various Artists*

COTÉ MOUNE YO   *Super Jazz Des Jeunes*

INDEPENDANCE CHA-CHA/RUMBA LIBERTE   *Tabou Combo*

----

is particularly visible in Haitian music and culture. The Haitian experience is unique in the Caribbean: a defiant black republic, a nation of slaves who under the leadership of Toussaint L'Ouverture overthrew their masters and who stood firm against the might of Napoleon's France. For these slaves, culture, tradition and belief were vital: these were the things that connected them to their past and told them who they were. When the slaves rose up they consciously rejected white gods and white religion, embracing beliefs and culture that reaffirmed their separate identity, This meant vodou religion and vodou drumming. Vodou has been much misrepresented in Hollywood movies: it's not some form of dark witchcraft. Those who practise vodou (or voodoo) believe that there is a visible and an invisible world, and that these worlds are intertwined. Spirits (loas) act as intermediaries between the two worlds. People can connect with these spirits through rituals that involve drumming and dancing.

If you're looking for a recording of ritual drumming, I recommend a CD released on a small British independent label, Red Eye Music. Haiti Vodou: The Voodoo Drums of Haiti was recorded by two Welsh musicians, Christopher Rees and Steve Garrett, who later told their story to the Guardian newspaper:

> "Rees... says the complexity of the rhythms astonished him; they sounded far more intense than similar music from west Africa. A drummer would kick off the ceremony, standing up and using a stick to define the beat, before other drummers joined him. Then new time signatures and textures would find their way in. 'The music had the intensity of drum'n'bass, but the people would dance calmly to it, as if they were totally at ease. Then something would suddenly move them, as if they were connecting to a communal heartbeat. For that to still exist in that form shows its intensity.'" [1]

Haitian drums also feature in various forms of commercial music, but if one had to codify all the music genres that have taken root in Haiti over the last hundred years, then probably the only conclusion that could safely be drawn is that there's no common cultural denominator. It's through embracing other cultures, and being open to change, that Haitian music has grown strong. So, the string-based music méringue (known in Creole as mereng) had a history closely intertwined with merengue, the music of the Dominican Republic. In the mid-1950s méringue was still hugely popular – not just the music, but the couples' dance. But the music ruffled political sensitivities. In the Dominican Republic, Rafael Trujillo had made merengue the national music, and its popularity had mushroomed. Now Haitian musicians were listening to Dominican musicians and Dominican radio.

Then, in 1955, the saxophonist and band leader Nemours Jean-Baptiste began to play a new dance, which he called compas direct. He slowed the rhythm down and brought in a lot of brass. Audiences loved it, and it quickly overtook méringue as the country's most popular dance, though how far it can be described as a Haitian music is something that's debated to this day. Nemours was familiar with jazz and Latin music, and these influences can be heard in compas direct.

One of Nemour's musicians, Webert Sicot, left the band and formed his own orchestra. They played a slightly different rhythm, which Webert called cadence rampa to differentiate himself from his former colleague. This was the start of an impassioned rivalry that was to dominate Haiti's music for a 10-year period. Each band had thousands of followers, who would express their allegiances very much like football fans. Nemours:

> "took red and white as his colors, and when he died in 1982, he was buried in his red and white clothes, with the red and white flag of kompa-direk laid out on a bier resembling a carnival float. During carnival, Sicot's and Nemours' fans would often clash. Partisans could be recognized by the colors they wore to identify with their favourite band." [2]

Gradually, though, the era of the big band was coming to an end, as a new brand of smaller groups arrived to replace them. They were known as mini-jazz, but don't let the name mislead you. The music was an exuberant mix of rock, funk, jazz and Latin grooves, and while it also drew on existing Haitian dance styles it redefined Haitian music. For the first time the electric guitar took on a dominant role. In the new mini-jazz bands the guitarists would typically be supported by just one horn player and one drummer.

Several mini-jazz combos are featured on an excellent compilation released by Strut in 2014: Haiti Direct: Big Band, Mini Jazz & Twoubadou Sounds, 1960–1978, among them Les Loups Noirs, Les Frères Déjean, Les Fantaisistes de Carrefour, Ibo Combo, and Les Difficiles de Petion-Ville. The track I've picked out here was recorded in 1962 by Super Jazz Des Jeunes. Unlike the new groups forming in the 1960s, Super Jazz Des Jeunes had already been around for a couple of decades, outliving their name which had been chosen when they were still teenagers. Led by saxophonist René St Aude, the band coined the term vodou jazz to highlight the fact that they were introducing Haiti folk songs and traditional rhythms into the dance music that they played. According to the liner notes, "sung by Gerard Dupervil, **COTÉ MOUNE YO** is a big band setting of a traditional Haitian folk song, adding the traditional vaksin to the line-up". The vaksin is a single-note bamboo trumpet.

On 12th January, 2010, Haiti was struck by a category 7 earthquake with its epicentre just 16 miles from Port-au-Prince. Tens of thousands of people died and even greater numbers were made homeless as vast numbers of buildings were severely damaged. Rich and poor alike were affected: even the presidential palace and the National Assembly building were laid to waste.

If only broken buildings were Haiti's only problem. The crumbling monuments were symbolic of Haiti's failed institutions: the lack of a stable democracy, the rampant corruption while millions lived below the poverty line, the failed education system (Haiti's literacy rate and primary school enrolment are among the lowest in the world). A year after the earthquake, Haitians went to the polls: it wasn't the smoothest or easiest of elections, but it did result in the first democratic transfer of power from one party to another in Haiti's history. And the new president, 50-year-old Michel Martelly, was a compas singer, and a very good one at that, known to many by his stage name, 'Sweet Micky'.

Martelly launched a high-profile programme to deliver free education in schools. As I write, this programme seems to be unravelling, mired in serious allegations while teachers who've been receiving no pay are on indefinite strike. Of particular interest here, Martelly also made a big personal commitment to setting up music schools. A close ally of Venezuela, he admired Venezuela's publicly funded musical education programme, El Sistema, and aimed to replicate it in Haiti. The first year of Martelly's programme, 2013, was planned to cost $7 million, with subsequent years costing between $4 and $5 million. The article in the Christian Science Monitor that quoted these figures explained that the programme's supporters anticipated that this investment would be repaid with interest by way of higher school attendances, more social development and lower crime. [3]

On this at least, Martelly's vision chimed with what many people wanted. Several small non-profits and aid agencies were already getting involved in this kind of work, and largely through their help a lot of music schools were being set up and musical instruments procured by one means and another. The flagship school, l'Institut National de Musique d'Haïti, officially opened in February 2014. And for a large number of young people who'd had little formal education, musical training provided them with a new self-discipline and sense of achievement.

At a time when Haitian popular music has lost its way, when compas direct has become just another brand of urban pop, perhaps this new generation of classically trained musicians can help forge a new identity. I'm not the only one who feels that something's lacking. Here's Fanfan from the band Tabou Combo:

> "Today's generation has no ideals... yes, in the '60s and '70s there were political, social and cultural questions, and we had to take up a position. Between the war in Vietnam, the US Civil Rights movement, the Black Panthers, we had things to think about and reflect on... and through music we could express ourselves about all this... But I don't understand this obsession with fashion... apparently some young compas artists don't have much to say." [4]

Today's generation could certainly take some lessons from Tabou Combo, the band who, since their formation in the late 1960s, have virtually come to define Haitian music. Forget the labels: their goal is to make feel-good dance music, to see audiences enjoying themselves, and to popularise the music of Haiti and the Caribbean. Their tunes are a heady mix of méringue, vodou drums, zouk, soukous, funk and much else besides, and they sing in several different languages. They currently list 13 band members on their website, including a horn section, a percussion section, a rhythm and bass guitar and a keyboard. Fanfan (Yves Joseph) is the band's manager, spokesperson and main songwriter. He says, "we consider ourselves more of a Carribean band than exclusively a Haitian band, so we try and raise whatever musical influence that floats into the Carribean." [5]

Now in their fifth decade, Tabou Combo's brand of high-energy music sounds as fresh as ever. How do they do it? They're a hard-working band who continue to play festivals around the world. A few younger musicians have been recruited to play alongside the old-timers. The enduring popularity of compas music has meant that they've not needed to update their style too radically. (Fanfan says that, "as far as rap is concerned, we've been doing rap since 1978" – and he's only half joking. [6]) And they generally do have something to say. Kompa to the World (2010) is a consciously outward-facing album, sung in five languages. The track **INDEPENDANCE CHA-CHA/RUMBA LIBERTE** commemorates 50 years since Congolese independence, a significant date for a band very proud of their African roots. It's a cover of a number by Le Grand Kallé, the father of Congolese music, with the lyrics updated to draw links with different struggles.

NOTES

1. http://www.theguardian.com/music/2010/mar/03/haiti-voodoo-drumming
2. Gage Averill – A Day for the Hunter, a Day for the Prey: Popular Music and Power in Haiti (University of Chicago Press, 1997), p87.
3. http://www.csmonitor.com/World/Americas/2013/0112/Music-schools-drum-up-new-hope-for-students-in-Haiti
4. http://afrozap.com/2013/06/22/ma-rencontre-avec-lun-des-maitres-du-konpa, retrieved February, 2015 (my translation)
5. http://www.africasounds.com/Tabou_Combo.htm retrieved February 2015
6. Ibid.

HONDURAS

Guillermo Anderson (1962–2016) was Honduras's most loved singer, and his song En Mi País has been described as a second national anthem. The lyrics, though, are rather interesting. Anderson is from the town of La Ceiba on the Caribbean coast, a place with a character all its own. Unlike other cities, such as Tegucigalpa and Comayagua where you can't go far without seeing imposing reminders of Honduras's colonial past, La Ceiba is a town with few pretensions, which sprang up in the late 19th century around the banana and pineapple trade. This stretch of coast is where the country's minority Garifuna population mostly lives, and they're just as much a part of La Ceiba's life as the majority mestizo population. In the song there's an ambiguity as to whether what he's describing is his country (mi país) or the more multicultural life of La Ceiba. There's a mass of musical references in the lyrics: guitar and accordion suggest European influences; the marimba was introduced to the region by African slaves, though it's become very much part of Latin culture; while the caramba (long wooden bow) and caracol (conch shell) are strongly associated with the Garifuna. But the biggest signal of all is that in a song about his country, he mentions Africa: for Anderson, Honduras is unimaginable without its Garifuna culture.

EL AMOR ASI	*Grupo Kazzabe*
SIELPA	*Aurelio*

Make no mistake: in the 21st century Afro-Hondurans are still victims of discrimination and prejudice. As in America, though, sweeping out racist attitudes is a long process, one that advances most of the time in innumerable tiny steps but that can accelerate during times of social upheaval. As in America, music had its part to play. Punta music and dance was performed at family funerals as part of traditional Garifuna ritual. Men would play large drums, maracas, caracols and perhaps other percussion too, and dancers would chant as they moved. In recent decades this ethnic ritual dance has been widely embraced by Honduran people, who see it as perhaps the most important indigenous Honduran dance. Some credit for this can be taken by the Garifuna themselves for setting up new organisations and promoting their culture, and by enlightened individuals like Anderson, but that is not the whole story. Perhaps the real turning point was when Garifuna music broke into the mainstream.

Punta rock came about when merengue groups began incorporating Garifuna drumming and chanting into their music. The music made its way from Belize to Guatemala and to Honduras, where after 1991 the group Banda Blanca suddenly found themselves the most famous band in the country thanks to the huge international success of Sopa de Caracol (conch soup). This was good-time music, with modern instruments at the fore, and was aimed more at clubs than at funerals. If Garifuna traditionalists had any misgivings about the music, their concerns were amplified by the video to Sopa de Caracol, in which women dancers wore bikinis and short skirts, but they might as well have tried to hold back the sea tide: gyrating women in short skirts were to become just as much a part of punta rock as the electric guitar.

Among the new bands that sprang up in the 1990s was one called Grupo Kazzabe, based in the northern city San Pedro Sula. In a country crippled by external debt and high poverty levels, no place has a worse reputation than this:

"For the fourth year running San Pedro Sula, Honduras' *second-largest city, has earned the title of most dangerous* *place on Earth outside of a war zone, with a 2014 murder* *rate of 171 per 100,000 people. Entire blocks of the city are* *abandoned for fear of gangs. Nearly every citizen is forced to* *pay what has come to be known as a 'war tax,' or extortion* *fees to the various street gangs that have overtaken the city...*

The grave situation in San Pedro Sula is largely a result *of criminal violence between the Mara Salvatrucha (MS13)* *and Barrio 18 street gangs... Many children are orphaned* *because their parents were killed or left to the United States* *to find work or flee the gangs. These children become prey* *for the gangs, who patrol schools to extort teachers, sell sex* *and recruit children to join their ranks.*

Last year's child migrant humanitarian crisis at the US- *Mexico border is a symptom of this dynamic. The majority* *of the more than 18,000 Honduran children apprehended* *at the border attempting to enter the United States were* *from San Pedro Sula."* [1]

Kazzabe's Victor Goza explains the broad appeal of their brand of punta in this way: "It makes people very happy, because it forces you to move the whole body." [2] For a younger generation starved of hope, this cheerful music offered an escape from the cares of daily life and was something they could call their own. It wasn't pure escapism, though, argues Victor Goza; it was a music rooted in Garifuna culture. They sang in Garifuna (and Spanish, with a bit of Miskito thrown in), they used a lot of percussion, and in their eyes there was no Chinese wall standing between traditional punta and the new punta rock.

What I like about **EL AMOR ASI** (Love Like This) is that, although it has this fast, heavy dance beat, it's sung almost like an acoustic ballad. So the song has a warmth and a humanity to it, as well as being a dancefloor filler. Two decades on, Kazzabe are still going, still bringing happiness in venues from Miami to Madrid and making people dance. To me their positive outlook speaks volumes about the spirit of the people of San Pedro Sula.

Now listen to **SIELPA** and hear the contrast. This is laidback, gentle, soulful music. The guitar playing suggests a Spanish influence – yet this also is Garifuna. The song, which is about a man who consults many doctors as he tries to diagnose a mystery illness, is sung in the Garifuna language. The style is called paranda, and his interpretation of it has made Aurelio Martinez a big star on the world stage. The song's taken from the 2017 album Darandi. Recorded completely live at the Real World Studios in England after Aurelio and his band had been playing at the Womad Festival, the album is something of a retrospective of his career to date, but the hard cover book that accompanies the album pushes the idea that it's something more than this: Aurelio's mission is to preserve the culture of the Garifuna people, and the book has much to say about the Garifuna and their history.

Aurelio grew up in a community totally without electricity, in the village of Plaplaya on the Caribbean coast. In later years he would come to appreciate the value of being raised in traditional culture more or less free from the pervasive influence of modern media as he saw Garifuna culture and ways of life coming under threat. Music was vital to him from an early age – "My first toy was a guitar I built for myself from wood taken from a fishing rod." [3] – and by the time he began attending secondary school in La Ceiba, aged 14, it had become a passion. Now he had the chance to fill in the gaps in his musical education, bringing himself up to speed on other Latin music genres.

By his mid-20s he'd already achieved a lot by most standards. His own group, Lita Ariran, had released an album of exceptionally good paranda music. Other projects included the punta rock band Los Gatos Bravos, with whom he did his first tours to the United States. Then, in 1997, a formative moment in his life: his first meeting with Andy Palacio. Andy was a few years older, but the two of them found in each other a kindred spirit and a burning commitment to Garifuna culture, and they became life-long friends. Through Andy, Aurelio also met Ivan Duran, the founder and director of Stonetree Records (see my chapter on Belize for more about Andy Palacio and Ivan Duran). The collaboration with Duran was to be instrumental in Aurelio's later career.

Aurelio announced himself on the world music scene with the release of his debut solo album, Garifuna Soul, on Stonetree in 2004. In 2006, he became the first of his people to be elected to the Honduran National Congress: effectively he was now both cultural ambassador and political tribune for the Garifuna. He was working as a congressman when he heard the devastating news of Andy Palacio's death. At that time, recalls Duran, "he hadn't been playing guitar for months because of his intense political commitments. But after Andy's passing, he gave a few concerts and he knew he needed to start recording right away." [4]

Both Aurelio and Andy had dreamed on playing in Africa. And now Aurelio had the opportunity, thanks to being selected as a finalist in the Rolex Arts Initiative and getting personal mentoring from the Senegalese musical giant, Youssou N'Dour. For a black

Honduran musician, seeing West African bands performing close up was very educative in itself. And Youssou seems to have had plenty of wisdom to impart: "Of course Aurelio needed to learn better arrangement, production and voice techniques. But it was in a different way that I could be most useful to him. He had to be himself, sure of himself, proud of his music and ready to take on the world." [5] Aurelio's next album, Laru Beya, was made partly in Honduras and partly in Africa, and the music is coloured by his African experiences.

Landini (2014) was marketed as a 'return to the roots' album. The title song is about Aurelio's home village, Plaplaya, and the place where the boats come in. Aurelio's mother was another big source of inspiration, and she even contributed a few songs herself. Aurelio says the album, which tells of some of the joys and sorrows of rural life, is "purely Garifuna". Yet it also shows how far he's travelled since that first album with Lita Ariran, nearly 20 years earlier. Landini was recorded at the Stonetree Studio in Belize, and it bears with it the stamp of Duran's production, a diverse group of musicians, and Aurelio's own musical journey.

It seems fitting to let Aurelio have the final word:

"We face discrimination and oppression. Yet, we are keeping this culture alive. My band takes our pride around the world, we convey to people a culture that is both powerful and rich. The soul of Garifuna is about bringing people together, in peace and harmony. I am a spirit, the music comes through me. I want to be true in my music. I sing what I feel." [6]

NOTES

1. http://securityassistance.org/blog/san-pedro-sula-honduras-nearly-war-zone

2. http://olanchitototheworld.blogspot.co.uk/2013/07/kazzabe-embajadores-musicales.html
3. http://archive.rockpaperscissors.biz/index.cfm/fuseaction/current.articles_detail/project_id/532/article_id/14844.cfm
4. http://www.aureliomusic.net/bio
5. http://www.rolexmentorprotege.com/pairing/2008-2009/youssou_ndour_and_aurelio_martinez
6. http://worldmusiccentral.org/tag/honduran-music

JAMAICA

It was one of many bust-ups in one of the most colourful careers in popular music: Lee Perry walked out on top producer Clement 'Coxsone' Dodd and joined forces with Joe Gibbs. As was his style, he immediately cut a single to let people know that he wasn't to be jerked around – I Am The Upsetter.

The year was 1966 – a seminal moment in Jamaican music. Ska music had encapsulated the joyful spirit of independence – but now the riddims were changing. With unemployment rising and fears of crime and gang violence, the government launched a mass eviction of squatters from Kingston's shantytowns. Rocksteady started as an offshoot of ska, as producers slowed down the beats. The lyrics were changing too as the rude boy subculture began to influence musicians. In 1967, 007 (Shanty Town) by Desmond Dekker and the Aces came out, as did Prince Buster's immortal Judge Dread. The birth of reggae was just around the corner.

Perry was now more his own master, and he produced a number of hits for Gibbs, notably Long Shot by The Pioneers. By 1968, though, he'd become dissatisfied with his treatment by his latest business partner, so he went independent. Once again a track was released to mark the occasion, People Funny Boy. On this, for the first time, we see something of the wild rush of ideas

BLACK PANTA	*The Upsetters*
NONE SHALL ESCAPE	
THE JUDGEMENT	*Johnny Clarke*
WISDOM	*Prince Far I and the Arabs*
BLACKMAN TIME	*Sister Carol*
BETTER MUST COME	*Buju Banton*
SLIDE MONGOOSE	*Blue Glaze Mento Band*

that's become his trademark, including one of the very earliest uses of sampling (a baby crying).

Whether Perry was any better a boss to work for than Coxsone or Gibbs is open to debate. His house band, The Upsetters, only lasted a matter of months before being replaced by a new Upsetters with a completely different line-up. The bands that he produced didn't show him a lot of loyalty; they all moved on after a time. What rankled most was the departure of the Wailers.

Bob Marley's Wailers cut two albums with Lee Perry's label, Soul Rebels and Soul Revolution, which I would argue are superior to all the later world-famous releases for Island Records. Perry recognised the special quality in Bob Marley's vocals and the force of his character, and rebuilt the Wailers sound around this:

> "Bob's lead vocals were transformed into something more urgent and raw, devoid of pretence and smooth edges. Out went the old-fashioned Wailers doo-wop harmonies, to

be replaced by terse but melodious back-up parts. Perry
dropped horn sections from the Wailers music... Now the
dark and primitive bass was the lead instrument, offset by
the metronomic chop of electric guitar." [1]

There were many great songs: Soul Rebel, 400 Years, Kaya, Duppy Conqueror. Some would be re-recorded later, but would lose a little of their magic with Chris Blackwell's more rock-oriented arrangements.

When the Wailers left, they took with them brothers Aston 'Family Man' Barrett and Carlton Barrett, who had been core members of The Upsetters after the group was reformed. "Was Bob who organised that, with Chris Blackwell's money," Perry told NME in 1984. "They took away my musicians. But I don't get vexed with Aston or Carlton because money talks very loud. Aston still checks me every day." [2] Perry was less charitable in some of his comments about Blackwell. However, both Blackwell and Marley remained appreciative of Perry's many talents – and Perry himself wasn't too proud to sign a lucrative distribution deal with Island in 1975.

Of course, Blackwell deserves massive credit for having the vision to invest serious money in Bob Marley when no one else would. He also had the nous not to make too many changes to what he found. A key reason why Bob Marley and the Wailers continue to inspire so many people to this day in every corner of the globe is that the music, as much as the message, is real and direct.

Rasta-inspired roots reggae wasn't the only thing happening in Jamaica in the 1970s. Within and alongside the reggae explosion a musical revolution was taking place that was to have a profound influence on modern digital music and hip hop. This new music was called dub, and its two great pioneers were Lee 'Scratch' Perry and King Tubby.

This revolution started in the most unlikely of ways. Jamaican

recording studios back then were fairly primitive. Songs would
be recorded on two tracks, the vocals on one and the rest of the
band on the other. By accident DJ Rudolph 'Ruddy' Redwood got
hold of one of these backing tracks, so he played it to an audience,
and they loved it and started singing along. The producer Duke
Reid quickly picked up on this, and began releasing singles with
the instrumental mix as a B-side. DJs found they could play these
B-sides in the dance halls and sing, chant or improvise words to
them. This became known as toasting. U-Roy is a legend among
DJ/toasters, a huge, influential character, someone who was
in there from the very start and who spent years working with
King Tubby. There's a lovely YouTube video of U-Roy meeting DJ
Kool Herc, the father of modern hip hop. Kool Herc was born in
Kingston and lived in Jamaica to the age of 12: he carried his roots
with him, and his love of Jamaican DJs like U-Roy and Big Youth
would later help to guide his way when he started making music
in New York.

At first, record producers probably saw instrumental versions
as a convenient way of saving money. Musicians only received
a session fee, so if different mixes of a track were released the
musicians wouldn't get a penny extra. But then in the early
1970s it got more serious. King Tubby and Lee Perry both got
themselves new studios where they could play around with these
instrumental tracks to their hearts' content. Dub was becoming
an art form.

BLACK PANTA (also released as Blackboard Jungle Dub – long
story) is the opening track on The Upsetters 1973 Blackboard
Jungle album. From Lee Perry's opening invocation to the meek
and humble, it's like entering in to this darkly exotic world. Sirens
are howling, drums are clattering a riddim, and there are bursts of
strange sound effects. The track riffs off the original riddim of The
Upsetters' song, Bucky Skank, creating something entirely new
and, in this case at least, far more memorable.

For the next few years Perry worked in his own Black Ark

Studio, and by common consent this was his most productive period. As a producer he received huge and justified acclaim for Max Romeo's War Ina Babylon, Junior Murvin's Police and Thieves, and The Congos' Heart of the Congos. The more groundbreaking adventures in dub were mainly saved for his own recordings. I like this tribute by Max Romeo:

> "Perry was using a 4-track at the Black Ark studio, but he could get about a hundred other tracks bouncing in and out of there by using stones, water, kitchen utensils and whatever else was available. He makes his money by being crazy, but he's no crazier than I am. All geniuses are mad. I remember Chris Blackwell… sitting on a couch and saying, 'Scratch, the tape is spilling over. You can't do that!' Scratch just said, 'The album is called Super Ape, and so I need a Super Tape!' He is a wizard, there is nobody else like him." [3]

Elsewhere, Perry claims with a twinkle in his eye: "It was only four tracks written on the machine, but I was picking up 20 from the extraterrestrial squad. I am the dub shepherd." [4]

From around 1979, Perry's world came crashing down. As events seemed to conspire against him, his behaviour turned from zany, erratic and insightful to obsessive and deranged. The Black Ark was trashed, and later burned down to the ground, apparently by Perry's own hand. Perhaps he knew what he was doing; he had to exorcise his demons, for his spirit has survived to carry on entertaining us well into the 21st century. Now in his 80s, he still tours and makes new music. His later output is variable in quality but is never dull. And he never fails to give great value in interviews with his mix of humour, philosophy, surprising metaphors and wordplay and soaring flights of fancy. How does he keep doing it? Let's let Scratch have the last word: "As an example to prove to people that God is still alive. He keeps me well to this age." [5]

King Tubby had none of Perry's ebullient extrovert nature. Whereas Perry loved nothing more than to stamp his personality all over his records, Tubby was ahead of his time in making music where the artist was almost invisible. A former radio repairman, he understood the technology and constructed his own equipment. His speciality was making dub 'versions' of tracks for release as B-sides, and these usually had a pared-down, understated feel to them. They were the product, though, of an intensely creative process. Not only did they make use of devices such as faders, echo and reverb, all of which had been pioneered by Tubby himself, they were also laid down live at the mixing desk. A student of jazz, Tubby believed in improvising even when recording, and trusting his instincts.

A King Tubby B-side would often be more highly prized than the actual A-side, as Johnny Clarke recalls:

> "Usually them 'ave the B-side, is when you turn over an' play the real tune or the number one tune or them cream of the crop song... Tubbys change that now an' mek the B-side be more exciting, more as I say 'interesting'. Man na play the tune done an' it no flip it over. Ca' years ago man used to play a tune an' when 'im done play the tune, jus' change a next, put on a next record an' no t'ink 'bout the flip. But after a while, no way 'im a go tek off the A-side an' don't flip it over, to the B." [6]

Johnny Clarke's big breakthrough had come about almost by accident. The producer Bunny Lee was recording a song by Earl Zero called **NONE SHALL ESCAPE THE JUDGEMENT**, and he cut a version of it with Clarke on backing harmonies. There are various conflicting accounts as to why the Earl Zero take was dropped, but a few days later another session took place at Duke Reid's studio, this time with Johnny Clarke as lead vocalist. Dave Hendley takes up the story:

"Bunny had chosen to rebuild the rhythm from scratch and None Shall Escape's revolutionary flying cymbals sound came about almost purely by accident. The Soul Syndicate band were... jamming prior to the start of the session when the drummer suddenly switched from his snare and began to play the beat off of his cymbals. When the time came to lay the rhythm he started by drumming in the conventional style. Bunny Lee stopped the session and asked the drummer to play the rhythm off the cymbals again like he had during the warm up... The young singer laid his guide vocal and it became immediately obvious that they had a huge hit on their hands. According to Johnny, Duke Reid came into the studio... and in his excitement fired a shot from his rifle into the wall." [7]

The percussion, and Clarke's vocals, turned a great song into a classic. None Shall Escape became a big hit in Jamaica, and the song that defined Clarke's career. Spare a thought though for Earl Zero, who wrote the original song. Hendley says that he's "searched for a copy of Earl Zero's version for over 25 years, but like the Holy Grail there is no certainty that it even exists."

For the next four or five years Clarke was just about the biggest name in Tubby's stable. I've read that during this time he was selling more records in Jamaica than Bob Marley – the kind of stat that it's almost impossible to verify, but he certainly released a vast number of records during this period, from roots to love songs. And as he supplied the hits, Tubby kept supplying the dub versions. The early 1980s was marked by gang violence, the rise of dance hall music and, for Clarke, declining record sales. He emigrated to England for a few years, returning to get his career back on track. He doesn't get anything like the credit he deserves these days, even in Jamaica, for helping to popularise roots reggae. But for him, more important than this is the way in which the Rasta message has taken off: "Rasta gets more respect...

The youth dem really play dem part, as far as seeing that Rasta is never ending, continually, non-stop, 'pon a global basis, too." [8]

The techniques of dubbing and toasting were opening up new sonic possibilities. By modern standards, WISDOM is a very primitive production, but before hip hop came along how many artists were nicking instrumental versions of songs and slapping new vocals on them? In Jamaica, in the 1970s, it was not uncommon. Here, the backing track is a mix of Satta Massagana by The Abyssinians, and the vocals are those of Prince Far I. I'm tempted to say that when you have a voice as good and as deep as that of Prince Far I, you could read out the telephone directory and get away with it. The Prince never quite went that far, but he had earlier released an album which consisted of readings from the Psalms. Wisdom is in the same vein, packed with biblical references, especially to the Book of Proverbs. Far I's voice is rich and powerful set against the reggae beat: this is spiritual enlightenment in dub. It's probably not to everyone's taste, but for me a lot of the best reggae is the heavy stuff – reggae that was written for a purpose.

Reggae artists who sing songs with a serious message are called 'conscious'. They don't see themselves as protest singers: they don't seek political involvement but they do want to encourage their followers to become enlightened and to live in the right way. Reggae's reputation as a politically engaged art form owes much to the songs and the philosophy of Bob Marley. Again and again his lyrics remind you that the world he knows is that of the Kingston ghetto; that the history of black people is one of slavery and oppression.

Although he flirted with pop music on a couple of recordings, this need in him to speak out never lessened. Rastaman Vibration (1976) contained War, a song with lyrics adapted from Haile Selassie's speech to the United Nations in 1963. And his 1979 album, Survival, was his most overtly political, a passionate call for African unity and African freedom. True, there were others writing songs and singing on these themes, artists such as Burning

Spear, but Marley was able to reach millions more people. Album sleeves and posters reinforced the idea of Marley not only as a cultural icon but as an icon of social rebellion.

The 1990s saw the birth of a conscious reggae revival. Jamaican music of the time was dominated by dance hall, a genre noted for its 'slackness' (explicit lyrics) and frequent references to sex and violence. Conscious artists, by contrast, took pride in giving 'positive messages' in their songs. They included a few big dance hall stars who'd taken to promoting Rastafari; new artists were also emerging. In the 1990s – and again in the 2010s – optimism flickered about the future of Jamaican music. My own assessment is less sanguine. Jamaica will always be the home of reggae music, but if we want to know what the future of reggae may look like we might have to look elsewhere. In the country that gave us Tommy McCook, Prince Buster, Desmond Dekker, Lee Scratch Perry, King Tubby, Bob Marley, Toots Hibbert and so many more truly original artists, today you'll struggle to find innovative producers making cutting-edge music, or musicians interested in more than what will sell in the American market – artists who can make roots music crucial again.

One way in which reggae can change is by doing better at reflecting the voices of women.

In the 1960s, what Lee Perry went through, every female singer had to go through the same or worse. The producers (all men) all robbed the musicians blind. Thirty years on, Phyllis Dillon was still bitter about her lost royalties: "You have money for me, you know where I am, send it to me. I think they like when you beg. And I going to die, you know, because I refuse to beg. Especially if it's mine in the first place, you know, I shouldn't have to ask for it." [9]

In Rastafari, women were respected and honoured, but their primary role was seen as homemakers, and they were expected to be deferential towards men. Judy Mowatt was one of many who felt uncomfortable with this: "What I saw for myself in some of the Rasta groups was that women were not supposed to play a dominant role. When I was living in Bull Bay, a man said to me that women don't speak, women don't ask questions, women listen. I felt really bothered, but I had to listen because he was an elder." [10] Rasta culture is said to have changed over the years, and I've no reason to doubt this, but the 2011 census throws up a surprising statistic: 25,325 men put down Rastafari as their religion, but only 3,701 women did the same.

In wider society, Jamaica was becoming a byword for high levels of guns and violent crime, and domestic abuse was also rife. Women in music were raising their voices, but getting heard was still difficult. Judy Mowatt left the I-Threes to make a thoughtful militant album, Black Woman, but despite her high profile the album never quite got the level of attention that it deserved. At least women reggae artists kept their dignity. Women artists in dance hall soon found that if they wanted to get their music out there they had to dress sexily and speak the language of the street. Sister Nancy, who did care what she was singing about, was the first female DJ to make a mark, but her career was soon to be eclipsed by the more commercially minded Lady Saw.

Sister Carol found her reason to sing in the slums of Kingston:

"Well, back in Jamaica growing up as a youth, whenever I recognised things that I'm against, like there's a lot of political crime in the area, sometimes shooting involved with politics, things like discrimination and racism... I always felt like Cinderella, not being able to have the chance to do or to have certain things I might have desired as a child. I was never really seeking a Prince Charming, per se, to redeem me; I was more looking for something to happen by the Creator. And I knew that it would always be music, because as a youth, that's what brought joy to me, the music, every time." [11]

She was just a teenager when her family emigrated to Brooklyn, and for most of her career she lived in New York, part of a large Caribbean community. She sings in patois; her songs are written first of all for Jamaican people and her Rastafari faith. But the songs are so strong, full of knowledge of history and lyrics that resonate with women's everyday lives, that they speak to a very wide audience. **BLACKMAN TIME** is Sister Carol in full flow: righteous and strong and confident, and I particularly like how the quick-fire lyrical assaults are punctuated with a melodic chorus as the dance hall and reggae riddims meld perfectly together.

It wasn't long before a yet more potent female voice arrived on the scene: Queen Ifrica. The daughter of Derrick Morgan, a ska king who had jousted with Prince Buster back in the early 1960s, she was raised in a Rastafarian community by her mother and stepfather. From the very start of her career she looked for inspiration to conscious artists: she wanted to sing songs that had a purpose. She has little time for female artists who use sex appeal to sell their music, which she sees as very short-sighted: "You have an artist that will be famous today, you have another that will be famous tomorrow, another one next week, another one next year and another one that will be famous in ten years time. It is what those individuals do with their fame…" [12]

Each of her albums bristles with issues and messages. Fyah Muma opens the lid on social conditions in her home town, the tourism hotspot, Montego Bay. Other songs deal with subjects not so commonly seen in reggae music. Daddy is a song about incest – "Many people, especially young, helpless people who would not normally have the courage to say to somebody that this is happening to them have now gotten that chance and acted upon it. And that is enough for me." [13] And Mi Nah Rub is about skin bleaching: "There is no label on these products and the smell is beyond terrible. The government doesn't intervene and there is nobody coming in to combat the importation of these products. The insecurities is what they are feeding on. I have so many ladies who come to me and tell me about the problems it has caused them. I tell them – love yourself, look at yourself in the mirror and love yourself." [14]

Ifrica has a huge following in Jamaica. Outside Jamaica, though, some know her for one thing only: homophobia. A few of her overseas concerts have been shut down by protestors, but this has only led her to defend her position – which she believes is consistent with her faith and with her role as a champion for victims of abuse – all the more vociferously.

She is not alone. Many of Jamaica's top dance hall stars are being targeted by the international gay community, in some cases for violently homophobic lyrics. This, however, is only one aspect of the problems afflicting dance hall. Violent and obscene lyrics may be bad enough but the dance hall scene has a multitude of links with organised gangs and in recent years this has had some horrific consequences. Several MCs have been shot at, have been involved in shootings or have been arrested for one reason or another. The high-profile feud between Vybz Kartel and Mavado (Gaza vs Gully) wasn't just some publicity stunt: there were competing gangs involved, and they meant business. The former Jamaican police commissioner Owen Ellington claims that: "Vybz Kartel led a gang that was responsible for well over a hundred murders." [15] Certainly violence seemed to follow him wherever he went. Since 2011, he's been incarcerated by the state, and has been tried for two separate murders, getting a not guilty verdict in 2013, but then a guilty verdict and life imprisonment in 2014. None of which seems to have dented his ability to sell records, though in 2014, the Jamaican parliament took a symbolically important step by passing the Anti-Gang Act, which prohibits the performing or recording of music that promotes killing or serious acts of violence.

Buju Banton epitomises the conflicts and contradictions of modern Jamaican dance hall. At the age of 15 he wrote Boom Bye Bye, a song with extremely violent lyrics that appears to incite violent attacks on 'batty bwoys', a derogatory term for gay men.

In his early 20s his career changed direction with the release of 'Til Shiloh (1995), which confirmed a new-found commitment to Rastafari and to conscious lyrics. From this time on, Banton wore his dreadlocks with pride, and his name was always linked to Jamaica's conscious music revival. He told Dorian Lynskey: "I knew that I was here for a greater purpose than to sing songs to make people gyrate, drink and enjoy themselves. I was here to sing songs that can uplift, educate and eradicate negativity." [16]

And yet he was unable – or unwilling – to shake off the ugly legacy of Boom Bye Bye. Gay activists who protested at his overseas concerts grew increasingly frustrated at his reluctance to engage with them, Peter Tatchell saying that, "Banton has been given so many chances to drop his incitements to kill LGBT people. He has refused, or agreed and then gone back on his word." [17] This shouldn't be so surprising: Banton would have been hearing, probably from people close to him, dark mutterings about 'gay agendas'. He was a product of a society where negative stereotypes of gay people were continually reinforced and harmful myths seldom challenged, a society in which there is still overwhelming opposition to the decriminalisation of gay sex. Despite the controversies surrounding him, in February 2011 Buju Banton received a Grammy award for best reggae album. Days later, a jury in Tampa found him guilty on drugs charges and he was sentenced to 10 years.

BETTER MUST COME is Buju at his best, as he'd want to be remembered. The driving reggae rock beat and deep gravelly singing call to mind the music of Bob Marley and the Wailers. It may not break any new ground but it delivers a positive message and is performed with great conviction.

Jamaican music may be going through its trials, but its greatest strength is its own incredibly rich legacy – much of which I've barely touched on in this short chapter. So I'm going to finish by going back to where it all began: mento music. Jamaica's answer to calypso, mento emerged as a rural music that used basic, often improvised instrumentation. The music was upbeat and cheerful, but it was also a genuine folk music, rooted in the lives of the black population, with humour, sexual innuendo and topical references enriching the lyrics.

SLIDE MONGOOSE is a glorious example of all these things. The Blue Glaze version has Sly Mongoose going into Bedward's kitchen, taking a chicken and putting it in its coat pocket. As you may surmise, the song is not really about a mongoose: it's a sexual satire on Alexander Bedward, a Jamaican preacher who proclaimed himself to be a reincarnation of Jesus Christ (which is more than Haile Selassie ever claimed for himself, but that's another story). Although Bedward passed away in 1930, the song outlived him, as later singers rejigged the lyrics to make it more relevant. Blue Glaze keep it mainly real with banjo, drum and percussion, though on this track Dean Fraser guests on sax.

The heyday of mento was the early 1950s: its popularity never really survived independence and the invention of ska. It was a key, necessary part of Jamaica's music revolution, yet it's often been the forgotten part of the country's musical heritage. The 21st century has seen the release of a number of compilations of original mento, so at least the music is now widely available. The Blue Glaze Mento Band released their debut album in 2011 – despite having been going since 1967! For most of that time they did the same as other mento bands: played the hotel circuit, performing for tourists. In more recent years they backed veteran mento singer, Stanley Beckford, on two records and a European tour. Then out of the blue they were approached about taking part in a film.

The documentary was to be called Pimento and Hot Pepper, and the two men behind it were Bill Monsted, a real-estate developer from New Orleans, and British film-maker Rick Elgood. They'd read up everything they could find about mento, and "we knew," says Monsted, "who and where the important mento bands were." They went round the island filming the bands and interviewing musicians some of whom they knew would not have many years to live.

> "The end of this tour brought us back to Kingston and a film/recording session with Blue Glaze Mento Band at Tuff Gong Studios. While filming in the studio was meant to provide a different surrounding to showcase one of the bands, it would also give us a high quality, non-field sound, and I felt Blue Glaze was the best band to provide that. After listening to the results, however, I was convinced that the three or four completed songs could be the foundation for a new audio project. Thus began a three session recording that eventually brought in some prominent guest singers and instrument players." [18]

Not just any guest singers either: Toots Hibbert and Bunny Wailer. For the ageing Blue Glaze musicians, this must have felt like validation at last.

NOTES

1. Stephen Davis – Bob Marley: The Biography (Panther Books, 1984), p116.
2. http://www.uncarved.org/dub/scratch.html
3. http://www.rollingstone.com/music/news/reggaes-mad-scientist-20100708
4. Various sources, e.g. http://www.washingtoncitypaper.com/news/article/13014152/dub-in-dub-out
5. https://www.theguardian.com/music/musicblog/2016/mar/21/lee-scratch-perry-at-80-birthday-reggae-interview
6. http://www.reggae-vibes.com/concert/jclarke/jclarke1.htm, retrieved September, 2016
7. Liner notes to A Ruffer Version: Johnny Clarke at King Tubbys 1974-1978
8. http://www.largeup.com/2016/01/14/largeup-tv-african-roots-with-johnny-clarke
9. http://incolor.inetnebr.com/cvanpelt/dillon.html
10. http://bombmagazine.org/article/2624/judy-mowatt
11. http://sbffranktalk.blogspot.co.uk/2016/02/sister-carol.html

12. http://www.manlikemarvinsparks.com/2009/05/queen-ifrica-interview.
    html, retrieved September, 2016
13. http://www.reggaenews.co.uk/interviews/queen_ifrica.asp retrieved
    September 2016, also quoted at https://clw75.wordpress.com/2013/03/01/
    get-down-with-the-beat/
14. http://www.afrobella.com/2009/08/04/afrobella-of-the-month-queen-
    ifrica/#ixzz1jWy3jMBP
15. http://urbanislandz.com/2014/04/27/jamaica-police-head-vybz-kartel-
    responsible-for-over-100-murders
16. https://www.theguardian.com/music/2003/mar/03/artsfeatures.
    popandrock
17. http://www.santacruz.com/news/one_hate_one_fear.html
18. http://www.bilmonproductions.com/about.html

MEXICO

In the USA Mexican music is enjoying an unprecedented boom. I'm a statistics nerd, so here's a couple of facts that startled me. Daniel Sheehy, director of the Smithsonian Center in Washington, DC, and a specialist in mariachi music, told NBC that at least 500 US public schools now offer mariachi as part of their music curricula. [1] The commercial category known as "regional Mexican" comfortably outsells all other music styles included in the Billboard Latin music charts.

Meanwhile, over in Mexico the traditional music scene has been wilting at the roots for a long time now. As I hope to show, there have been a few artists emerging who are trying to change this, though theirs are not the names most familiar to American audiences. But first things first: how did we get to where we are now?

One effect of the Mexican Revolution was a resurgence of nationalist sentiment and national pride. In 1920s and 1930s Mexico, writes John Chasteen, "everything national had become fashionable – folk music (corridos) and dance (jarabes), traditional dishes (tamales and moles), old-style street theater (carpas), and artisan objects." [2] Several of the main singing styles then – ranchera, corrido and bolero – were quite similar, a common characteristic being the highly expressive and at times

LA ZANDUNGA	*Chavela Vargas*
LA BAMBA	*La Negra Graciana*
EL CASCABEL	*Los Utrera*
QUÉ VIVA EL FANDANGO	*Patricio Hidalgo y el Afrojarocho*
SAN PEDRO HERMOSO	*Alejandra Robles*

melodramatic vocals. People strongly identified with these styles, and none more so than the ranchera. Ranchera was Mexico's answer to country music. Like country music, it had humble rural origins, and like country music it repackaged itself into a nostalgic, sentimentalised version of the country's past. The golden age of the Mexican film industry started in the mid-30s, and some of the biggest screen stars of the age were also popular ranchera singers: Pedro Infante, Jorge Negrete, Antonio Aguilar.

In an age of musical icons and larger-than-life characters, many of whom are still admired today, Chavela Vargas (1919–2012) was like a dangerous presence: a rebel, a mould-breaker. She carried the pains of the world on her back, but also knew many of its pleasures. She had a turbulent childhood in Costa Rica, which she describes in her own inimitable way – "I never got to know my grandparents. My parents I got to know better than I would have liked. They never loved me and when they divorced, I stayed with my uncles – may they burn in hell!" On her uncles' farm she learned all about hard labour, spending long hours on tasks like picking oranges. She dreamed of having a life and a career of her own, and then at the age of 14 she ran away, ending up leaving her home country and travelling to Mexico.

In Mexico she sang, she got to meet some of the stars of the day and she lived for a time with Diego Rivera and Frida Kahlo in their Blue House. But could such a strange, unconventional creature ever hope to have a singing career? Chavela was a lesbian who had little interest in hiding her inclinations (when she finally came out publicly at the age of 81 it was a surprise to no one). She dressed in men's clothes, carried pistols, smoked cigars and drank on stage. Her voice was already deep, though not yet like it was to become in later years. The song that made her famous was called Macorina. Marvette Perez, a curator of the Smithsonian Museum says of it: "I don't think there could be a more queer song for a woman to sing. The song says, 'Ponme la mano aqui, Macorina.' Put your hand right here, Macorina. And whenever she sang the song, she put such sexuality, desire and kind of sensuality into it that you knew why she was singing, and to who she was singing it. She was singing it to a woman." [3]

Chavela's career was outrageous. Stories and myths abounded about her exploits, scandal never seemed too far away. And her performances continued to defy convention as she adopted a male persona. But when she sang, people were mesmerised. Often a song would never sound the same again after you'd heard Chavela's version. **LA ZANDUNGA** was an old Oaxaca song in the son istmeños style that would have been familiar to Chavela's audiences. But by slowing the song down and transferring the emphasis from the melody to her own raspy vocals, she's brought out the tragedy underlying the song.

It couldn't last – and it didn't. When she fell, she fell hard, with no soft landing. Her alcoholism had caught up with her. Chavela had been a fighter all her life, and this was to be her hardest fight, but after many dark years out of the public eye she made a triumphant comeback. Even she could hardly believe the amount of love that was now coming her way: "It's like a miracle. If there are miracles in life that is one of them because there are singers who take a break for a year or two and don't come back, they can't do it. I retired for fifteen, I came back and they opened the gates, hoping for a sight of me." [4]

Popular singers frequently drew on regional folk culture, taking the songs and melodies and putting them in a new context. The musicians wore colourful folk costumes, but a lot of this was window dressing: these were professional groups who'd learned how to cater to the demands of the record and film industries. In the 1960s and '70s small kindlings of interest started up in the roots of this folk culture. The folk revival that followed was centred on the port city of Veracruz.

Veracruz's situation as the main port on the eastern seaboard has led to an eventful history, an ever-changing ethnic mix and a rich culture. The city was founded by Spanish conquistador Hernán Cortés 500 years ago. The Totonacs joined forces with Cortés: many of their descendants still live in Veracruz today. Later, after the slave trade began, Veracruz became the main port of entry for African slaves. Yanga, a town in the state of Veracruz, is named after Gaspar Yanga, an escaped slave whose followers took refuge in the mountains where they frustrated the Spanish authorities for many years. After repelling an attempt by the army to crush them, they forced the government to negotiate with them, and eventually to cede them the right to form a free black settlement. Elsewhere in Mexico, slaves worked in the sugar cane fields and the mines and as personal servants.

The music of Veracruz is called son jarocho, and it's traditionally played at a fandango: a community celebration with good music, poetry, dance and liquor, in which all are encouraged to participate. Don Esteban Utrera (whose dates, I saw with surprise, mirrored Chavela Vargas: 1919–2012) was one of a dwindling number trying to keep the dying tradition alive, organising fandangos in his own home and passing on his knowledge. Gilberto Gutierrez (born 1958) got to know him in the late 1970s. The young Gilberto was impressed by this hard-working man who in addition to raising a large family reared cattle, lived in a sustainable way off the land, and had this deep knowledge of folklore, taking care to preserve ritual and tradition. Just playing songs with him was an education in itself.

In 1977, Gilberto and his older brother, José Ángel Gutiérrez, formed the group Mono Blanco, who almost singlehandedly introduced traditional son jarocho to a new generation of Mexicans. Among the musicians they recruited was one legendary figure – Don Arcadio Hidalgo (1893–1985), a black man who'd fought in the Mexican Revolution. Having his time-worn voice on Mono Blanco's early albums did wonders for their credibility.

Another group with similar objectives, formed in 1985, was El Siquisiri. More were to follow, all from Veracruz or the neighbouring area: Son de Madera, formed in 1992 by Gilberto's younger brother Ramon, after a few years playing with Mono Blanco; also in 1992 the Utrera family band Los Utrera; Los Cojolites in 1995; and Grupo Estanzuela in 1997.

Alongside all these young bands, a mother of eight children well into her 50s was about to start her career. Graciana Silva García (1939–2013) grew up in a musical family. When she was 10 years old her father hired a blind harpist, Don Rodrigo Rodríguez, to teach her brother, Pino Silva, how to play. The sound of the harp was the most beautiful thing she'd ever heard. She listened in attentively to the lessons, learning as much as she could. Pino Silva never mastered the harp, but his sister did. As her playing improved she joined her father's band as they performed at fandangos and other events in the Veracruz region. And decades later she was still playing harp in the bars of Veracruz when the music producer Eduardo Llerenas walked in one night and realised he was seeing something special. Two weeks later La Negra Graciana, as she was now known, was recording an album of son jarocho music for him, accompanied by her brother Pino Silva on jarana (a guitar-shaped instrument unique to Veracruz).

Among the 18 tracks on the album is **LA BAMBA**. This most

recognisable of all Mexican songs is in fact a traditional son from Veracruz, and this is how Veracruz natives will tell you it's supposed to be performed, in a lively fashion, to the music of the harp and the jarana. One might argue that the song's no longer the property of Veracruz: millions of people of Latin heritage around the world have taken it to their heart, and the countless versions that have been released feature artists as diverse as Joan Baez and Wyclef Jean. But it's not merely a song. Gilberto Gutierrez once said, "Without the fandango this music loses its meaning." [5] The dancefloor at a fandango is a wooden platform and depending on which sones are being played, solo dancers or groups of dancers will take the stage. These are dances where people keep rhythm with their feet – like tap dancing, but the direct origin is Spanish flamenco. La Bamba is a couples' dance, and when its fast rhythms are played fancy footwork is essential.

Los Utrera, the group formed from the sons and nephews of Don Esteban Utrera, understand the centrality of the fandango. Several of them are expert dancers, and teaching people the dance steps and preserving the rituals of the fandango are just as important to them as the music itself. Wendy Cao Romero, who's not a family member, describes how Los Utrera became as important to her as family:

> "They have taught me how they work in the community, how they live, how they get together in the fandangos, how they share their expertise, experience, and how Don Esteban is a 'flowering oak' who doesn't fall, in spite of his age and delicate health. We have organised countless fandangos where people no longer played, we have recorded old musicians who had never recorded... I produced the book and video 'Son Estos Pasos' which is a journey through seven regions in the south of Veracruz and examines the different ways of dancing, playing and celebrating." [6]

The track featured here is another old favourite that appears on most son jarocho compilations, **EL CASCABEL**. The musicianship and singing is superb, but again I must leave you to imagine the dancing: it would be one of a set of well-choreographed flamenco-style zapateado dances involving whole groups of suitably attired men and women (white lace dresses are traditional for the women).

The oak finally fell in 2012. Shortly after this, Los Utrera learned that they were to receive an award from the government – the National Prize for Arts and Sciences in the arts category. The award was made jointly to two musical dynasties that had formed just a few miles apart in southern Veracruz and were linked by many bonds of friendship, marriage and musical partnership: the Utrera and Vega families. At the ceremony there was tremendous applause for the two patriarchs, Don Andrés Vega and the absent Don Esteban. Don Andrés also received congratulations from President Felipe Calderón for being one of the architects of "nuevo son jarocho", to which he retorted "¿Nuevo? ¡ Uy! Yo que pensé que tenía como 400 años o más" (New? What! I thought we'd had it for 400 years or more). [7]

Patricio Hidalgo (born 1966) belongs to another musical dynasty: his grandfather was Don Arcadio Hidalgo. The family farm where he grew up was in Apixita, a mainly Nahua community – one of Mexico's ancient indigenous peoples. There was no electricity and no TVs, so they would entertain themselves by singing and playing music. At the age of 12 he visited Minatitlan, where he met his grandfather for the first time. This was around the time when Don Arcadio had just begun collaborating with Mono Blanco. Gilberto Gutierrez and Juan Pascoe of Mono Blanco played for the youngster. "That was my first Son Jarocho show; then we took a ride back to Apixita. Gilberto asked me if I knew my grandfather was famous," telling the boy about all the places he'd been. "I did not know what being famous was, for I saw that the jaraneros [jarana players] no longer played at funerals in

Apixita; and I never knew that they could travel on the road, or earn money from playing." [8] Within a few years, Patricio had learned everything they could teach him about the fandango, and joined Mono Blanco himself, touring Mexico and going to festivals abroad, and earning money for playing and singing.

In the early 1990s, Patricio formed his own group, Chuchumbé. The group's African-sounding name was significant: already Patricio was looking deeply into the roots of son jarocho and making some surprising discoveries: "Seventeen years ago, an antique manuscript was found in the church archives of Puebla (Mexico) with the words of a proscribed song of that era. We took the name 'Chuchumbé' from the lyrics and then worked on putting it to music." [9] Why was it banned? Because it was being sung by Cuban slaves and was associated with a sexually provocative dance. For Patricio, this was part of a hidden history of son jarocho. He applied himself to learning more about the African origins of Veracruz's traditional instruments, to uncovering what he could regarding jarocho's links to slavery and resistance to colonial rule, and to writing new songs that recreated this dark past.

Patricio's latest band, Afrojarocho, are as much a project as a band. All the music serves a purpose: to open the door on this hidden history, on the African roots of son jarocho. "The African element that we have has not been studied nor historicised nor taught – it has been ignored," he claims. "So for me to achieve this – in knowing my grandfather was black and that he lived in Opalapa and that in Opalapa the blacks came from Angola – it was to unveil the African in Son Jarocho." [10] (Don Arcadio's father was a black Cuban immigrant to Mexico, hence the connection to slavery and to West Africa.) The first album, El Regreso de la Conga, is a collection of jarocho congas. Congas had been introduced to the culture of Veracruz by former Cuban slaves who settled in the Sotavento region. This was followed by Subterráneo, an album with a very different feel from your traditional son jarocho album, with its African drums, politicised lyrics and diverse rhythms. QUÉ VIVA EL FANDANGO is almost like a song that's been deconstructed, driven in its first phase just by vocals and a steady percussive beat. A celebration of the fandango wouldn't be complete without hearing the strings strike up a rhythmic melody, and happily this isn't too long in coming.

Veracruz has been the centre of the folk revival, but there have been signs of life elsewhere. In north-eastern Mexico son huasteco trios have been quietly re-emerging. A trio huasteco will typically play a five-stringed jarana huasteca, an eight-stringed bass guitar called a quinta huapanguera, and a violin. Remember Eduardo Llerenas, the guy who 'discovered' La Negra Graciana? He also worked with some friends over a number of years recording the music of the region, and the resulting two CD compilation, El Gusto – 40 Años de son Huasteco, was released in 2012 by his Discos Corason label. I don't think any of these groups are big stars even in Mexico, but the album should be a wake-up call for anyone who thinks that quality Mexican string band music is a thing of the past.

Yet another release on Discos Corason, La Tortuga, Sones Istmeños, is a wonderful introduction to the son istmeño music characteristic of the Isthmus of Tehuantepec region of Oaxaca state. Some songs are sung in Spanish and some in Zapotec, an old indigenous language.

These aren't the styles of music – or the artists – that are making it big in the USA. Mariachi and norteno have serviced the American market for many years now, and the American market and the tourist trade are what drives their development. It's more than likely that the next kings of mariachi will be made up of people living in and probably born in the USA. So for me it's the regional sones that are the beating heart of Mexican music. It's here that the roots of the music are at their most visible, that the African and indigenous influences can be seen; here also there is scope for reclaiming the old traditions and giving them a 21st-century makeover within a Mexican framework.

For some Mexicans at least, learning about and connecting with regional music is more than just a musical project: it's a personal journey, a chance to touch base with aspects of their own identity. Here's the fusion singer-songwriter Lila Downs (born 1968):

"In Mexico... there are many signals warning against identifying yourself too closely with your indigenous roots. It's a barrier to social mobility, so everyone fantasizes about being güerito. My father was a white Anglo-Saxon man... my mother always insisted that I spend a lot of time with him, which took my mind away from my Indian origins. It was only much later, after his death, when I began to reconnect with the culture of my mother and feel proud of my roots." [11]

The fact that Lila – an educated girl who'd spent time living in the USA and whose father was an academic – could have felt this way about her origins speaks volumes about the racism that was endemic in Mexican society. What gave her confidence as an adult was the revolutionary Zapatista movement that since 1994 has been a voice for indigenous peoples and the voiceless poor. Racism is still present, if not always acknowledged. Afro-Mexicans – Mexicans of black African descent – chafe at the fact that indigenous people, although discriminated against, at least enjoy some official status, while their status is barely acknowledged and seldom discussed. They describe themselves as Mexico's 'third root'. In 2008, the Mexican government released a rare study that confirmed that Afro-Mexicans suffer from institutional racism. For Mexico's blacks, though, most of whom live in the southern states of Oaxaca, Guerrero and Veracruz, changes have been slow in coming. The kidnap of 43 students on the night of 26th

September, 2014, took place in Iguala, a town in Guerrero, and the students were mostly from rural and indigenous backgrounds. In their battle to learn the truth, relatives of the missing students allied themselves not with the police or the authorities but with the Zapatista EZLN.

Yes, racism still existed, but anti-racism had found its voice. There was now a movement to defend the rights of minority groups, a movement that deepened as artists and musicians found their own ways of expressing support for its aims. Questions of identity were being widely debated. This was the context in which the Oaxaca singers, Lila Downs and Alejandra Robles, chose to celebrate rather than deny their ethnic origins.

Alejandra Robles (born 1978) is from the Costa Chica region of Oaxaca. Costa Chica is home to one of biggest concentrations of Afro-Mexicans in the country, but anthropologist and author Bobby Vaughn claims that: "all but the most educated people in the Costa Chica pueblos in which I have worked have had little consciousness of Africa and even less of being part of any African diaspora." [12] He could also have added that there is little sense of common cause with the indigenous peoples who also live in the region. The music of the region is not his main concern, but he notes that there are three types of rural music in Costa Chica – tropical, chilenas and corridos – and of these the rock-based tropical genre is the most popular. Or to put it differently, traditional music is not very popular, which is to be expected among populations that lack a strong self-identity.

However, there are people trying to turn this situation around, and what is of interest here is that one of the ways in which they are doing this is through music. There's now an annual black people's cultural festival in the town of Huazolotitlán, which sets out primarily through music and dance to celebrate and raise awareness of black history and culture. And artists like Alejandra Robles are trying to revive the chilena – a music steeped in local history, brought to the region by Chilean sailors in the 19th century along with the cueca dance; perhaps black dockworkers would have been among the first to pick it up and hear the music before it spread among the Afro-Mexican population.

Alejandra took classes in contemporary dance at the School of Fine Arts of Oaxaca, afterwards majoring in opera at the Universidad Veracruzana, while also studying African and tap dance. Dance is very important to her: it's a tradition that runs deep in her family, and that she associates with Afro-Mexican culture. Her songs are from Oaxaca, Guerrero and Veracruz, but again and again she returns to chilenas – this is what she identifies with the most. SAN PEDRO HERMOSO is a nice example of her style. It's lively and fun, and an affirmation of her love of dance rhythms, but it's far from being traditional. Additional instruments have been added, and then afterwards Alejandra injects her own style, her own personality. It's one of the most joyous moments on an album, La Sirena, which covers a lot of musical ground – alternating continually between the slow and the fast, different ideas and style combinations.

She believes that the black people's festival in Costa Chica is brilliant – the Afro-Caribbean Festival in Veracruz also – but it's not enough to hold multicultural festivals in these regions: "I'd love there to be ones in Queretaro, Mexico City, Tamaulipas, Nuevo Leon, Jalisco. Each state to have a festival dedicated to the black race." [13]

NOTES

1. http://usnews.nbcnews.com/_news/2012/05/04/11526485-mariachi-has-changed-my-life-mexican-music-grabs-us-students?lite
2. John Chasteen – Born in Blood and Fire: A Concise History of Latin America (W.W. Norton & Co, 2001), p226.
3. http://www.wbur.org/npr/131295564/chavela-vargas-the-voice-of-triumph
4. http://www.letraslibres.com/revista/artes-y-medios/les-dejo-de-herencia-mi-libertad-entrevista-con-chavela-vargas

5. http://www.banderasnews.com/0604/ent-sonjarocho.htm
6. http://losutreraintegrantes.blogspot.co.uk
7. http://periodicoperformance.blogspot.co.uk/2013/06/los-vega-y-los-utrera.html
8. http://www.musiquesdumonde.net/Patricio-Hidalgo-Belli.html
9. http://www.speroforum.com/a/2049/Chuchumbe-music-to-bridge-the-gap#.Vew_8anxrQk
10. http://www.voyageofsound.com/post/54217431410/revolution-and-rhythm-patricio-hidalgo-reviving, retrieved Septenber, 2015
11. http://www.letraslibres.com/revista/artes-y-medios/lila-downs-musica-americana-sin-fronteras
12. Bobby Vaughn – Afro-Mexico: Blacks, Indigenas, Politics and the Greater Diaspora, from Anani Dzidzienyo and Suzanne Oboler (eds) – Neither Enemies nor Friends: Latinos, Blacks, Afro-Latinos (Palgrave Macmillan, 2005), p125.
13. http://guerrerocultural87.blogspot.co.uk/2011/09/alejandra-robles-el-canto-de-una-morena.html

NICARAGUA

Bluefields is the largest town on Nicaragua's Atlantic coast, also known as the Mosquito Coast after the indigenous Miskito people. It's also by far the most ethnically diverse community in Nicaragua, which has much to do with the town's colourful history. Bluefields is named after a Dutch pirate called Abraham Blauvelt. In the 17th century, the Caribbean was awash with pirates and one of the great prizes was the rich Spanish city of Granada on the shores of Lake Nicaragua. Blauvelt established a settlement on the relatively less well defended Mosquito Coast, and after the region became a UK protectorate in 1655 the British called the town Bluefields. It remained a UK protectorate for 200 years, during which time the British allied themselves with the Miskito kings, and English is spoken in Bluefields to this day. In the latter part of the 19th century an agreement was drawn up to set aside part of the Mosquito Coast as a self-governing Miskito reserve, but in 1894 the region was annexed by Nicaragua.

Geographically, Bluefields has remained very isolated from the centres of population on the east coast:

"To get to Bluefields from Nicaragua's capital of Managua, first you take a bus for about six hours. At the last stop you

move to a boat: either a speedboat that will bounce over the
river for two hours or a slower one that takes six hours, Mark
Twain-style. It's either that, or a ride on a bouncy dirt road
that was supposed to be upgraded to asphalt years ago." [1]

Those who can afford it can also fly. This isolation has helped to preserve its unique ethnic make-up and independent character. Long starved of support from central government, the people draw strength from one another. They speak a few different languages, but they all seem to get along pretty well. I've mentioned the Miskito people; other indigenous groups are Ulwa, Mayangna, Rama and Garífuna. If you're not indigenous, you probably identify either as mestizo or Creole.

Natural disasters are no stranger to Bluefields. In 1988, the town took the full force of Hurricane Joan and the houses that were made of wood collapsed like matchsticks. Press reports quoted a Red Cross nurse at the scene saying, "There isn't enough left of the houses to make a fire." [2] Afterwards concrete was used in a lot of the rebuilding.

For years Bluefields has also been home to some of Nicaragua's most distinctive and exciting music. The focus of this is Palo de

Mayo, or the Maypole Festival, which runs through the entire month of May, culminating in a street parade after sundown on 31st May known as Tulululu. Community groups join in the parade as it passes by; maypole trees are carried aloft festooned with ribbons while people shake and dance behind.

Maypole is a curious amalgam of British and African traditions. British May Day traditions have pagan roots, and the ritualistic, magical character of maypole dancing must have struck a chord with the local Creole population. Numerous descriptions of Palo de Mayo inform us that the festival is a celebration of Mayaya, an African goddess of fertility. This seems dubious: if it relates to an African religion I've not been able to find it, it's more likely that Mayaya is a variant of Maia, the Greco-Roman goddess of spring. The most respected living authority on maypole tradition is Bluefields resident Lizzie Nelson (born 1922):

> "The maypole dance was first celebrated south of here in Greytown, sometime in the 17th century by British colonists. It spread from there with slave owners to the Corn Islands and later the lagoon. It has since become more multicultural. Every May my mother and aunts used to dance around a green tree hung with little fruits. Since the 1960s, the tree has been substituted for a ribbon pole, but the steps remain the same. We call the dance a mento or soka, but the steps are basically those of a polka. Another group dance we call the shotise, and it is a kind of quadrille." [3]

Despite Lizzie's best efforts, maypole dancing has moved away from this traditional model over the years, becoming more and more sensual.

Maypole music is street festival music, its core elements being heavy drumming and calypso type songs with a repeated refrain.

Modern groups will use horns, electric guitars and electronic instruments to beef up their sound. Some modern composers have tried their hand at writing maypole songs with varying degrees of success, but the traditional songs have a magic that's hard to beat. Some are little stories of everyday life, usually four lines or a verse sung repeatedly. Judith Drownded is a song that tells how gossip can spread – in the song Judith is still alive. Anancy Oh references a spider character from African folklore. Others like Tulululu or Mayaya (Lost the Key) direct the movements of the dancers (though there may be other meanings: the search for the key may be symbolic of the changing of the seasons, and so on).

The group who've come to define maypole music and have introduced it to the lives of people around the world are Dimension Costeña. They started out in the 1970s in the Old Bank neighbourhood of Bluefields under the name Grupo Gamma. Founder member and vocalist, Anthony Matthews, had grown up selling fish and shining shoes for a living. Before the group was formed he used to sing Beatles songs in English. The new group did their research and soon became experts on maypole. At first they set their stall playing traditional instruments such as the bongo drum and donkey jawbone, "but public demand forced us to recruit other musicians to play saxophone, trombone, synthesizer, and the group now has 11 members". [4] This was maypole as it had never been heard before. The repertoire wasn't new, but the big band sound was, and there were a few new rhythms too. By the 1980s, Dimension Costeña were the most popular band in the country, and in demand internationally.

SOUP ON THE TABLE is a celebration song. It tells of a great party where there's an abundance of food on the table. The refrain is 'finga nail'. Someone has found nails in the soup – a disaster! But the fast frenetic pace of the tune and the light tone of the song leave no doubt that we're supposed to smile. We all know what it is to struggle to put soup on the table, is the subtext. Let's shrug off life's difficulties and be joyful while we can.

In the 1980s, under the Sandinistas, there was a change of direction of cultural policy. The radical priest and poet Ernesto Cardenal was made minister of culture, and he had a strong vision that strengthening regional identity was an essential part of discovering and defining national identity, that cultural struggle had a key role to play in this, and that it was the duty of central government to give support where it was needed. Cardenal gave backing to a variety of indigenous cultural projects. The Palo de Mayo Festival was expanded and the research and promotion of maypole tradition was given government backing. As a result, interest in and knowledge of maypole began to grow apace.

Three decades on, Bluefields is still a hub for lovers of roots music. Driving things forwards is a new non-profit project called Bluefields Sound System (BSS). BSS is a community recording studio, a multimedia skills centre, a school of music and a cultural preservation project. Their offices are provided rent-free in government buildings but they're independently run and have to find their own funding. At the school, young artists learn about traditional maypole music, but they also learn graphic design, web design and production skills, equipping them to take on the challenges of the 21st century. Already they've done a few crowdfunding projects, there's a few promising artists emerging, and BSS are in a position to release all recordings through their bandcamp page. The project's credibility is greatly enhanced by the involvement of veterans such as Mango Ghost (who died in 2012) and Sabu.

Sabu's nickname is El Hombre Gato – 'the catman' – and I love this description of him: "The 65-year-old performs with the energy of a gatito (kitten); showing off his wild leg kicks and dance moves that would make the artist formerly known as Michael Jackson jealous." [5] The explanation for his demonic energy, according to BSS, is that he: "according to folklore was born a monkey, and sold his soul to the devil to receive the powers to inject audiences with his music." [6] He only made one album in the mid-1980s:

fortunately the master tapes survived the onslaught of Hurricane Joan, to be remastered and re-released to the world by BSS nearly 30 years later. It's not a maypole music album and there are a few changes of pace, but it's the maypole song that is the most irresistible. On **CHACALIN** the high quality production brings out the earthiness of his voice, and if you close your eyes, you may just be able to see Sabu's feet flying in all directions as he sings.

NOTES

1. http://www.ticotimes.net/2015/06/02/bluefields-the-dream-of-independence-for-a-forgotten-colonial-harbor
2. http://www.nytimes.com/1988/10/24/world/hurricane-kills-111-in-caribbean-and-leaves-thousands-homeless.html
3. https://www.theguardian.com/uk/1999/may/08/3
4. http://www.monimbo.us/files/Anthony.pdf
5. http://www.parisdjs.com/index.php/post/Martin-Perna-of-Ocote-Soul-Sounds-presents-Afro-Nicaraguan-Music-from-Bluefields
6. https://bluefieldsound.bandcamp.com/album/live-your-life-vive-tu-vida

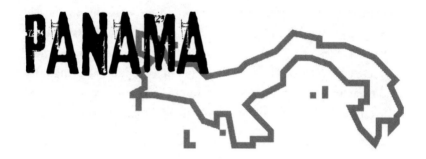

PANAMA

On 15th August 2014, the 100th anniversary of the opening of the Panama Canal, President Juan Carlos Varela visited Corozal American Cemetery, where he laid a wreath in honour of all those who contributed to the construction, operation and maintenance of the canal. Most of the news media made perfunctory reference to the 25,000 who are said to have died during the construction of the 50-mile canal. These reports, however, did not see fit to mention the colour of their skins.

The influx of West Indian labour to Panama began in the 1850s, when contractors for the American-owned Panama Canal Railway Company recruited thousands of Jamaicans to work on the new railway. The employment practices from the railway were adopted wholesale by the French when they started construction on the canal in the 1880s. During this abortive phase of the construction, the main causes of the appalling death rate were diseases such as malaria and yellow fever. No one was safe, but the Jamaican blacks who were compelled to live in filthy insanitary conditions were hit disproportionately hard. West Indians earned $0.10 an hour, and the work was pitilessly hard. Few stayed longer than a year.

When the Americans began work on the canal in 1904, they did more than retain an exploitative labour system: discrimination

TAMBORITO SWING	*Los Silvertones*
EL PAJARO ZUM ZUM	*Ceferino Nieto*
TU CUMPLEANOS	*Oswaldo Ayala*

became institutionalised. They did this through what was known as the gold and silver roll system.

Gold-roll workers enjoyed higher pay, sick leave and home leave entitlements, better housing, better schools, better health care, and so on. Silver roll, on the other hand, lived in ghettos and enjoyed few rights. Initially the gold roll included any skilled and semi-skilled workers. But after a few years this changed: in a political move West Indian workers were barred from the gold roll and many were demoted. At the same time the Canal Zone enacted a policy of not hiring any American blacks. So it was that racial segregation became a fact of life in Panama. In the areas assigned to the blacks – predominantly in Colón Province – permanent towns grew up, known to this day as silver towns.

The Jamaican government, still sore at having to bear the cost of repatriating its citizens after the French project collapsed in 1889, imposed a prohibitive tax on anyone wishing to leave to work in Panama. So, instead, the Canal Zone recruited heavily from Barbados, and to a lesser degree from the French islands of Martinique and Guadeloupe. Culebra Cut symbolised the dangers under which silver-roll workers toiled. Working in brutal heat, under the threat of mud slides that could engulf anything in their path, they not only drilled rock but had to transport extraordinary quantities of dynamite, and many a fuse was set off accidentally.

Those West Indians who stayed in Panama after 1914 – and there were many of them – would remain subject to silver-roll regulations for many years. They would also play a significant part in shaping the country and its culture.

Before talking about the music, I feel that I should acknowledge a huge debt to the three-volume series compiled by Roberto Gyemant and released by Soundway:

- *Panama! Latin, Calypso and Funk on the Isthmus 1965–75 (2006)*
- *Panama! 2, Latin Sounds, Cumbia Tropical & Calypso Funk on the Isthmus, 1967–77 (2009)*
- *Panama! 3, Calypso Panameño, Guajira Jazz & Cumbia Típica on the Isthmus 1960–75 (2009)*

These albums are essential listening, and laid down here are the many components of a musical heritage that's as exciting as anything to be found in Central America. Gyemant himself has no doubts as to why Panama has produced such a variety of floor-filling music: a major reason is the country's unique racial make-up, and the influences brought to the country by the black immigrant workers who built the canal. [1]

One obvious influence was calypso. According to Panama-based journalist Aliyya Swaby, it was in the coastal region of Bocas del Toro that Panamanian calypso took root – "A large wave of Caribbean workers migrated to Bocas del Toro to work on the banana plantations in the 1920s, and they brought calypso with them. They played in the streets, in bars, and in restaurants, from night until morning – for audiences of all ethnicities." [2] Panama certainly had its share of fine calypso singers. One of these, Lord Cobra, was a former bartender who grew up in Bocas del Toro but who made his name in Colón Province. He sang about everyday events but he sang with such grace and wit and humour that the people loved him.

El tamborito, Panama's national dance, was first introduced to the country by African slaves several hundred years ago. El tamborito means 'little drum', and in a traditional performance three drums beat the rhythm while spectators clap and stomp their feet. It's a courtship dance: the male dancer, called montuno after the straw hat he wears, holds his arms aloft and moves his feet in a rapid shuffle. The female dancer or empollerada (after her long skirt) holds the skirt out wide and lets it swish gracefully as she moves around the floor.

TAMBORITO SWING, from the Panama! 2 album, is like a full force gale hurling the traditional elements of the dance up in the air and seeing where they land. This is music born in the swinging nightclubs of Colón, where people would dance to anything that moved. In Los Silvertones's tamborito it's the horn players, not the drummers, who take centre stage; it's all about finding the pulse of the audience, which they do brilliantly with this tune. This is just one example of what can happen when different cultures meet.

For the first half of the 20th century, the dominant instrument in Panama had been the violin. A growing thirst for hotter dance grooves drove the pace of change. Before long another instrument was to come to the fore that would become indelibly identified with Panamanian music. Perhaps surprisingly, this was an instrument that originated in Europe: the accordion.

It's even more surprising when you learn that, at the time, the accordion was regarded as a bit of a vulgar instrument. It was played mostly in bars to working-class men who didn't know any better, whereas men and women of refinement prided themselves on a taste for the more respectable violin music. The man who did most to popularise the accordion in Panama came from a peasant background, and though he was of Spanish stock his band called themselves Las Plumas Negras (the Black Feathers), in acknowledgement of the fact that many of them were dark-skinned. Rogelio 'Gelo' Córdoba was the first accordionist in the isthmus to make recordings, and the success of these paved the way for other conjunto musicians to adopt the instrument. Gelo did not live to see the full fruits of what he'd started: he died of a stroke in 1959 at the age of 43.

Ceferino Nieto (born in the Azuero province of Herrera in 1937) was one of many superb artists emerging around this time. Although his father had been an accordionist, Nieto started out as a violin player, but once he decided at the age of 15 to move to the capital it was inevitable that he would soon pick up the accordion. His brother helped him get a job at Café Durán, and before long he had a night job working as a musician. As the money started coming in he bought himself his first couple of accordions at $173 each. By 1953, he'd formed his first band, and by the 1960s his rivalry with another band leader, Dorindo Cárdenas, had made him famous. From their musical contests the two men became close friends.

On the track **EL PAJARO ZUM ZUM** the looping drum rhythm and the sound of shaking maracas should tell you that this is cumbia music. Although cumbia is most strongly associated with Colombia, its roots in Panama are just as old and as deep. For generations the cumbia dances had been popular. In the 20th century cumbia's popularity was growing across Latin America. Until this time the music had kept a very traditional form, played with a small number of instruments with the flute providing the melody. But in Colombia, as larger bands began playing cumbia, horn sections, guitars and accordions were being added. Soon more modern versions of cumbia were sweeping across Panama too: this was what packed the dancefloors, and what self-respecting band doesn't want to get their audiences dancing away?

Panamanian folk music is called musica tipica, and this too has evolved much over the years. Many musicians come from the

Azuero peninsula on the Pacific coast, and this was the birthplace in 1952 of my third featured artist, Osvaldo Ayala. Ayala is also known as El Escorpión de Paritilla after the village where he grew up. He's an internationally acclaimed accordionist who, in 1996, won a Grammy for a collaboration with the king of Panamanian salsa Ruben Blades. Tipica is a broad genre encompassing the old and the new. Currently successful tipica act, the brother/sister duo Samy y Sandra Sandoval, draw on a wide range of musical influences. Ayala by contrast has a deep respect for tradition and I can think of no better introduction to the music of Panama than his song **TU CUMPLEANOS**, with its slightly slower rhythm.

For most Panamanians, the country's proudest hour was not 15th August 1914, but 31st December 1999. On this date the country assumed total control of the canal, following a treaty signed by US president Jimmy Carter in 1977. In the eyes of many this was the moment when the country finally achieved true independence. It was a day of national celebration: "The streets of the city, on the east bank of the Pacific entrance to the canal, and Colón, on the west bank of the Caribbean approach, are decorated with bunting, buildings are plastered with commemorative posters, and the airwaves are filled with exultant salsa songs. Even Coca-Cola cans carry a slogan celebrating the handover." [3] Among the events on the day, Ruben Blades played an open-air concert to an audience of thousands, while Osvaldo Ayala was performing with the national Symphony Orchestra in the Canal's main administration building.

NOTES

1. http://www.sfbg.com/2009/07/01/isthmus-insanity
2. http://www.ozy.com/performance/panamanian-calypso/30055.article
3. http://www.nytimes.com/1999/12/26/travel/what-s-doing-in-panama.html

PUERTO RICO

In June 2017, Puerto Rico held a referendum on the island's future. The three options: independence, statehood (becoming the 51st US state) or retaining their present status as a US overseas territory. My initial reaction was probably the same as yours: independence seemed a logical choice for an island with a strong cultural identity, and where most people speak Spanish as their first language. In fact, 97% voted for statehood. OK, the result didn't mean much, mainly because opposition parties boycotted the ballot, which they said was rigged, and turnout was only 23%. But the ties to the USA run deep. All Puerto Ricans are US citizens and carry US passports, and if they want to settle in the USA there's no wall that can stop them. More Puerto Ricans live in the USA than live in Puerto Rico: by recent estimates over five million live in the USA, a large proportion of these in New York City and Florida. Would they really want to trade this freedom for the freedom of independence?

Just three months later, Puerto Ricans were given a rude wake-up call. Hurricane Maria hit the island with full force, creating the worst natural disaster in its recorded history. The entire power grid was destroyed, leaving the island with no electricity; in a disaster for one of its main cash crops, 18 million coffee trees

PORQUE NO PUEDO SER FELIZ   *Héctor Lavoe*

PARAÍSO BORINCANO   *Ecos de Borinquen*

were destroyed; overall, 80% of the territory's agriculture was lost. Now more than ever Puerto Rico needed American support. But they discovered that actually the USA didn't care very much about them. Coverage of the disaster in American media was scanty, and President Trump's initial response was a highly unsympathetic tweet saying that Puerto Ricans faced a financial crisis of their own making.

All this is grist to the mill for those who argue that statehood would mean more Americanisation and an erosion of the island's cultural distinctiveness. Puerto Rico knows all too well what cultural assimilation can do. When Columbus arrived, the island was inhabited by thousands of Taino Indians, but their numbers were decimated by diseases carried by the Europeans. The Taino still have a ghostly presence: Puerto Ricans have borrowed many words from the old Arawak language, and surprising numbers of Puerto Ricans carry Taino DNA. Today Taino is a dead culture. But Puerto Rico does have its living cultures that aren't American-inspired. Bomba and plena are the music of black Puerto Rico, a meld of African and Caribbean influences. Jibaro, on the other hand, has a very Spanish flavour: it's played on stringed instruments, most notably the cuatro, and typically follows a song format called the décima, which is descended from old Spanish ballads.

Jibaro is also a national myth, a myth just as potent in its way as that of the American cowboy. For the term also refers to the campesinos: Puerto Rico's poor farm workers. These simple, poorly educated men of the mountains became icons, supposed to represent all the purest and most essential qualities of Puerto Rican identity – honest and hard-working, also a proud people, who revolted against Spanish rule, then stood up to the Americans after the Spanish had been ejected. It's a romanticised view of history that airbrushes out the mighty part played by black slaves in shaping the island's story. More generally, it takes no account of the many ways in which the Puerto Rican character has been enriched through exposure to other cultures.

Héctor Lavoe (1946–93) was often spoken of as a jibaro, yet his life could hardly have been further removed from the stereotype. The young Héctor Martinez grew up not in a mountain farm but in a working-class barrio of the city of Ponce. At the age of 16, against his father's wishes, he boarded a plane to New York to pursue his dreams of becoming a singer.

> "On the jet and for many years after, Lavoe was haunted by the... last words of his father, 'If you go to New York, forget you have a father!' Hector realized that he had to prove himself, so right then and there, he made himself a promise..." [1]

The promise was to achieve money and success, whatever it cost him. Before long he'd already sung in several bands, and acquired a new stage name – Lavoe, which meant La Voz (The Voice). Then in 1967 fate (in the person of Johnny Pacheco) brought him together with a young Nuyorican called Willie Colón. Willie's debut album El Malo, with Héctor's vocals, was an instant hit, and a defining moment for a new musical genre called salsa. The title was significant. El Malo means 'the bad one' and Willie and Héctor played off a bad boy image: they were the kids from the barrios, from the margins of society, and they made music that appealed to the Nuyorican youth. Unlike New York's Latin orchestras this music was fresh, it was swinging and it was contemporary.

Héctor inhabited two worlds. He was the voice of Puerto Rico while also representing the New York scene. Willie Colón remembers him as: "basically a hick from Puerto Rico [who] wanted to come to New York and be part of this 'West Side Story' kind of thing. I was raised by my grandmom in the South Bronx, who told me, 'Don't forget you're Puerto Rican.' He taught me Spanish, I taught him English." [2]

They were as close as brothers. But, like many things in Héctor's life, the partnership was not to last. By the mid-1970s they had gone their separate ways. Héctor, already a legend, recorded many more albums both with his own band and with the Fania All Stars. **PORQUE NO PUEDO SER FELIZ** is everything that one could ask in a salsa tune: a strong dance rhythm, full of brass and fast guitar work and dripping with emotion. It's feel-good music, but with an undertone of sadness – the title means 'why can't I be happy'. Sadly, the title was all too prescient.

Héctor's tragic life has been the subject of several biographies, and of a Hollywood film, El Cantante, in which real-world couple Marc Anthony and Jennifer Lopez play the singer and his wife. For many years Héctor fought the demons of drug and alcohol addiction, while personal tragedies seemed to follow him around. There had been warnings: his brother died of a drug overdose on the streets of New York City, and this was part of the reason why his father had been so desperate to keep him at home. His home in Queens was burned down by a fire, almost wiping out his entire family. Back in Puerto Rico, his mother-in-law was brutally murdered, and his father died. His 17-year-old son was accidentally shot and killed by a friend. In 1985, he was diagnosed with HIV, an occupational hazard for intravenous drug users. He continued performing, but his emotions were in turmoil, his life turned upside down. In 1988, after giving what he thought was his last concert, he attempted suicide by jumping off the ninth floor of the Regency Hotel Condado in Puerto Rico. He survived to see five more painful years before his AIDS-related death in 1993.

The funeral took place in New York. Thousands of the city's Latin community came together for what must have been a truly memorable occasion:

"The funeral procession to St Raymond's cemetery lasted six hours. And during this time the crowd and those following the caminata (procession) played, sang and danced to Héctor Lavoe's music. At the cemetery, many climbed on top of mausoleums and continued to sing Plena music in tribute to him during the final benediction and hours after the lowering of the coffin into the grave." [3]

Miguel Santiago Díaz was born the same year as Héctor Lavoe, 1946, in the heart of jíbaro country, and jíbaro music was in his blood. "As a child, he often heard his father improvise décimas at local town competitions, where trovadores would compete in fiery duels known as controversias." [4] His father taught him what he knew, but Miguel was eager to improve his skills, so he raided the library to discover more about the art of the jíbaro. The controversias especially appealed to him: "a pico a pico is what we call an encounter, a controversy between singers. Each singer might be improvising six, seven, eight décimas… If there is not a run-in between singers, an encounter, a give-and-take, as we say, well, then the fiesta is lacking." [5]

Unlike Héctor, he wasn't interested in the pursuit of fame and fortune. He fell into his career almost accidentally through his interest in education. Ecos de Borinquen began life as a radio show, which Miguel used to raise awareness of traditional music and promote young singers. The show needed a house band, and so the group Ecos de Borinquen was formed. That was in around 1980, and ever since then Ecos de Borinquen have been tireless ambassadors for jibaro music both in Puerto Rico and on the world stage. Miguel remains very much part of the group, making sure that it remains faithful to his original vision while also providing lead vocals on many tracks.

Of the group's many recordings, the two released on the Folkways label are most likely to be familiar to European and American record buyers: Jíbaro Hasta el Hueso: Mountain Music of Puerto Rico (2003) and El Alma de Puerto Rico: Jíbaro Tradition (2016). They are a great introduction to jibaro music, but they're by no means entirely traditional. There's a lot of creative input from the band: musical director Ramón Vázquez Lamboy writes arrangements, and Miguel himself writes a lot of lyrics. PARAÍSO BORINCANO is a track from the 2016 album, sung by Yezenia Cruz, who cut her musical teeth some years back singing on Miguel's radio programme. The song, written in décima format, is a homage to the island's natural beauty.

Much has changed from the time when Miguel Santiago Díaz began making his radio programmes. The cuatro is staging something of a comeback: there are many more young cuatristas now, cuatro orchestras, cultural festivals. In these ways the music can act as a jumping off point for those interested in exploring aspects of their cultural identity. And these explorations are set to continue, whatever the decision is that Puerto Ricans make on their island's future.

NOTES

1.   http://www.salsamagazine.com/index.php?page=14
2.   http://www.nytimes.com/2006/08/13/movies/13beal.html
3.   Agustín Laó-Montes and Arlene Dávila (eds) – Mambo Montage: The Latinization of New York City (Columbia University Press, 2001), p217.

4. Jaime Bofill, sleeve notes to El Alma de Puerto Rico: Jíbaro Tradition, http://media.smithsonianfolkways.org/liner_notes/smithsonian_folkways/SFW40570.pdf

5. Daniel Sheehy, sleeve notes to Jíbaro Hasta el Hueso: Mountain Music of Puerto Rico, http://media.smithsonianfolkways.org/liner_notes/smithsonian_folkways/SFW40506.pdf

SAINT KITTS AND NEVIS

The word 'carnival' comes from the Latin 'carne vale' – farewell, flesh. The reason being that early carnivals were a time of feasting and merrymaking before the deprivations of Lent. In several countries, such as Trinidad, the carnival season strictly precedes Lent to this day.

Not so in St Kitts and Nevis. The St Kitts carnival is a Christmas event, officially starting on Christmas Eve and carrying through to the start of the New Year. So the question is: why the difference? What's that all about?

The first Englishman to start a colony in the Caribbean was Sir Thomas Warner, on St Kitts in 1624. An old colony, it also inherited a few old English traditions. The settlers associated Christmas with feasting, processions and mummers plays. This is the origin of the street theatre that is such a distinctive part of Kititian culture, though it's doubtful whether the early settlers would have recognised the Christmas Sports of modern-day carnival! One carnival tradition is at least loosely based on the mummers, and that's the mummies plays. But in general the Christmas Sports as they exist today are a mix of African, European and Caribbean influences. As a crude guide, the moko-jumbies (stilt walkers) are based on African mythology, the clowns are probably a take on the jester of European folklore, while the Bull Play is inspired by an incident that took place on St Kitts a mere 100 years ago. Masquerade dances are an even more bewildering cultural potpourri:

> *"The Quadrille, which has its roots in 17th century France, is the first dance. It is a slow, structured couples dance. The second dance, the Fine, picks up the pace. It demands greater skill as the dancers work their way, on one foot, towards each other in the centre of the ring. There they perform a Fertility Dance that is traceable to the mating dance of Africa.*
>
> *The real spectacle comes when the masquerades break into a frenzy of Wild Mas, throwing their tomahawks into the air. This dance is typical of the African war dance that has been performed over millennia. The next dance is the Jig. Here the dancers display their skill with the tomahawk, with their right foot hooked behind their left.*
>
> *This dance follows right into the Boillola, another dance movement where the tomahawk is held between the dancer's legs, while the dancers jump and clap to the music,*

moving from side to side. European roots are put on parade
when the dancers pair off into couples and perform the
Waltz to a moderately fast triple meter." [1]

All performed, of course, in colourful and lovingly crafted costumes evocative of West African culture.

Carnival music, on the other hand, isn't markedly different from that of other Caribbean islands; so soca is the dominant genre but people also still dance to the beat of calypso and steelpan music. Back in 1962, when soca hadn't yet been invented, and the island's music still retained something of its diversity and uniqueness, Alan Lomax visited Nevis and recorded chantey-singing fishermen, calypsos accompanied by guitar and cuatro, and string bands, fife players and drummers performing quadrilles. But St Kitts and Nevis are small islands with a tiny population, and, in an era where music – and indeed people – could cross oceans at will, it was perhaps inevitable that their music would follow a similar path to that of their Caribbean neighbours.

The undisputed king of carnival today is Konris Maynard (born 1983), who performs under the name King Konris: he's a six time winner of the St Kitts National Calypso Monarch and a three time winner of the regional Leeward Island Calypso Monarch. He is from musical stock: his father and his uncle both took themselves seriously enough to acquire their own nicknames (Mighty Contenda and Mighty Director). From his teenage years Konris applied himself to his music – but he also applied himself just as diligently to his studies. So in between battling for those Junior Monarch titles he was in college in St Kitts. Then while studying for his BA at the University of the West Indies in Jamaica he decided that the senior competition needed a new lease of life – and that he was the man to provide it. So in 2005 he entered a song, winning the Monarch title at the first attempt. This was to be the first of an unprecedented four successive victories, during which time he also collected a first-class degree in electrical and computer engineering and enrolled for a master's degree in the same field from the University of Waterloo in Canada.

FINISH DE SONG is a light-hearted track in which he makes fun of his own trait of trying to 'pursue perfection':

> "Whenever I'm doing my songs, I take a bit of time to finish them because I go over them and make sure they are what they're supposed to be; the music, the theme, making sure the whole song come together. I told myself I can make this into a song and talk about some of the things that I have songs about that maybe up to this day I still can't finish them. Because of my little curse of trying to be perfect, trying to avoid any problems, I don't think it's finish, so my fans, friends, family, they tell me finish de song." [2]

Behind its fun exterior this was a very personal song. Konris sang of his desire to make a difference, to write that one song that could unite the nation, and warned the politicians that if they failed to get their act together then next time round he could be running for president. This was no idle threat: in 2015 he was elected to parliament as a member of the opposition Labour Party.

Konris is a worthy champion who still has much to give, many songs to write. I have to note the fact, though, that, whether you call it soca or calypso, he is singing to a fast, synthesised beat. There's nothing on show here that resembles a traditional musical instrument. The music lacks the richness, the subtlety, the human touch that traditional instruments can give it. By way of comparison, Ellie Matt, the previous generation's carnival king, was a multi-instrumentalist, and if you listen to his early hits you can hear the sound of a full band. Taking stock of Kititian music today, the ageing calypsonian admits that "the music has deteriorated over the years", [3] though this is a criticism that could equally be levelled at other Caribbean countries.

NOTES

1. http://www.stkittstourism.kn/love-st-kitts-culture-history-arts-culture.php
2. http://www.sknvibes.com/news/newsdetails.cfm/67091
3. http://www.sknvibes.com/islandfacts/sitepage.cfm?p=167

SAINT LUCIA

"My country heart, I am not home till Sesenne sings,
a voice with woodsmoke and ground-doves in it, that cracks
like clay on a road whose tints are the dry season's,
whose cuatros tighten my heartstrings."

Derek Walcott, from Homecoming

When the Nobel judges awarded Derek Walcott the Nobel Prize for Literature it was an extraordinary achievement, not just for him, but for the Caribbean island where he was born, an island with a population 2,000 times smaller than that of the United States. This though was no freak occurrence: Walcott's poems and plays drew depth and colour from their connection to a surprisingly rich strand of Caribbean culture. The lines quoted brim with nostalgia for St Lucia. Ground doves are tiny birds familiar to the Caribbean islands. The cuatro is a guitar like instrument widely played on the island, at least when Walcott was writing. And Sesenne was – and still is – St Lucia's best loved singer.

Sesenne Descartes was born in 1914 in a small village community. For many years she was a simple entertainer unknown outside her local region. Then Harold Simmons came to hear her sing. This was before independence, when St Lucia was still under British rule. There was no heritage industry at the time. Simmons was a folklorist with wide-ranging interests in music, dance and folklore, and a defender of Creole culture. He wrote that: "Art in itself could not be called Art unless it springs from the people." [1] Simmons took the singer under his wing and made many live recordings of her performances. Following on from this she was invited to represent St Lucia at the Expo 67 Festival in Grenada. Her performance there was greeted by rapturous applause and repeated encores. Unfortunately, the only commercial recording of her singing was made in 1991, by which time her cracked voice could no longer be compared to ground doves.

Sesenne lived to the age of 96, and in the twilight of her life her name became closely linked with projects honouring St Lucia's Creole heritage. In 1973, the Folk Research Center opened in the capital, Castries, started up by people who'd been inspired by the work of Harold Simmons. A number of folk groups started up, including the Hewanorra Voices, who were led by a close friend of Sesenne, Joyce Auguste. In her day job, Auguste was music supervisor for the St Lucian school system with responsibility for introducing folk singing into the school curriculum – what an interesting way of making a difference. Now, as well as the Folk Research Center there is a school of music, and at the end of October every year there is a festival of Creole culture (Kwéyòl). (Sesenne herself opened the first Creole Day in 1984.) In 2012, the Folk Center launched the Harold Simmons Folk Academy, with a remit that included research, workshops and the promotion of Kwéyòl language and culture.

Musical Traditions of St Lucia, West Indies, is a 1993 Folkways album that came about following a long period of planning and collaboration involving the Folk Research Center. Jocelyne Guilbault's liner notes create an impression of a country that's gone some way to coming to terms with a mixed heritage of African and European cultural influences. [2] The colonial rulers, and at the time the Catholic Church, had a negative attitude to African-derived musical traditions, mirroring the official attitude to the Kwéyòl language, which was not formally taught in schools prior to independence. The Creole revival was therefore a cultural nationalist movement. Within the movement, as Guilbault tells us, there were voices arguing that all European-based culture was tainted by colonialism. An example was the kwedril dance, derived as its name suggests from the French quadrille. The argument that prevailed, though, was that kwedril is unique to Lucian culture; it has a number of features distinguishing it from its European antecedent and so it's a part of national culture. As a result, kewdril was revived and the tradition survives to this day. There are five kwedril dance tunes on the album, and on my featured song, **GWAN WON,** which is a happy, upbeat number, the heavy use of the chakchak (shaker, or rattle) helps to give the music its island feel.

I leave the final word to another poet, John Robert Lee, reflecting on Sesenne's death:

"There is something about St Lucian folk music that moves its writers in ways we can't explain easily. St Lucia is at heart a Creole/Kwéyòl society, neither English nor French. And the music of Sesenne, her folk singers and musicians, call to that. Call from that. Are that! And yes, the heartstrings tighten, deep under the sound: the melancholy 'La Commette', the dancers' flaring skirts, the insistent shac shac... And we celebrate even as we lay to rest Sesenne Descartes of Mon Repos, our Queen of Culture. And we celebrate too as we learn that musician and musicologist Joyce Auguste is now drawing on her archives to produce new, never-heard-before recordings of Sesenne Descartes." [3]

NOTES

1. http://www.stluciafolk.org/folkPersonalities/view/18
2. https://folkways-media.si.edu/liner_notes/smithsonian_folkways/SFW40416.pdf
3. http://caribbeanreviewofbooks.com/crb-archive/23-september-2010/woodsmoke-and-ground-doves

SAINT VINCENT AND THE GRENADINES

Vincy Mas is carnival: it's St Vincent's moment in the limelight, the country as it wants to be seen and remembered, a riot of colour, music and imagination. It's also of huge economic importance to this tiny country: St Vincent has about the same land area as the Isle of Wight, and a significantly smaller population. Vincy Mas is a great occasion that more than lives up to the hype; its problem, though, has always been that it's competing with several other Caribbean carnivals that offer a similar experience but on a larger scale. The majority of the thousands of visitors who come from overseas for the carnival are people from the Vincentian Diaspora. Is this enough, or could Vincy Mas be doing better?

The carnival's present incarnation goes back to 1977. In that year the recently formed CDC (Carnival Development Committee) moved the festivities from their traditional pre-Lenten slot to a 12-day summertime celebration. It was a commercial decision, aimed at avoiding the clash with the Trinidad carnival and maximising tourism footfall, and a decision made with the future growth of carnival activities very much in mind. Vincy Mas attractions include a Calypso and Soca monarch, a Carnival King and Queen based on best individual costume, beauty pageants, steel bands, mas (masquerade) bands and a Mardi Gras parade on the final day.

Back in 1977, a young calypsonian's career was just taking off. Alston 'Becket' Cyrus was born in the island of St Vincent. His biography drops the intriguing nugget of information that he served in the US army as a young man, so he must already have been a resident then (green card holders are entitled to join the military). [1] We're not told if he ever served in Vietnam but we do know that he was already performing while he was a soldier, and left intent on taking up a singing career. New York in the 1970s was a magnet for Caribbean immigrants and the source of some of the most exciting new trends in Caribbean music, and it was here that Becket met another Vincentian immigrant, the producer Frankie McIntosh. Becket asked McIntosh to help him out on a few of his arrangements, and this turned out to be the start of a 40-year collaboration.

McIntosh was an early pioneer of soca music. A synth-driven, speeded-up, dance-oriented variant on calypso, soca has always been a fluid genre, able to absorb other musical styles, and McIntosh had the versatility to match. Becket–McIntosh compositions have shaped and defined Vincy Mas and have made soca into the dominant force that it is in St Vincent today. It's party music, but this didn't deter Becket from expressing his views in song from time to time on a range of subjects (Carnival History; Oppression; I am an African; Say No to Drugs, etc.).

On **VINCY MAS** Becket lets the music do the talking. Listening to it feels like as close as you can get to carnival without being there: you're aware of all the layers of sound around you, the fast, insistent beat, the horns, the drums. The lyrics reflect the Vincy Mas experience from the point of view of a festival goer. It's just one exuberant ride.

I'm not sure that Vincy Mas needs to change greatly. But if the CDC decide to give it another shakedown, I hope that they'll look at ways of making it more reflective of St Vincent's unique heritage.

St Vincent was one of the last outposts in the Caribbean to be settled by Europeans, and the reason for this was the Black Caribs. Would-be settlers in the 17th century were confronted by people of black skin: African slaves who'd either escaped from other islands or were survivors from transportation ships wrecked off the coast. They mixed freely with indigenous Caribs, giving rise to a new ethnic group: the Garifuna people of today. And they fought to keep their freedom: for much of the 18th century St Vincent was a bastion of resistance against colonialism and slavery. Their most famous leader, Joseph Chatoyer, was so successful in battle that the British were forced to sign a treaty with him. This unprecedented success was not to last, however: the British failed to honour the treaty, rebellion broke out and although the British suffered some heavy setbacks the Black Caribs were eventually forced to surrender. Some 5,000 defeated Caribs were rounded up and shipped out to a nearby 300-acre island called Baliceaux, where they were left to starve. Over 2,000 died before they were shipped on again, this time to Honduras.

Garifuna people today live in Honduras, Belize, Guatemala, Nicaragua and the USA. To them, Baliceaux is a deeply important place; Garifuna representatives travel there every year to pay their respects. Baliceaux is privately owned, and proposals to sell it off for tourism development have met with loud protests from the Garifuna.

A small number of Black Caribs were never deported, and their descendants still live in St Vincent today. Garifuna culture in St Vincent had virtually disappeared, and people had been growing up ignorant of their own Carib roots, but this is all changing now. A Garifuna Heritage Foundation has been set up to spread the word in St Vincent about Garifuna culture and history, and they do a lot of work with community groups in pockets where there are still people of Carib ancestry.

One of these communities is Rose Hall, who have an admirable website that explains all about who they are and what they're trying to do. [2] It's an eco-tourism resort dedicated to protecting the natural environment, but visitors can also expect opportunities to learn about Garifuna culture, language, crafts and music. Central to the community is a drumming group. The Rose Hall Drummers acknowledge that their music is a synthesis of different influences, but their self-made drums are authentic enough, and the music sounds great. They've performed around the world but they also take time out to teach drumming to Vincentian children. They're keen to carry on and to record more albums – "we want to change people's mindset about our culture and help to revive our sense of pride as a mix-cultured people."

The American film director, Andrea Leland, would share these sentiments. Having spent 20 years working with the Garifuna diaspora, she was very moved by the emotional reaction when one of her documentary films played in St Vincent. And so, to help bridge the disconnect between the people and their culture, she made another film, Yurumein, which is all about the Vincentian Garifuna.

NOTES

1. https://www.becketmusicsvg.com/bio
2. http://rosehallculturalorg.wixsite.com/drummers

TRINIDAD AND TOBAGO

In 1943, when Invader wrote the words to **RUM AND COCA COLA**, the USA had just set up large naval and air bases in the northwest of the island of Trinidad, having been granted the rights for this by the British government. The meaning of the song is unambiguous. American servicemen were living it up and taking advantage of native women, creating a trade in prostitution. 'Rum and Coca-Cola' is a clever double- : Invader saw that the GIs liked to drink rum with Coke as a chaser, but the title is also suggestive that there were other kinds of mixing of fluids going on.

I've often found that real life can be stranger than satire, and that certainly proved to be the case here. This little anti-American ditty was about to get expropriated and become a hit in America, and it would take a protracted court case before Invader saw a cent of the Yankee dollars that his song had earned.

The song spread across the island like wildfire; soon it was being played everywhere. Later that year, a USO (United Service Organizations) show arrived in Trinidad to entertain the troops. The MC was a comedian called Morey Amsterdam, and when he left for home he had in his pocket some verses of a song to do with rum and Coca-Cola. A year later, having 'cleaned up' the song, he copyrighted it, complete with some of those lyrics

RUM AND COCA COLA	*Lord Invader*
MONEY IS KING	*Growling Tiger*
WEAPONS OF MASS DIS-ILLUSION	*Mighty Sparrow*
JUMP HIGH	*Phase II Pan Groove*

that he'd appropriated. The true meaning of the song was now obscured, so much so that the Andrews Sisters didn't think twice when given the song to record. Rum and Coca-Cola by the Andrews Sisters became the top-selling single of 1945 in the USA: in one of many ironies it was especially popular among American GIs.

There were actually two court trials, as Lionel Belasco, who claimed to have written the melody, also brought a suit. In the first trial Amsterdam's claims to authorship fell apart and the judge ruled in Lord Invader's favour. Finally, after the Belasco case had been settled, Invader received a handsome cheque (one informed estimate is $30,000 after taxes). [1] What he then did with the money, according to Kevin Burke, "was spend it as quickly as possible on his entourage by opening a nightclub (the Calypso Club) in Port of Spain which was operated with a total disregard for financial controls." [2] Within a year he was hard up for cash. Tragically, it seems that he sold the rights to the song, which had been restored to him by the New York judge, to Amsterdam in 1950 as part of the final disposition agreement, and from that day on, "every time Invader sang the song, as his audience demanded, Morey Amsterdam collected a fee."

Recorded in 1935, **MONEY IS KING** is in my book one of the greatest howls against social injustice, not just of the Depression era, but of any era. There is so much vivid imagery and human experience packed into its three minutes. But its real power lies in the song's shocking message that for those without money "a dog is better than you", which still resonates 80 years later.

You thought that Trinidad was the home of the happy-clappy feel-good carnival tune? Perhaps it's time to introduce a bit of history…

Colonial Trinidad in the 19th century had a well-established social hierarchy. Beneath the whites who owned the plantations, coloureds, Indians and blacks each had their own social status. People were routinely judged on their racial characteristics, which could determine what work they could do and what other privileges they may be able to claim. Back then, carnival was run by whites and street festivities were restricted to certain social groups. Following emancipation, black ex-slaves created their own street entertainment, which they called Canboulay. The word comes from cannes brulées, a direct reference to a brutal practice that would still have been vivid in the minds of many blacks: when a fire started up at night in a sugar cane field, drivers and overseers equipped with whips, cow horns and blazing torches would herd up the slaves, get them to extinguish the fires and salvage the canes before the juice became soured. Canboulay, then, was a celebration rooted in the dark side of the life of slaves: it involved torch-lit midnight processions with drumming, singing and dancing by masked men and women.

The white establishment perceived Canboulay as a threat and found plenty of cause to condemn it. It attracted the dregs of human society – the poor and the criminal classes. The popular stick-fighting dances were aggressive and warlike; other dances were too sexualised. The Trinidad Chronicle called the event "a barbarous din that disgraces the entire nation", while the Trinidad Sentinel went one better, describing it as an "orgy of every species of barbarism and crime". [3] As tensions grew, a new police chief was appointed who made it his business to 'do something' about this shocking state of affairs. His name was Captain Arthur Baker. In 1880, participants were asked to come without their drums, sticks and torches. The event passed peacefully enough, but the following year groups of blacks defied the police and serious rioting ensued. The troubles continued over the next couple of years, and the skin drums and the sticks were banned completely.

But the torch that had been lit in 1881 could not be so easily put out. Every year at carnival time black people took to the streets and made their own celebrations, and again and again these celebrations showed the amount of pride and spirit of resistance that existed. Calypso singers would satirise the powerful even during the height of repression. Instruments were fashioned from whatever materials came to hand. Skin drums were replaced by bamboo tubes, which in turn would later be replaced by another invention, the steel drum. As a result of all this, carnival became over time exactly what it should be: a genuine coming together of peoples and mixing of cultures.

Within a few years of the riots the attention of the authorities was drawn to a new problem – calypso songs. As more and more calypsos were sung in English Creole instead of French Creole they could no longer be ignored. Before the days of radio and mass media, the calypso singer was the mouthpiece of the people, a purveyor of news and gossip and scurrilous allegations, a commentator, a satirist and a clown. Calypso was the hip hop of the day: it was all about the words, and about pushing boundaries of what could be said. No subject was too sacred or too controversial to be taken on. During times of censorship, though, it was also about being subtle and quick-witted. Jumping ahead briefly, in 1972 the government tried to bring in censorship by introducing the Sedition Act. This was met with an inspired response by Chalkdust, Ah Fraid Karl. A long charge sheet of allegations against the government is drawn up, but Chalkdust evades responsibility for it. This, he says, is what 'they' say: I'm too 'fraid; I couldn't possibly comment.

The 1920s and '30s were a great era for calypso, most of the great singers were from Trinidad and Tobago, and any compilation of early recordings from this time is well worth getting. While the compilations focus on the more famous songs, in truth, the music was of variable quality. A lot of songs would be written at short notice, they were banal more often than they were brilliant, and the music was often clearly something of an afterthought. King of the extempore song was Lord Executor (1884–1952), who's honoured in this fine (unsigned) tribute on the Roaring Lion website:

> "Lion admired Executor and considered him to be the most educated, intelligent, well-read and witty of all the calypsonians of his day. Lion undoubtedly considered him a genius in the art form... According to Lion, Executor wrote about 1,000 songs in his lifetime, but he seldom completed a song before rendering a performance... Lion has related countless confessions by top calypsonians who met humiliating defeat and devastation when the 'Lord' walked in late, and unexpectedly into a competition, and left 'Mocking Pretenders' baffled, and in shock." [4]

An example is given of a carnival competition in 1935:

> "On the cast that night there were singers like King Radio, Attila, Beginner, Growler others and myself – we were the resident singers. While the last competitor was on stage, Lord Executor walked right in, and as the competitor sung his last verse, the audience shouted, 'we want Executor', over and over. The manager of the Tent called Executor and asked him if he would like to compete. He replied that he would, but he did not know what it was all about. He was

told that it was about Dancow Milk, and that the winner would be given a prize. Then he was given a leaflet with the advertisement, and the names of the agents, product info etc. The Lord then went on stage, and told the musicians what key he wanted to sing in and then he improvised a song there and then."

He won, of course.

All the competitors were men. For a very long time there were scarcely any female calypsonians. Lady Trinidad is generally credited as being the first, but she didn't write her own material. Male lyrics made much of the so-called war of the sexes, and women were almost always portrayed in negative terms. King Radio may have sung "Man Smart, Woman Smarter", but the song's real message is in the lyrics: women are conniving; they'll fool you and cheat on you. Attila's Women Will Rule the World lists the achievements of women but there's a twist in the tail as the singer issues a tongue-in-cheek warning to men. If we allow this to happen, Attila is saying, we men will have to mind the baby, and he's only half joking.

In the run-up to independence national consciousness grew. Some artists began calling themselves 'kaiso' singers, a reference to the Africanised term for calypso, to distinguish themselves from apolitical 'calypso singers' such as Harry Belafonte. After independence they wouldn't be afraid to hold the new government to account.

Mighty Sparrow didn't start out as a political singer: as he acknowledges himself, his main desire was to entertain. Sparrow was born in a fishing village in Grenada in 1935, but had lived in Trinidad ever since he was a baby. In his early days he dealt with his nerves by constantly moving around when he was on stage. One night the MC said to him during a performance: "Why don't you stand still? You look like a sparrow," and the name stuck. His reputation established by the 1956 hit Jean and Dinah (the first of his eight Road March wins), the following year he led a high-profile musicians' boycott of carnival. Meanwhile, Sparrow had been persuaded of the need to offer his support to the new government of Dr Eric Williams and the People's National Movement. However unimpeachable his motives, it's hard to get so excited about a calypso song that urges people to pay their taxes so that they can get better schools (PAYE).

By the time of independence Sparrow was churning out hits on a regular basis. The most remarkable thing is that he has remained on top of the game for another 50 years, seeing off rival after rival. What's his secret? He himself is a larger-than-life character, able to assume many personalities and points of view, and he's developed a very good ear for what people are thinking and feeling, and because of this he's adept at changing with the times and capturing the mood of the day. So it was that the same person, who in 1970 was appealing for national unity, was in 1983 railing against corruption on Capitalism Gone Mad.

Sparrow has also moved with the times musically, working with larger bands, integrating big rhythms to his songs and embracing other styles like soca and chutney. But he's never lost sight of the fact that in calypso music the song is the message, and every song should have a point, a reason for existence. Sometimes they're light-hearted and semi-humorous; sometimes they deal with social issues. He doesn't move around so much these days when he's on stage, but he can still pack a punch. In 2008, he won plaudits for Barack de Magnificent, his homage to Barack Obama, written some 45 years after he'd mourned "A Death of Kennedy". But the song on the album that impressed me the most was his outspoken anti-Iraq War anthem, **WEAPONS OF MASS DIS-ILLUSION**, with its mocking chorus.

Though the Road March title remains a vital part of carnival, the dominant music at carnival time for many years now has been soca. And for all that soca is a home-grown music with a feel-good vibe, there is little in it to appeal to traditionists. Caribbean rhythms are meshed together and overlaid with a synthesised drum beat to create a product lacking in much regional character, its vacuous pop lyrics in stark contrast to the wit of calypso. This said, it's intriguing to learn that the acknowledged father of soca music, Ras Shorty I (previously Lord Shorty), had a conception that is at odds with the way in which the genre later developed. "I came up with the name soca," he says. "I invented soca. And I never spelt it s-o-c-a. It was s-o-k-a-h to reflect the East Indian influence." [5] Trinidad and Tobago is split between people of African origin and people of Indian origin. Shorty had wanted to develop a form of dance music that had a recognisable Indian influence, and on songs like Indrani you can hear the dholak and the tabla. It's another tale of what might have been...

Since 1963, Trinidad's steel bands have vied against each other in the Panorama competition, and a carnival without steelpan music would be unthinkable today. I've briefly alluded already to the history of the steel drum. Steel drums were improvised instruments and at first it was a craze that spread like wildfire through the poorest neighbourhoods of Trinidad. People experimented with any kind of metal container that they could get their hands on – garbage cans, paint cans, the large drums used for shipping biscuits. The tops of the containers were pounded outwards into a convex shape and beaten with wooden sticks. In 1946, Elliott "Ellie" Mannette discovered that making a concave surface allowed him to play more notes while helping the drum to retain its sound for a longer time. Numerous more innovations followed, but the process that was developed still sounds very labour intensive. Each drum has to be hammered into shape and shapes beaten into the surface for the individual notes, then the drum is tempered by being heated – traditionally over a burning tyre – and cooled. Now the tuning can begin, which is done today using an electronic strobe tuner.

Phase II Pan Groove are seven-time winners of Panorama, and JUMP HIGH is the tune that carried them to success in 2014.

The outfit was formed in 1973 by Len 'Boogsie' Sharpe, born 20 years earlier to a Jamaican father and Trinidadian mother. His experience of steelpan goes back even before he learned to talk: the Crossfire steel band carried out nightly rehearsals beneath where he slept. His winning song in 1988 was called Woman Is Boss – a timely rebuke to the misogyny of calypso singers. "We don't give women the recognition they deserve," he said at the time. "I believe that woman is boss because of the important roles they play in our lives." [6]

Steelpan is all about the music though, and, while the recorded version can't possibly compare with the live carnival experience, Jump High is an exciting listen. The exuberant rhythms and the ringing of the steel drums carries with it the feel of street music; after a time you realise that the music isn't just repeating itself, it's a very elaborate composition. Boogsie is a brilliant composer, arranger and producer, and over eight minutes he gives us quite a ride.

Trinidadians believe that they do carnival better than anyone else in the world, and if reputation is anything to go by they may not be far wrong. It's integral to the lives and identity of the peoples of Trinidad and Tobago. It's also an important part of the islands' economy. Over 40,000 people come from abroad every year for carnival week, and the government estimates that total revenue from the event is in excess of $100 million – and the numbers are growing. Even this it seems is not enough: in December 2014 the government distributed $9.7 million to regional carnival committees with a view to holding additional events throughout the year.

There are always some who say that carnival has become too commercialised, and that it's lost a lot of its original character. They have a point. The famous street parade is no mere community event. To become part of the parade – to 'play mas' – you need to join a band. The bands are run as enterprises. It can cost anything between $200 and $1,000 for a costume and having your needs catered for over the two days. Makers of wonderful traditional costumes are dismayed by people's willingness to purchase cheap and tacky alternatives: "We call it two-piece and fries, the bikini and the bras. The costume comes like a fast food. To them, the bottom line is profit. It has nothing to do about country or culture anymore." [7] The inevitable consequence of this: working-class Trinidadians are increasingly excluded from active participation.

Since 1991, the National Carnival Commission have served as the custodians of carnival, with a brief that includes protecting its cultural integrity. This goal has been not sacrificed but traded off against the goal of optimising economic potential and, although some money has been invested in training traditional skills such as costume making, it pales into insignificance alongside the money invested in income generating activities.

But traditional culture has not been lost. It lives on in the people of the islands. Knowledge of the history of carnival runs deep. There's a rich fund of collective memory, which includes an appreciation of how much carnival has taken from slave culture, an awareness of past acts of resistance from the stickfighters to the Canboulay Riots, and a knowledge of the traditional characters that were once central to carnival folklore. The desire to connect with this fund of tradition expresses itself every year in activities taking place around the fringes of carnival, and at times spills over into the main carnival programme. For example, the Canboulay Riots pageant, which takes place on the Friday before carnival and is a theatrical re-enactment of the riots, is a 21st-century invention that came into being as a result of the research and ideas of carnival commissioner, John Cupid.

NOTES

1. http://www.rumandcocacolareader.com/RumAndCocaCola/Calypso_on_Trial.html
2. http://scarlettproject.com/wp-content/uploads/2013/09/KEVIN-BURKE-new-essayfinal.pdf

3. John Guzda – The Canboulay Riot of 1881: Influence of Free Blacks On Trinidad's Carnival (2012), p3–4. http://digitalcommons.buffalostate.edu/cgi/viewcontent.cgi?article=1002&context=exposition
4. http://roaringlioncalypso.org/lord-beginner-and-executor
5. http://www.sibetrans.com/trans/articulo/265/the-politics-of-labelling-popular-musics-in-english-caribbean
6. http://www.panonthenet.com/articles/pan_mag/boogsie_1988.htm
7. http://www.nytimes.com/2011/03/09/world/americas/09trinidad.html?_r=0

UNITED STATES OF AMERICA

Murder on Music Row is a song about the death of country music, how its true spirit has been killed by commercialisation, to the point where even the steel guitars have been silenced. The song had been previously released by Larry Cordle, who co-wrote it with Larry Shell. But what really got everyone talking was Strait and Jackson performing the song at the 1999 CMA awards show. At the time these were two of the biggest stars in the country music industry, so not even the most cynical could accuse them of having any personal axe to grind. The song echoed what many people were feeling, and its favourable reception left no doubt as to the depth of these concerns.

The USA has an extraordinary musical heritage. Jazz, blues and country music all originated here, cross-fertilising with a strong folk tradition and with African-American spirituals. These in turn were to be the foundation of innumerable genres and sub-genres of modern American music: gospel, soul, disco and funk; rock and roll and rock music in all its incarnations. They also shaped the development of pop music and folk music. But here's the thing: for all the great music that still comes out of America every year, musicians generally are atomised. Their influences are

I'M STILL IN LOVE WITH YOU	Steve Earle & The Del McCoury Band with Iris DeMent
THE TALKIN' SONG REPAIR BLUES	Alan Jackson
OLD VIRGINNY	Jean Ritchie
THE ANGELS LAID HIM AWAY	Rhiannon Giddens
GOING AWAY BABY	Cedric Burnside Project
ANYTIME IS SATURDAY NIGHT	Meschiya Lake & The Little Big Horns
INTERTRIBAL 4	Wild Band of Comanches

likely to be very diverse, things they've picked up from the radio and from digital media. They're more likely to be hooked into current musical scenes than to feel that their musical roots lie in a community, a place, a particular tradition. The lift-off point of a musical career is often seen as the moment when the artist starts to assert their individuality, whether this be by developing their style or writing their own songs.

Murder on Music Row expresses this feeling of rootlessness: the sadness of tuning into country music radio and hearing songs aimed at the pop market, songs with nothing much to say and with little or no awareness of the legacy of past giants such as Jimmie Rodgers, Bob Wills, Hank Williams, George Jones, Merle Haggard and Johnny Cash. The point was not to attack the industry. After all, the goals of the industry (making hits and profits) were still the same as they had been in country's heyday, even though the industry itself had changed. The point was to provoke a reaction and get people to think about where country music was headed. Traditional country music is far from dead, but the proof will always lie in artists who remain true to country's roots, and people's willingness to go to their concerts and buy their records.

Away from music award ceremonies, talent shows and pop charts there is another America, an America with a deep respect for its musical roots and an interest in music that sounds authentic, that speaks of America's past. Evidence of this can be found in the popularity of bluegrass, alt-country and Americana music, interlapping genres that draw from both country and folk music – which is well represented by the website and print journal, No Depression. It can be found too in the growing number of consciously revivalist old-time music festivals, and in the rising numbers taking up traditional instruments such as the mandolin and ukulele. This is the America that I'll be exploring in this chapter.

The first song that I want to introduce is from 1999, the same year that Strait and Jackson did their duet at the CMA Awards, and it features no fewer than three inspirational musicians: Steve Earle, Del McCoury and Iris Dement. Steve Earle is an outsider, a Texan kid who showed up in Nashville in 1974 with a guitar, an attitude and an admiration for the songs of fellow Texan Townes van Zandt and of the Outlaw Country movement whose biggest stars, Willie Nelson and Waylon Jennings, also hailed from Texas. This – rather than the more mainstream Nashville sound – was what resonated with the young Steve Earle and made him want to write music. In fact, Townes van Zandt was such an influence that Steve named his firstborn after him

(Justin Townes Earle, one of the most consistently good singer-songwriters in the USA today). As it turned out, the drug- and alcohol-addicted van Zandt was a great songwriting model but a less good lifestyle model. By the early 1990s Steve had become a heroin addict, blowing $500 to $1,000 a day on his habit and selling off almost everything that he owned. Eventually he was busted and sentenced to a year in jail. He served only 60 days before going into rehab: that was in 1994, and he's kept away from the drugs and the alcohol ever since.

When Steve returned to making music, he did so with the support of his peers, who saw in his work much of what they most valued in country music. I'll let Emmylou Harris speak for them:

> *"Steve is so understanding of all that great core tissue that is the real pulse of country music, and that is completely invisible in what is happening in country music right now... You know, that generic, bloodless stuff that is churned out? I'm completely mystified by it. We've now become musical producers of what is comparable to the Big Mac—you know what you're going to get every time you open up the wrapper." [1]*

So when Steve Earle decided he wanted to make a bluegrass album, he had no shortage of offers to help. His friend, Del McCoury, was an obvious choice. Del knew everything there was to know about bluegrass: right at the start of his career back in 1963 he had the amazing good fortune to be hired by the father of bluegrass himself, the leader of the very first bluegrass band, Bill Monroe. (This is just one of two remarkable events that bookend his career. Half a century later, McCoury was handpicked by Woody Guthrie's daughter, Nora, to work on some songs from the Woody Guthrie archive for which no music existed. So he wrote some music to the songs, and in 2016 the album Del and Woody was released.)

Love songs may not be his stock in trade, but Steve Earle certainly knows how to write them (remember Galway Girl?). I'M STILL IN LOVE WITH YOU is a duet with Iris Dement. The song has a strong melody and hook, the lyrics have a touching honesty to them, there's plenty of heart in the vocals, the instruments are real, and it's got the twang of a traditional country tune.

THE TALKIN' SONG REPAIR BLUES is also unmistakably a country song – but what kind of country? Alan Jackson's reference to talkin' blues evokes a particular tradition to which my first introduction was through early Bob Dylan songs such as Talkin' World War III Blues. Dylan's inspiration came from an album compiled by John Greenway and released on Folkways in 1958, Talking Blues, which included tracks by Chris Bouchillon, Woody Guthrie and Joe Glazer. Talking country songs are an entirely separate tradition that reflects the close bonds between early country music and folk music. Examples of talking country are Tex Williams – Smoke! Smoke! Smoke! (That Cigarette), Jimmy Dean – Big Bad John, and Johnny Cash – A Boy Named Sue. Talking country songs tend to be more plain spoken, whereas the talking blues is spoken to the beat; also there is often more of a storytelling element in talking country.

Despite its playful use of harmonica, the Alan Jackson song (written by Dennis Linde) is, in reality, country rather than a talking blues. It's well-written, witty and funny: the kind of qualities that you hope to find in a good talking country.

Alan Jackson has earned the right to criticise soulless modern country, because his many hits draw on a splendid variety of country tradition, bringing George Jones-style ballads and honky-tonk into the mainstream. In 2015, his Keepin' It Country tour, which celebrated 25 years of hitmaking, treated large audiences around the USA to an amble through his musical career. The tour proved so popular that it was extended into 2016, then 2017, when it was finally put to pasture to make way for the Honky Tonk Highway Tour.

When Alan Jackson declares his support for traditional country, what is it that he means? After all, country music has been changing ever since it started back in the 1920s; it has never stood still. But one thing it has always been proud to associate itself with is the working class. Its origins lay in the music of the rural working class, it was at its best when songs reflected the lives and concerns of working-class folk, and its stars were never more revered than when they remained true to their working-class origins. (Loretta Lynn actually was a coal miner's daughter; Tammy Wynette, Dolly Parton and Merle Haggard were also among those who celebrated their poor working-class roots.) Alan Jackson is one of many who believes that money is changing this ethos, and changing the very nature of country music. The country music industry – symbolised by Nashville – has become so large and powerful that the idea of another Bill Monroe coming along in the future and changing the way that country music is played seems fanciful: the producers are now the gatekeepers who ultimately decide what kind of music will get played on country radio.

We tend to think of country music not just as working class, but as southern white working class. Rhiannon Giddens, as we shall see, goes against this stereotype. More to the point, though, the idea that hillbilly music – a key element of early country – is some form of unadulterated white working-class culture is frankly nonsense. In the 19th century the banjo and the fiddle were part of the stock-in-trade of black musicians in the south. At the time when early record companies made the decision to market hillbilly to a white audience, black hillbilly musicians were still common, according to Eric Brightwell:

> *"Take the case of DeFord Bailey. Bailey was the first black musician to play on the Grand Ole Opry, had a grandfather who'd been a champion Tennessee fiddler in the 1880s, and as a child played alongside relatives at the Wilson County Fair with The Bailey Family Band. In 1975 he revealed to an*

interviewer, 'I never heard the blues till I came to Nashville to work. All I heard as a boy back then was what we called black hillbilly music.'" [2]

Other black folk artists of note (the term country wasn't then in common parlance) included Elizabeth Cotton and Gus Cannon, though the influence of black musicians extended beyond recordings: Eric Brightwell also informs us that A.P. Carter, Bill Monroe and Hank Williams all received training from black musicians.

Kentucky has always had a strong country music tradition, from Loretta Lynn and Merle Travis to Dwight Yoakam and Sturgill Simpson. And the roots of this lie in Appalachian folk music, hillbilly and bluegrass: the music of the rural poor. Coal Miner's Daughter is just one of many songs inspired by Kentucky's coal mining industry: other notable ones include Which Side Are You On?, Sixteen Tons and Jean Ritchie's The L&N Don't Stop Here Anymore. Kentucky's known as the bluegrass state after its wide expanses of bluegrass, and that's why the boy from Rosine, Kentucky, Bill Monroe, named his band the Blue Grass Boys. Today, Kentucky bluegrass has a whole other meaning: in Bill Monroe heartland, the International Bluegrass Music Museum in Owensboro draws crowds from around the world, especially in late June, when it hosts the ROMP Festival.

Kentucky's old-time folk singers led hard lives, had interesting personalities, and some very individual singing styles. Buell Kazee, Roscoe Holcomb, Aunt Molly Jackson, Lily May Ledford and Jean Ritchie are all worth exploring, though I don't have space to write about them all here. Aunt Molly Jackson was among the singers recorded by Alan Lomax in eastern Kentucky in the 1930s: these recordings of "farmers, laborers, coal miners, preachers, housewives, public officials, soldiers, grandparents, adolescents, and itinerant musicians" have recently been digitalised and made available online by Nathan Salsburg and the American Folklife

Center. [3] More influential in its time was the album Mountain Music of Kentucky, compiled by Folkways and released in 1960, which featured traditional banjo playing by Roscoe Holcomb and others.

Perhaps the one thing above all else that makes Kentuckians feel connected with their musical heritage is the Renfro Valley Gatherin'. John Lair was a local man made good who returned to Renfro Valley to build an ambitious entertainment complex in this small community. Since 1939 it's been host to the Renfro Valley Barn Dance, a country music show that has helped to unearth many stars of the industry, and since 1943, The Gatherin' show has been broadcast on American radio stations. For many years it was a live show with John Lair as host. It's seen a few changes since those days but it still bears the imprint of its creator. John Lair was a big fan of bluegrass music, and for many years now his centre has played host to the Old Joe Clark Bluegrass Festival.

For Jean Ritchie (1922–2015), connecting with Kentucky's musical past involved a very personal journey. Her family was from a place called Viper in the Kentucky mountains, their lives had always revolved around song and not having a radio doesn't seem to have bothered them at all:

> "They had songs to accompany nearly all of their activities, from sweeping to churning to working in the fields. When they got together in the evening to sing as a family, they chose from a repertoire of more than 300 songs. Among them were hymns, traditional love songs and ballads, and popular songs by composers like Stephen Foster. For the most part, these songs were learned orally and sung without accompaniment." [4]

The youngest of 14 children, Jean soaked it all in. As a kid she learned songs quickly, and learned to play the mountain dulcimer by imitating her father. She went to college and university (no mean achievement for a girl of her background), ending up with a degree in social work. She moved to New York in 1946 to work at the not-for-profit Henry Street Settlement. For someone with an ear for folk music, this was an exciting time to be in New York. The American folk revival was in its infancy and New York was its epicentre. Woody Guthrie and Pete Seeger sparked off these regular informal musical gatherings that they called hootenannies, which drew in not only white folk singers but blues artists such as Leadbelly and Josh White. Jean's singing was to open all their eyes to the richness of the Appalachian folk tradition. It certainly made an impression on the folklorist Alan Lomax, who made extensive recordings of her for the Library of Congress.

In 1952, Jean, now married to George Pickow, successfully applied for a Fulbright scholarship to travel around Britain and Ireland collecting folk songs. George was a professional photographer, which was very fortunate, because it allowed the young couple to travel and work together. The journey was motivated by a desire to discover more about the musical heritage of the Ritchie family, and more generally of the Appalachian region where almost any family you spoke to was of Irish, Scots or English descent.

"Where I came from, we had some Irish, and some English, and some Scottish, mainly Scottish. The Ritchies came from Inverness. But we began our collecting in Ireland. It was fascinating to visit there and hear the same tunes that we sing in Kentucky, but maybe with different words. Then I'd go to Scotland and hear the same words with maybe an Irish tune. Therefore, in the mountains of Kentucky, we seem to have taken what we thought was the best of everything. If we liked the words we would put a pretty Irish tune to them. Everything sort of got wedded together. Pity that human beings can't do the same. It's part of my

heritage, and it's been thrilling my whole life to be able to
discover, more and more, the roots of the music, what folk
music really is." [5]

Back in the USA, Jean released a regular stream of albums
through the 1950s and '60s, also publishing several books –
Singing Family of the Cumberlands (1955), The Dulcimer Book
(1963), Folk Songs of the Southern Appalachians (1965), etc.
During this time she was a frequent performer at the Newport
Folk Festival, also serving on its board of directors. She remained
faithful throughout to the traditional way of performing that she'd
grown up with – singing unaccompanied, or sometimes with
a guitar or a dulcimer. She was never very popular or famous,
but her influence was enormous. She, as much as anyone, made
America aware of its debt to Appalachian folk music, and she's
probably also responsible for thousands of people playing the
dulcimer today. Jean and George set up a workshop where they
started making their own dulcimers, George doing the finishing
and Jean doing the tuning, and their sales ran into the hundreds.

OLD VIRGINNY was an Appalachian folk standard. All the old-
time Kentucky singers recorded versions of it (mostly under the
title East Virginia): Buell Kazee, B.F. Shelton, Roscoe Holcomb,
Lily May Ledford. But Jean Ritchie, by hitting the high notes and
drawing them out slowly, gives the song a haunting beauty that
none of the others can match. For her, the song is associated with
her father – "In that time, anything that wasn't church singing
was sinful, and the fiddle was without question the instrument of
the Devil. Old Virginny was one of the songs that was thus saved
by my 'sinful' father…" [6]

Dom Flemons, Rhiannon Giddens and Justin Robinson, the
three original members of the Carolina Chocolate Drops, first met
in 2005 at the Black Banjo Gathering in Boone, North Carolina.
Their shared interest in the role of African Americans in the history
of the banjo was the spark that led to the band being formed.

Their guide and mentor in those early days was a grizzled old fiddle player called Joe Thompson (1918–2012). Joe's father was a fiddler too, who'd learned the instrument from his own father, a slave, and Joe's uncle was a banjo player; so Joe grew up playing the fiddle as black musicians had played it for generations in that part of North Carolina. In his teens he formed a band and they quickly became part of the Appalachian string band scene. Then came the war, and after the war black string bands were no longer in demand. But Joe carried his knowledge in him, and after many years as a factory worker he picked up his career and got to perform on stages across America.

From Joe, the three young musicians learned about different playing styles: "black fiddlers played in a style that was more rhythmic, syncopated and African in character, and called the tunes 'Negro jigs." [7] Hence the title of their exuberant 2010 album, Genuine Negro Jig, which while celebrating the music of black Appalachia was full of creativity and ideas, and won a Grammy in the traditional folk album category.

Rhiannon is the only founding member still in the band, which is perhaps surprising given the breadth of her own roots and interests. Her father was black and her mother was white and in Greensboro, NC, in the 1970s there was no place they could get married, so they had to go to Winston to get their marriage licence. Her ethnic heritage defies ready-made labels: there's British/Irish blood in there, and Native American blood apparently too. "When I was in high school," she says, "I was a part of a pow wow drum group… After college I found Gaelic singing from the islands of Scotland, which was very similar to what my memories of pow wow singing had been. All of these cultural connections are a big part of who I am." [8] She also believes that the true identity of North Carolina is built on precisely this kind of cultural mixing: "The history of North Carolina is so interesting, there's so – we're never one thing or the other. We're never red or blue. We're never black or white. We're just really a mixed state." [9] Note the 'we':

Rhiannon identifies as North Carolinan rather than as a member of any one ethnic group. Just to complicate matters further, though, she's now married to an Irish musician and they've decided to split their home life between Greensboro and Ireland.

Freedom Highway (2017) is Rhiannon's second solo album, and the whole album is a testament to African-American history and song. It's an album to fill you with anger at the brutality that this population has so often endured, but also to inspire you with the courage and strength that's revealed in the female characters who are at the centre of most of the songs. Rhiannon shifts between folk, blues, R&B and gospel: she wants this to be an album for all African Americans, not just those who would buy a folk album. The track that caught my attention, though, is a classic country blues, first recorded by Mississippi John Hurt in 1928. The original song is called Louis Collins; Rhiannon's version is entitled THE ANGELS LAID HIM AWAY. A mother weeps to see her son taken to his grave. Who shot him and why? These questions are never answered, and in a way this makes the song all the more poignant: there have been so many mothers in the south who've had to shed tears for their sons. Rhiannon does the right thing in not trying to do too much with the song. She keeps its stripped-back feel, its gentle pace and its melodic structure, and her voice has in it all the compassion and sorrow that the song requires.

As we leave the mountains and head south, we come to a region of north Mississippi that borders on Tennessee. We are now in Hill Country, a place that claims to have its very own blues music tradition, distinct from that of the delta blues. Hill Country is not part of the Mississippi delta. This is not flood-plain land; it's a mixture of flatland, forest and rolling hills.

It was here in Senatobia in 1942 that Alan Lomax recorded a blind musician and son of a slave called Sid Hemphill. What he was hearing was a hangover from slave culture played with primitive instruments that had never been recorded before. It was called fife and drum music and it blew Lomax's mind.

Half a century later, the memories were still vivid: "In vaudou ceremonies, dancers make pelvic gestures toward the drum to honor the holy music that is inspiring them. I never expected to see this African behavior in the hills of Mississippi, just a few miles south of Memphis." [10]

Sid Hemphill was keeping the culture alive along with a handful of others: Otha Turner and Ed and Lonnie Young. It wasn't the blues, but it helps us to understand the powerful sense of local identity which enabled a sub-genre of blues to emerge. Hill Country blues took its form from the blues of Mississippi Fred McDowell (1906–72) and a generation of artists who emerged in the 1960s and were strongly influenced by him: R.L. Burnside (1926–2005), Junior Kimbrough (1930–98) and Sid's granddaughter Jessie Mae Hemphill (1923–2006). Though none of them achieved commercial success or recognition on the scale of the Chicago blues singers, I recommend them highly. Their calling card was a rhythmic guitar style (in contrast to the fingerpicking that we've just heard), with drone effects and minimal chord changes.

Junior Kimbrough spread his seed liberally: he had 36 children and never left a penny to any of them in his will. I'm not sure that his musical legacy was the first thing on his mind when he made all them babies, but a couple did go on to become musicians. R.L. Burnside was no slouch himself – "I got 12 kids and you need a damn computer to count my grandkids." [11] All eight of his sons played with him in his band, and two of them, Duwayne and Garry, have appeared on several Mississippi blues recordings. The torch has now passed on to two grandsons, Cedric Burnside and Kent Burnside, who are proudly keeping the Hill Country blues tradition burning.

Cedric Burnside had an incredible musical upbringing, playing drums with some of the meanest blues musicians north Mississippi has ever known.

"When I was 8 or 9 years-old, I started playing drums at the house parties they used to throw. By the time I was 10 or 11, I was playing in the juke joints. I just kind of looked and learned, you know, playing behind my Big Daddy (R.L. Burnside) and Mr. Junior Kimbrough." [12]

"The police used to come in the juke joints, and they would have to hide us behind the beer coolers. They fed us cheeseburgers, and when the police left, we jumped back behind the instruments and started jamming again." [13]

During his teens he often toured with the band to the detriment of his formal education, but the musical education he was getting was second to none, performing with the best and building up his own confidence and knowledge. By the time that the Cedric Burnside Project was formed in 2010, Cedric's CV was starting to fill out: he'd recorded an album with his uncle, Garry Burnside, and a couple with Lightnin Malcolm, he was known as one of the best drummers around and was always in demand. The new band saw Cedric team up again with Garry Burnside, and they were joined by Cedric's younger brother Cody. After Cody tragically died in 2012, Cedric reformed the band with long-term buddy Trenton Ayers: "Trenton's dad, (Little) Joe Ayers, was one of the original bass players for Junior Kimbrough. So just like me, Trent had that in his blood." [14]

The aptly named Descendants of Hill Country (2015) is the second Cedric Burnside Project album since Trenton joined the band. Another old acquaintance, Amos Harvey, was made producer – "I knew if anybody knew our sound, it would be Amos… We went in the studio, and we recorded a CD in three days. It turned out to be pretty awesome." No technical wizardry was required – this is a lo-fi production. **GOING AWAY BABY** is lowdown dirt-encrusted blues rock, the guitar keeps ferociously pounding out the same riff, the driving rhythm has a raw energy that you don't hear so often nowadays. The album has a dual purpose. It's a tribute to the great Hill Country bands of R.L. Burnside and Junior Kimbrough, but it's also an announcement to the world that descendants of those musicians love the tradition and want to keep it alive, and that the music can still grab you with its rugged directness and its groove. "Everything I write," says Cedric, "is based on hill country. It might sound a little modern because I'm a little modern, but as far as keeping the hill country blues alive, I'm going to keep that tradition alive. I'm going to do that until the day I die." [15]

ANYTIME IS SATURDAY NIGHT sounds exactly like what you'd expect to hear if you randomly dropped into one of the countless live music events that take place in the city of New Orleans seven nights a week… no, it's better than that: it's what you dream of finding there. There's lots of brass, it's explosive, joyful, free-flowing, and the female singer is sassy and stylish. The band are called Meschiya Lake and The Little Big Horns; they know their traditional jazz but are not cast in any mould: they do their own thing and they know how to have a good time.

Meschiya Lake is a relative newcomer to the city and its culture: her childhood was spent in Oregon and South Dakota. At the age of nine she won a singing contest, earning her $500 and a regular paid gig. Back then she was singing country, but she quit when she was 13 – "I was getting into punk rock in high school. I was very rebellious." [16] After high school she joined the circus. Her job, as a member of Know Nothing Family Zideshow and End of the World Circus, included eating lightbulbs and insects, and fire dancing. She loved the rootless lifestyle and the companionship that the touring circus offered. But when one day she arrived in New Orleans she realised this was a place that she wanted to be. In New Orleans she began singing again – how could she not? – learned to perform jazz music and joined a band called Loose Marbles who were dedicated to street performance. Then she moved on again, from street music to a band with ambition. The Little Big Horns, which she formed in

2009, gave her that freedom to express herself and the means to reach a global audience.

Meschiya's story isn't as outré as it might sound: the story of Louisiana's music is very much a story of immigration, of cultural cross-currents colliding, and of the forging of a unique tradition that crosses boundaries of race and class.

New Orleans gave jazz to the world. The names of the jazz pioneers have passed into legend: Buddy Bolden (who started it all with his improvisational approach to cornet playing), King Oliver, Louis Armstrong, Jelly Roll Morton, Kid Ory and Sidney Bechet, all of whom headed north at one time or another during their careers, taking the Dixieland tradition with them. But why New Orleans? Was it accident, or was there something unique in the city's cultural make-up?

From 1682 to 1762, Louisiana was under French colonial rule. The French left behind a legacy that remains to this day: a Creole population, with shared cultural ties that included Catholicism and the French language. This was supplemented by thousands of refugees from Saint-Domingue and Haiti in the 1790s and early 1800s: mostly of African origin, these were Louisiana's black Creoles, and from them was to come zydeco music while the more Europeanised Creoles played Cajun. Louisiana was also home to a large African-American slave population, and to European settlers from various waves of immigration.

Above all it was in New Orleans that these cultures lived side by side, rubbing up against each other. Congo Square became the place where black slaves were licenced to congregate, play music and dance before abolition, and the Africanised chanting and dancing fascinated observers who'd never heard anything like this before. The year 1857 saw the introduction of the organised pageant to the city's carnival, which prior to that date had been more akin to a rowdy street party: this would evolve into the famous Mardi Gras parade. Meanwhile, military bands furnished with European brass instruments were becoming very popular.

This too was street performance – it could be heard at parades and picnics and on the riverboats – and it crossed divides (there were black brass bands too). The New Orleans jazz funeral was another tradition that predated the age of jazz. In the 19th century, black neighbourhood organisations would club together to provide insurance and burial services to members: from here it was a natural step to incorporating music into funeral processions, and from these processions the tradition of the 'second line' was born, in which bystanders with no connection to the deceased would join the procession and dance to the music.

Street music, brass bands, carnivals, all in a unique cultural melting pot: it was in this fertile ground that jazz was born. New Orleans honours its heritage in many ways. Preservation Hall opened its doors in 1961 in the heart of the French Quarter, operating as a non-profit music venue and a touring band. The Jazz National Historical Park was opened in 1994. As well as Mardi Gras itself, Louisiana has an abundance of music festivals, most notably the Jazz and Heritage Festival, which draws thousands of people to the state every year. But it's not all about honouring the past. Current bands such as the Pine Leaf Boys breathe new life into established genres with a spirit of innovation. For Derrick Tabb, a drummer with the Rebirth Brass Band, the dream was to pass on the gift of music to the next generation – "I saw the direction that our youth were taking in New Orleans and wanted to make a difference. I remembered my struggles as a kid and those that reached out to me... I knew what it was that kept me out of trouble and it was music." [17] In the aftermath of Hurricane Katrina, he founded a non-profit, The Roots of Music. Every year they enrol in their after-school programme over 100 students, young kids for whom the city's schools have failed to provide a decent musical education, and get them all playing music. Since 2009, a Roots of Music marching band has paraded the city every Mardi Gras. The goal is to encourage these kids to lead positive, self-reliant lives, with half an eye also on creating the musicians of the future.

In contrast to country music, blues and jazz, Native American culture has long been neglected and little understood (though perhaps less so in Canada, where the Polaris Music Prize was won in 2014 by Inuit throat singer, Tanya Tagaq, and in 2015 by veteran songwriter, Buffy Sainte-Marie). The year 2016, though, was to be a landmark, a year that changed everything. On 1st April the first resistance camp of the Dakota Access Pipeline protests was formed. The issue had already been brewing for a while. Indigenous activists were arguing that the proposed pipeline would damage the environment, pollute precious water resources and defile sacred sites. At first the camp was just a few teepees, and then, in ever increasing numbers, people started arriving from every corner of America. Soon there were hundreds, then this became thousands. Numerous GoFundMe campaigns were set up, which collectively raised nearly $8 million. Later, serious questions would be asked about how all this money was used; but it was invaluable to the Standing Rock protestors. Native American tribes gave generously too, but even more significant than the money was their moral support.

"My tribe is Crow, and our traditional enemies are the Lakhotas, and they shared a (peace) pipe together at Standing Rock," says rapper Supaman. "They haven't done that in a long time." [18] This experience was multiplied countless times. Those who spent time in the camps – members of the many tribes, political activists, veterans, celebrities – spoke of the sense of community and the love that they found there. For Native Americans everywhere it was like they were joined by a new bond, and one of the ways in which they expressed this was through music. Taboo, a hip hop artist from The Black Eyed Peas, put together a collective of Native American musicians to record a song for the movement, and Stand Up/Stand N Rock was released in late 2016. In September, when the winners of the 16th Annual Native American Music Awards were announced, it was also confirmed that nominees and winners had donated their songs to two free compilation CDs. There are 44 songs on the CDs and a big variety of musical genres, so it seems churlish to complain, but I was a bit disappointed that no nominees from the pow wow category were included.

For many Native Americans, pow wow is the music with which they identify most strongly. The term refers both to a music genre and the event with which it is associated. Pow wows are gatherings of Native American tribes – social events where people break bread together, but also celebrations of culture. Modern-day pow wows are highly organised events that follow a tight schedule and require an MC to call on each act in turn. All pow wows, says Becky Olvera Schultz, revolve around dance, and central to dance is the drum and the singers who form part of the drumming troupe – "The drum is the heartbeat of the pow wow." [19] Very broadly, the singing styles fall into one of two categories, the high-pitched Northern Plains or the tenor-voiced Southern Plains. Many songs have no lyrics as such: they use what are called 'vocables', which kind of makes sense when you remember that pow pows are where cultures are shared with other tribes who speak different languages. It is also common, though, for songs to have a meaning and a purpose. Some pow wows are centred on dance competitions and others aren't; every pow wow is a feast of colourful dance costumes and a showcase for a variety of dance styles.

The Wild Band of Comanches are a Southern Plains group from Oklahoma. According to their official bio, "We hail from the Great Comanche Nation and are deep in our Comanche culture and community. We all sing together at the 'center drum' and participate within the Native American Church and also Comanche Churches." INTERTRIBAL 4 is a typical piece of pow wow music with drumming and wordless chanting. Hear how the voices keep lifting and dropping away: these changes will dictate the moves of the dancers. This is music to be felt, to be physically experienced.

NOTES

1. http://www.theabsolutesound.com/articles/new-old-ways
2. https://www.amoeba.com/blog/2015/02/eric-s-blog/black-hillbilly-or-what-you-really-know-about-the-upper-south-.html
3. http://lomaxky.omeka.net/about
4. https://www.ket.org/education/resources/mountain-born-jean-ritchie-story
5. http://www.alternatemusicpress.com/features/jeanritchie.html
6. From Folk Songs of the Southern Appalachians (1965), extracted from, http://research.culturalequity.org/get-audio-detailed-recording.do?recordingId=12743
7. http://originalpeople.org/joe-thompson-fiddle-player-who-helped-preserve-the-black-string-band
8. https://indiancountrymedianetwork.com/culture/arts-entertainment/rhiannon-giddens-pure-folk-music-fire-from-a-good-ol-mixed-race-north-carolinian
9. https://www.ourstate.com/rhiannon-giddens
10. Alan Lomax – The Land Where the Blues Began (1993), extracted from, http://aliciapatterson.org/stories/african-american-music-mississippi-hill-country-they-say-drums-was-calling
11. https://www.theguardian.com/music/2003/nov/16/popandrock2
12. http://www.bluesblastmagazine.com/featured-interview-cedric-burnside
13. https://thesipmag.com/cedric-burnside
14. http://www.bluesblastmagazine.com/featured-interview-cedric-burnside
15. http://www.phoenixnewtimes.com/music/cedric-burnside-has-rls-tradition-on-his-side-7594330
16. http://www.myneworleans.com/New-Orleans-Magazine/April-2012/PERSONA-Meschiya-Lake
17. http://www.bulletmusic.net/features-1/keeping-music-in-childrens-lives
18. https://noisey.vice.com/en_us/article/nnemjg/native-artists-have-united-to-make-a-song-for-standing-rock
19. https://www.voanews.com/a/native-american-pow-wows-celebrate-patriotism-unity/3917859.html

SOUTH AMERICA

ARGENTINA

In Buenos Aires, tango tourism is big business. And when I say big, I mean leviathan-sized. The growth of the industry has been so strong that the city's economy and its cultural life are being radically transformed.

The number of international tourists coming to Argentina passed the two million mark for the first time in 1994. In recent years it's been over five million, around the same level as Brazil. But unlike visitors to Brazil, who are dispersed between several different destinations, most visitors to Argentina have only one destination: Buenos Aires. And, for a great many of them, the city's foremost attraction is tango dancing.

The city council saw its opportunity and threw its weight behind developing and marketing its tango culture. New and larger milongas (dance halls) were opened, tango schools started up, and since 2003 the city has hosted the Mundial de Tango (World Tango Dance Tournament) alongside the city's annual tango festival. The sheer numbers are staggering:

"The amount of people and institutions that are involved in the local dance scene of Buenos Aires has been increased tenfold since 2001. Approximately 300 milongas per week in

JUAN CHIFLA	Mario Bofill
COPLAS DE PENAS	Mariana Carrizo
SALTA EN MI VOZ	Chaqueño Palavecino
ESPERANDO HEREDAR	Marina Ríos y Javier Díaz González
ALMA EN PENA	Orquesta Típica Lunático 33

120 different locations take place in Buenos Aires convening more than 35,000 dance practitioners. Furthermore, there are estimated more than 300 places, where nearly 2500 dance instructors give tango lessons." [1]

Every evening thousands of tourists go to tango shows. Most will attend places where the entertainment is largely geared to the demands and expectations of tourists. For the city's economy it's been one long success story: tourist dollars have underpinned a rapid growth in the entertainment sector.

You can't commodify a culture without losing something of its essence. I'm uneasy about the direction of travel of Argentine tango, and I'll have more to say on this later, but this chapter is not exclusively about tango, and that's also important. Tango is one branch of Argentina's musical tree, and the showering of attention that it has been receiving has implications for other (often more deeply rooted) forms of traditional music.

Unlike older forms of folk culture, tango was an urban culture that sprang up in the poorer barrios of Buenos Aires and Montevideo. Immigrant communities contributed a lot to its development. It was influenced by Argentine folk guitar music (primarily the milonga, which was itself a composite of different styles), by European dance-oriented music such as the waltz, and by African dance rhythms. For years it existed as an urban subculture, unrespectable owing to its working-class roots and to the shockingly sexualised nature of the dancing (couples dancing together!). Not until the early 1930s was it fully embraced by polite society.

Before tango became part of national culture, other forms of folk dance flourished around the country. Zamba is a slow dance performed to the rhythm of guitar and the bombo legüero drum. It's derived from a Peruvian dance called La Zamacueca and is most popular in the north-western Andean provinces of Salta, Jujuy and Tucumán. Chacarera is a fun courtship dance for couples that doesn't involve any touching. It's claimed that it originated in Santiago del Estero, but it's long been popular throughout the northern regions. Chamamé is danced in pairs with the man and the woman literally cheek to cheek. The word Chamamé is from the indigenous Guaraní language; the dance has evolved over centuries, but it's associated most strongly with the north-eastern Corrientes province, where settlers from central Europe introduced the accordion and turned Chamamé into an accordion-based music. It's here, in the city of Corrientes, that La Fiesta del Chamamé is held every year.

Like the tango, Chamamé music has experienced something of a revival in recent years. Leading the revival has been Chango Spasiuk (born 1968) from Misiones province, a virtuoso accordion player with a bent for improvisation. Though he works with musicians from other genres, he still speaks lovingly of the old Chamamé musicians who first inspired him. The patriarch, says Chango, the real father of the music, is bandoneonist Transito Cocomarola (1918–74). [2] Cocomarola died on 19th September, a day that is now officially commemorated in Corrientos province as Chamamé Day. Tarrago Ros (1923–78) "created a style that's really simple… today there's a load of people who try to play that way because for all that it's simple, it's very popular, but they can't get the beauty of Tarrago's way of playing. And it's a real dance style, it's the most danceable of all. It's as if he were Glenn Miller." Isaco Abitbol (1917–94), "has a way of playing the bandoneon that's very intense. Intense both in terms of the sound and emotionally". And Ernesto Montiel (1916–75) "didn't just develop the music but also the way of playing the accordion." All these four greats are correntinos who were born and lived their lives in the Corrientes region, and one senses that Chango sees in them an integrity that is reflected in the simple directness of their music.

Mario Boffil (born 1948) is cut from the same cloth: a correntino himself and an honest character who writes songs that tell stories of everyday life and has an ability to make an audience laugh. When he was still a teenager he formed his first band with cousin Alberto, Los Hermanos Bofill, but since his mid-20s he's been performing mainly as a soloist. He's written over 200 songs, and the legendary Tarrago Ros is one of several folk singers who've sung covers. JUAN CHIFLA is a story of rural folk, sung with passion. The accordion playing adds an extra touch of drama.

Argentine folklore music draws on traditional dance styles, on Andean music and on the music of European immigrants. Its high point was in the 1960s and '70s, when many outstanding artists and groups emerged in the northern provinces: in Salta, Los Chalchaleros, Los Fronterizos and Los Cantores del Alba; in Santiago del Estero, Los Hernanos Abalos and, later, Los Manseros Santiagueños and Dúo Coplanacu, while Tucumán province still venerates Atahualpa Yupanqui and Mercedes Sosa.

Of all these artists, Atahualpa Yupanqui (1908–92) left the greatest legacy. His father was a Criollo descended from indigenous people, while his mother was Spanish by birth. The family moved north to Tucumán province when he was 10, and it was here that the child developed his life-long love of the land and its people and the music of the guitar. He joined the Communist Party and in 1931 took part in an unsuccessful uprising, following which he had to make a dramatic escape to Uruguay. Returning to Argentina in 1934, he went on an ethnological expedition to study the Amaichas Indians. Travelling by mule, and carrying his guitar everywhere, he learned new songs and grew familiar with the rhythms of the zamba, vidala and chacarera. Over the next decade he continued to lead a troubadour life, travelling around the region, doing more research and giving many impromptu performances, and getting imprisoned several times for his political activities. During this time he met his future wife and musical partner, Nenette.

In 1949, he left Argentina again, this time for Europe. In Paris he found a friend and a sponsor in Édith Piaf, while the leftist poets Louis Aragon and Paul Éluard and the artist Pablo Picasso, all inspired by the beauty and the moral passion that they saw in his poetry and his lyrics, became confirmed admirers. Back in Argentina, as the folk revival began to take root, artists such as Mercedes Sosa took inspiration from Atahualpa's life and from his vast collection of songs and poems and knowledge of traditional folklore culture. Atahualpa was also a key figure in the politically committed folk movement of nueva canción.

The influence of the folk movement on Argentine culture can still be seen today in peñas. Peñas are the equivalent of folk clubs: they're musical evenings held in bars and restaurants where communities gather to enjoy good wine, good food and live music. There may be a folklore band playing – though the style of music varies considerably from one place to another – but people will often will bring instruments as well, and there'll be music and dancing long into the night.

Peñas and folklore festivals such as Cosquin are life's blood for traditional musicians like Mariana Carrizo. She didn't have to visit a peña to 'discover' the music, though; it was already engrained within her:

"I was born in the Angastaco hills, San Carlos province, a village in the Calchaquí Valley where copla was like bread, a daily thing and the most essential part of life. We lived with my grandmother and her house was... 3,000 meters above sea level. It was two days walk to take our produce to town and sell it there or exchange it for sugar, yerba and other foodstuffs that we couldn't grow ourselves." [3]

The copla that she grew up with is a very old musical form with both indigenous and Spanish roots. Its roots were in rural northern communities like that in Calchaquí Valleys and for a long time they kept it alive. These days there are also copla festivals in the heartland areas. Even at the festivals, though, there are artists who'll take the copla, a sung poem, add too many instruments and make it into something different altogether. Not so Mariana. She doesn't depart too far from the tradition, because this is what's real to her. "When I sing," she says, "it's not just me." The coplas are a record of the lives of her ancestors, and the land where they trod. The song tradition is a way of remembering and honouring one's roots.

COPLAS DE PENAS keeps the simple structure of the rural song form, but Mariana performs it with an intensity of feeling that's all her own. The complete absence of stringed instruments is rather refreshing – clearly there's more to Argentine folk music than first meets the eye! Mariana's plans for 2018 include a book and a new album.

Chaqueño Palavecino looks the part of the gaucho singer in his wide-brimmed hats and ponchos. He's a superstar: every album he releases, and he's released a good many, piles off the shelves, and he's won countless awards and accolades. Personal glory, though, has no interest for him – it's the music that he cares about:

"We brag about it when tango music is played abroad, when Lionel Messi scores a goal... But sometimes we don't

put the same price – or take the same pride – in our folk
music. Often foreigners value what we have more than we
do ourselves. It hurts, but that's how it is." [4]

Chaqueño has paid his dues. He grew up in the Salta region in
the far north of Argentina, raised by his mother. After his mother
became ill they sold their few belongings and moved in with their
extended family in Tartagal. Here Chaqueño spent his teenage
years, attending school in the morning and working in the
afternoon, doing any odd job that came his way. His mother died
when he was 16. He moved to Salta city, where he got a job loading
and unloading bottles. By his mid-20s he was back in Tartagal,
now working as a bus driver. He formed a band and took his first
steps on his musical journey. But it wouldn't be until 1997, when
he was 38, that he would finally give up the bus driving.

He knows all the best folk tunes; performing zambas,
chacareras, cuecas. **SALTA EN MI VOZ** is the work of an artist in total
command, the song is about the landscape that he knows so well,
the music is equally innate to him, and his strong voice finds the
right groove easily.

Mariana Carrizo and Chaqueño Palavecino are among
the artists featured in Carlos Saura's 2015 documentary film
Zonda: Folclore argentino (or Argentina). It's beautifully and
imaginatively shot, all in the one physical space, and a good deal
of care has clearly gone into the choices of artists and genres of
song and dance. The film could have benefited, though, from
adding commentary.

The 1930s and '40s were tango's golden age. Dozens of tango
orchestras were operating in Buenos Aires, but it wasn't about the
numbers. In the cosmopolitan capital, tango had found its time
and its place. The large orchestras were perfectly suited to the
stylised dance music, adding professionalism and a dash of grace.
They were led by some of the most brilliant musicians of the day,
who were always innovating and finding ways to keep the music

fresh. Carlos Gardel had set the standard for lead singers, who were given free rein to express themselves. To name just a couple that I love, Mercedes Simone (1904–90) combined a tremendous sensitivity and a toughness in her vocals, while Edmundo Rivero (1911–86) had a striking deep bass-baritone voice.

Astor Piazzolla (1921–92) is generally heralded as a musical genius who kickstarted the renaissance in tango that has continued to this day. He was certainly a great innovator, but this is miles apart from the type of music that people had danced to just a generation earlier. Piazzolla dispenses both with the traditional orchestra – the orquesta tipica – and also the singer, to create improvised jazz-style arrangements that he called 'tango nuevo'. His work paved the way for other artists to explore different ways of introducing modern elements to the music. Some bands – like Bajofondo or the French-based Gotan Project – have gone the whole hog and combined electronic music with elements of tango, in so doing butchering the original art form. Others have proceeded with greater respect and sensitivity to classical tango, and it's on these that I wish to focus.

Marina Rios is a young singer in her 20s whose early experience of tango was listening to her father sing. In 2010, she formed a duo with the guitarist Javier Díaz González and they performed tangos, milongas and waltzes. On the album Tango, Trasnoche y Bohemia they seek to revive some 'tangos poco transitados', which charmingly translates as tangos less travelled. On ESPERANDO HEREDAR the vocals are strong and clear and the Spanish guitar adds a melodic feel, but this folk-tango hybrid somehow seems a shade insubstantial. Marina's latest collaboration with bandoneon player Costanza Besson could prove more interesting.

Orquesta Típica Lunático 33 were formed in 2008 in Córdoba, Argentina's second city. Their very name is a statement of intent: they want to rekindle some of the magic of the great tango orchestras of the 1940s, of which they claim no fewer than 50 existed in Córdoba alone. Presently they are the only one, and, though their numbers are limited to 10, venues struggle to accommodate them. Their instruments include guitar, bass, bandoneons and violins. The first album, called Tango a Primera Vista, consisted of eight tangos, a milonga and two waltzes, drawn from different periods. The featured track **ALMA EN PENA**, which is a Gardel cover, is from the second album Sueño y Orquesta, which follows a similar formula. Sofia Yannel's compelling vocals make you hang on every word. According to guitarist, Adrian Alzáa, the band's song arrangements are the real backbone of their music. You can't just take songs and try to copy them. In the 1940s each orchestra had its own identity and direction: "That is why the music has been creative, each orchestra had their own man, like Pugliese or Troilo, they were all unique. I think we have some of that." [5]

NOTES

1. Franco Barrionuevo Anzaldi – The New Tango Era in Buenos Aires: The Transformation of a Popular Culture into a Touristic "Experience Economy" (2012), http://www.academia.edu/1820107/The_new_tango_era_in_Buenos_Aires_The_transformation_of_a_popular_culture_into_a_touristic_experience_economy_
2. http://www.abc.net.au/radionational/programs/intothemusic/chamame/3070038
3. http://almagrorevista.com.ar/mundo-poetico-mariana-carrizo-la-pastora-saltena-lleva-la-copla-los-escenarios-del-mundo
4. https://www.clarin.com/espacio-clarin/chaqueno-palavecino-cantar-cerrar-boca_0_BkfS1DOce.html
5. http://latipicatango.com.ar/lunatico-33-tradicion-y-libertad

BOLIVIA

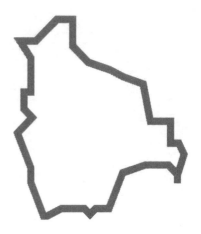

It turns out that I had Andean music all wrong. Instead of being this deeply traditional music that's been largely unchanged for generations, it's a modern hybrid.

In 1952, Víctor Paz Estenssoro was swept into power by a revolutionary movement and set about making some far-reaching reforms. Hitherto, the indigenous people who formed the bulk of the population were marginalised and excluded, their cultures ignored and belittled. Victor Paz brought in land reform, universal suffrage and much more. For the first time, Aymara- and Quechua-speakers had their own radio stations, and people in the cities could listen to their music. The universities were at the centre of a political awakening, and middle-class students identified themselves with the cause of indigenous rights: music helped to provide a bridge between the two communities.

Gilbert Favre was a Swiss musician who fell in love with an older woman whose story belongs in the chapter on Chile: the revolutionary singer Violeta Parra. Affair seems too tawdry a word to describe this passionate relationship that lasted several years. He also developed a passion for South American music, hanging up his clarinet and learning to play the quena (Andean flute). Early in 1965, he decided to walk away from Violeta: the

TU CASAMIENTO Y MI MUERTE	*Los Jairas*
IMÁGENES	*Luis Rico*
SOY SOLTERITO	*Alaxpacha*
WARMIKUNA YUPAY-	
CHASQAPUNI KASUNCHIK	*Luzmila Carpio*

arguments were getting too intense, and she'd just tried to commit suicide. "Taking my camera, my clarinet and my quena," he later wrote, "I went to the Embassy of Peru, where I was received as a dog by some female officials, I left immediately and went to the Embassy of Bolivia," and here he was met with smiles. So the decision was made to move to Bolivia. [1] Violeta was distraught and made several trips to La Paz to try and save the relationship. Two years later, depressed at losing Gilbert and by the knocks that she'd taken in her own musical career, she put a gun to her head and killed herself.

Gilbert, meanwhile, was busy reinventing Bolivian music. Los Jairas were formed specifically to play at Peña Naira, La Paz's new art gallery and cultural hub. Gilbert was teamed up with three of La Paz's finest: Ernesto Cavour (charango), Julio Godoy (guitar) and Edgar Jofré (drums). Despite the employment of quena and charango it wasn't a traditional ensemble, and that was the point: they wanted greater versatility and they wanted to recast folk music in a way that would appeal to the artists and intellectuals who frequented the Peña Naira.

Los Jairas's music crossed boundaries and did more than any other group to enhance the reputation of Andean indigenous music, both in Bolivia and globally. Judging by TU CASAMIENTO Y MI MUERTE it's not hard to see why. It's a yaravi, a fusion of indigenous rhythms with Spanish folk poetry, and it seems like we've got the best of both worlds. The vocals wax and wane in declamatory style, the softly played charango is ideally suited to the task, and the restrained use of the quena makes the tug on your heartstrings all the stronger when you hear its call.

Los Jairas spent a couple of years performing in Europe. When they returned, in 1971, Ernesto Cavour had left the band. No matter: they had shown the way for indigenous musicians to open up the global markets (and Simon & Garfunkel's 1970 recording of El Cóndor Pasa had also opened doors). Within a few years a family-based band from the Cochabamba region, Los Kjarkas, would follow them onto the global stage. Various other groups formed who followed in the footsteps of Los Jairas, though without quite the same level of artistry. The more successful of these were not village folk groups, but bands put together by indigenous university students (Savia Andina, Paja Brava). As for Cavour, he was on a mission of his own to promote the humble charango. Already, in 1962, he'd founded a charango museum in La Paz (which still exists today under the name Museo Instrumentos Musicales de Bolivia). In 1973, he co-founded the Bolivian Charango Society, and he's never tired of playing the instrument and telling people about its qualities.

As Bolivia was going through some turbulent years, other new genres were springing up. One of these was nueva cancion, of which Violeta Parra had been one of the architects. In 1967, Luis Rico was a happy-go-lucky university student who studied economics and played guitar when one day during a party he heard some news that would change his life. This is how he remembers it:

> "The dictator General Barrientos had ordered the killing of
> the miners and their families, who had gathered at Siglo

20 from all around Bolivia to morally and economically support Che Guevara's guerrillas... Eighty seven miners, women and children lost their lives that night. So I asked myself: what is it that I do? And, what is it that I should be doing? I dropped out of university, and started writing music and singing." [2]

The actual number who lost their lives that day remains hotly disputed half a century on. In any case, Luis never looked back. The songs poured out: miners songs, peasant songs, migrants' songs, women's songs, songs of struggles for democracy, and to protect the environment... and he wrote his share of love songs too! In 1971, Hugo Banzer Suarez became the country's president thanks to another military coup and Luis found out how tough the life of a protest singer can be: "In Banzer's time, I was arrested nine times, beaten, and lost several teeth." [3]

IMÁGENES is a beautifully written song that shows how seriously Luis took the craft of songwriting. Written like a poem, the words are spoken rather like one might recite a poem to a large audience – not normal speech but not singing either. The song describes in vivid detail a series of snapshots of the miners lives as they put away their work tools and head for the canteen to fill their bellies. Then the union siren sounds, summoning the miners to a general assembly. As the miners start to gather the song ends with a plea to keep the mines open. It's not unlike some of Bob Dylan's early political songs, which move from the telling of a story to the spelling out a few political messages.

Decade after decade, he carried on. As long as he could sing he couldn't walk away, it meant so much to him. He wanted to educate people and to stir their feelings, somehow to change things through his songs. The albums were almost incidental: it was when he was singing at protests and rallies that he was most alive. The rights of indigenous people was a cause particularly close to his heart. He spent time in Amazonia with indigenous communities there to get a better understanding of their way of life, their concerns, their culture.

December, 2005, saw a landslide victory in Bolivia's presidential election for an indigenous Aymara Bolivian and the son of a poor coca farmer, Evo Morales. It was a transformative moment for many reasons, not least of which being the improvements that Morales would bring to countless lives in Bolivia's indigenous communities. But the election result hadn't dropped out of a clear sky. It followed years of social unrest, of the growth of indigenous organisations, and of reforms made that failed to address the demands of the social movements. Luis must have shared in the excitement, but political affiliations had never been for him; he kept his independence. And when Morales decided to build a highway through an area of rainforest (Tipnis) that was also a protected indigenous territory there was never any doubt as to what side Luis would take. Tipnis, he argued, is "the lungs and the centre of the Amazon," and such, a project would not only do incalculable environmental harm but also threaten the way of life of the Tipnis Indians. [4] Morales countered his critics by stressing the economic benefits the project was supposed to bring. In 2011, activists embarked on a two-month-long protest march to La Paz. When Luis Rico met with the leaders the day before the rally in La Paz they asked for a song for the occasion. Luis didn't even know whether it would be possible to write a song from scratch at such short notice, but he said yes. The song was called Coraje and it instantly became an anthem of the movement. The government put the project on hold. There have since been attempts to resurrect it, but at the time of writing its future is still very much in doubt.

Bolivia, in the 21st century, is a country very proud of its unique cultural heritage. Evidence of this is everywhere, but suffice it to mention the Carnaval de Oruro. The carnival's overarching theme is based on religious ritual tradition, and while the music and dancing has a contemporary flavour it incorporates many elements that are centuries old. One of its most famous attractions is the Diablada, or the 'dance of the devils'. The big parade, in which thousands of dancers and musicians take part, retains features, we're told, from medieval mystery plays. It's Bolivia's most popular festival, people come from far and wide, and for 10 days every year leading up to Lent the Oruro city streets pulsate with sound and colour.

The Andean music model as popularised by Los Jairas and Los Kjarkas is slowly dying. Bolivia has gone through many changes in the past 25 years and the music no longer quite seems to fit. At the same time, there's a strong desire to make sure that Bolivian music keeps its Bolivian character – as a consequence, acoustic instruments and traditional rhythms keep popping up, sometimes in unlikely places. As artists search for new creative models, indigenous music has been combined with everything from Spanish music and Latin American musical forms to pop, rock and hip hop. It's exciting, but also disorienting – who's to say what's traditional and what's modern: where are the lines in the sand?

The disconcerting shriek at the start of **SOY SOLTERITO** sounds like something taken from a horror film. Alaxpacha are a band who want to play traditional rhythms but don't want us to pigeonhole them or their music as something stuck in the past. The barrage of sound, the high tempo, the calling out, the whistles – this is their way of reaching out to urban audiences. What brought the Alaxpacha musicians together, though, back in 1993, was a shared love of traditional Aymara music. They take traditional rhythms such as the morenada, the huayno and the ch'uta and inject them with new life. And they take a special interest in songs from the high plains, the altiplano of western Bolivia, "that's to say La Paz, Potosí, Oruro and most of all the morenada rhythm which has become our trademark," confirms director Ramiro Aguirre. [5] The track is taken from A La Paz – Maravilla del Mundo: an entire album dedicated to the region's music and dances. This alone should tell you how seriously they take their music research, and over the years they've travelled across South America promoting regional Bolivian music.

Adding to indigenous music a rare mix of wisdom, creativity and spirituality is the voice of Luzmila Carpio. She was born in 1949, in the tiny village of Qala Qala, high up on the altiplano. She was brought up speaking Quechua – she never heard any Spanish spoken until she was seven years old. "My earliest memories," she says, "are filled with music and of my mother carrying me on her back. She sang to me constantly, pointing out the birdsongs on our way." [6] She became adept at distinguishing the calls of the different birds. Her mother would also tell her many stories about Pachamama, the Andean deity who is Mother Earth. For her people, a spiritual way of life was inseparable from a reverence for nature. "We have to respect the spirits of the water, the air that we breathe, our mountains, our trees. This knowledge is very present in our culture. We live in harmony with the Pachamama, Mother Earth." [7]

In her teens she moved to the city of Oruro and began singing in Spanish, and made her first radio performances. Singing in Spanish was practically obligatory for anyone with aspirations for a successful career, but Luzmila knew it wasn't right for her. She began writing songs in Quechuan, playing the charango and studying the indigenous cultures of the Andes. She wasn't just interested in past tradition but in the present: through her songs she spoke up for the environment and the rights of women, and against injustice and hate.

In the early 1990s, now living in France, Luzmila was shocked to hear about all the planned commemorations for the 500th anniversary of the 'discovery' of the Americas. Her own language had been spoken in South America for at least 2,000 years! To her it was like a sign of the importance of preserving her language and culture.

"At that time I was working with UNICEF in Bolivia," she

recalls. "I was trying to educate our people in numeracy and literacy in our own dialects. Our languages have always been marginalised. On top of that reading and writing never really reached women." To this end, Carpio composed a series of songs to support the UNICEF project. Aesthetically, they showcased the tones, sounds, and instruments inherent to the musical forms of the Potosi region. Conceptually, they aimed to cultivate an awareness of the Aymaran and Quechuan languages and their rich associated cultures while continuing to tackle the issues she'd long rallied against. [8]

This collection of songs – all written by Luzmila – was called Yuyay Jap'Ina (Reclaim Our Knowledge). A set of four cassette tapes filled with songs was distributed among all the many communities who'd participated in the project, placed in libraries and learning centres and into the hands of many illiterate women. And there they remained until two decades later Luzmila released an album called Yuyay Jap'Ina Tapes on a French label. Now the world can hear 17 of the most powerful of the songs recorded back then by the younger Luzmila. The album is a homage to Pachamama; as a social document it's of considerable interest, but perhaps the main thing to be said is that it's a very intriguing and engaging set of songs, ranging from Ch'uwa yaku kawsaypuni, where she sings in a high falsetto to a frenetic chorus of charango and birdsong, to the slow, graceful Arawi. Luzmila tells us that WARMIKUNA YUPAY – CHASQAPUNI KASUNCHIK means "Women, we have to be respected". This is a song to dispel any stereotypes that you have about Andean music. The mood is euphoric, the music fast and hard-hitting. The combination of charango and Luzmila's voice has a jarring and engaging off-kilter quality once heard never forgotten.

When Evo Morales became president he appointed Luzmila Carpio as his country's ambassador to France. The new constitution, approved in 2009 following a national referendum, redefined Bolivia as a plurinational state and recognised Aymara and Quechua as official languages. For Luzmila, more than anyone, this was an enormous victory: she who'd had to battle prejudice just to sing in Quechua, who'd raised awareness of Quechua language and culture through her art and her public activities, and who'd worked with so many illiterate women, the victims of a discriminatory education system. She wasn't finished yet, though: when I saw her perform at Womad in 2015 she was celebrating the release of Luzmila Carpio meets ZZK, on which her songs are given the electronic treatment by several cutting-edge producers. Throughout her career she's always been ready to try out new ideas, and this was another challenge to be embraced:

> *"Of course I like the traditional way of playing my songs with flutes and bombos–the first clothes–but all this new light on my songs is very exciting. A good song can wear new clothes well even 30 years after. The fact that the lyrics are in Quechua don't mean the music has to be in traditional versions only." [9]*

NOTES

1. http://www.paginasiete.bo/cultura/2014/5/11/gringo-favre-21170.html
2. http://www.startts.org.au/media/Luis-Rico-Sings-for-a-Better-World.pdf
3. https://www.eldia.com.bo/index.php?cat=386&pla=3&id_articulo=95880
4. http://www.startts.org.au/media/Luis-Rico-Sings-for-a-Better-World.pdf
5. https://www.radioub.com/index.php/rcultura/2514-alaxpacha-y-sus-exitos-en-concierto
6. https://www.mindfood.com/article/pachamama-interview-with-luzmila-carpio
7. http://www.lanacion.com.ar/2025183-luzmila-carpio-la-chamana-que-canta-con-los-pajaros
8. http://www.dummymag.com/features/luzmila-carpio-meets-zzk
9. http://www.afropop.org/22271/luzmila-carpio-meets-zzk

BRAZIL

"I was born in Houmus, close to Vigario Geral. I saw a lot of friends die. Vigario Geral was the worst, most dangerous favela in the whole country. It was known as the Brazilian Bosnia because so many people died there." [1]

The speaker of these words is José Junior, and he's talking about a project that he initiated that has transformed the lives of many people in this notorious Rio slum. The project began life in 1993, after police massacred 21 innocent people in Vigario Geral in retaliation for the killing of four cops. One of the 21 dead was the brother of Anderson Sa. Anderson had been involved in drug gangs as a kid, but now he joined with José Junior to start Grupo Cultural AfroReggae (GCAR). A month after the massacre they opened a cultural community centre in Vigario Geral. With the aid of community volunteers and borrowed instruments they began providing workshops in Afro-Brazilian dance, percussion, soccer and capoeira. This model was then replicated in other favelas (shantytowns). And it's still going: in 2012, for instance, we're told that GCAR had 6,000 members in Rio with organisations in five favelas and 75 projects under way.

EU QUERO É SORONGAR	Elza Soares
ROXÁ	Clementina de Jesus
AGONIZA MAIS NÁO MORRE	Beth Carvalho
SÓ VIA FACA VOAR	Bezerra da Silva
MEU AMOR JÁ ME CHAMOU	Samba Chula de São Braz
NO MEIO DO PITIU	Dona Onete

The 'AfroReggae' label is misleading. The GCAR band fronted by Anderson Sa makes unremarkable urban fusion music with socially conscious hip hop lyrics. But what José Junior's organisation have achieved is something altogether more remarkable. They've given a positive focus to the lives of street kids who've known little but drugs and violence. They've inculcated in the favelas a culture of self-help. And they've helped revive belief in collective community action – all of which lessens the power of the drug gangs. All of this has been done though music. In late 2013, the drug gangs hit back, unleashing a campaign of violence against GCAR. Mere bullets, though, cannot destroy such powerful ideas and values once they have taken hold.

I came looking for the roots, the character, the identity of Brazilian music, but all these things proved surprisingly elusive. Brazilian musicians love drawing on a variety of influences, pushing themselves artistically, taking their music in different directions. So we see a lot of mixing of genres. Samba is the national music, but samba comes in so many different forms that the word is not a great deal more descriptive than 'rock music'. Many successful Brazilian artists sing in a jazz-inflected style, often with a very gentle samba beat. This, I came to learn, was bossa nova, but it could also be samba, because there's a lot of crossover between the two musical forms. Bossa nova has a refined yet easeful quality that has made it popular the world over. My search, though, was to lead me in a very different direction, back to the slums of Rio de Janeiro.

Why the favelas? Brazil is a country of contrasts, where wealth and extreme poverty exist side by side, and nowhere is this more obvious than in cities such as Sao Paulo and Rio de Janeiro. The first phase of explosive urban growth happened in the 1940s and '50s, when thousands of farm labourers migrated to the cities, many of them ending up on the hillsides of the then-capital Rio. Unwanted, they were treated as non-people, as the city refused to provide sanitation, electricity or other services. In fact, the only service that the new migrants saw much of was the police force. Poverty was institutionalised; the slum population were excluded from normal society and were regularly abused, harassed and criminalised. All of these are still live issues decades later. In 2009 the Rio state government began to build walls round some of the favelas to remove them from sight and to restrict their growth, thus making permanent their exclusion.

Most of the population of Rio and São Paulo are migrants, or descended from recent migrants to the city. In the favelas not only is the concentration of migrants much higher; there is also a larger black population, a product of Brazil's racial divide. So you have people of different ethnicity and cultural background thrown together in a small space. This can be (and often is) a recipe for conflict, but there is also always the potential that people will find common cause over the neglect and injustice that they experience at the hands of the authorities. In this environment music and football are powerful social tools. Both are democratic, open to participation by those with limited formal education, and both are transformative, capable of bringing communities together and instilling a sense of hope.

Decades earlier the city of Rio had given birth to samba music. And given samba's modern reputation as a cross-class, cross-cultural music, it's intriguing to learn that it began life as an extension of Afro-Brazilian culture. After the abolition of slavery in 1888, many former slaves headed to Rio, where they established their own communities. Among these immigrants were the Tias Baianas (Bahian Aunts), matriarchal leaders and priestesses in Afro-Brazilian culture and the Candomblé religion. Tia Ciata was the most famous of these, and at her home the early samba pioneers used to gather together and make music. So African dance and drumming were a vital part of samba in its earliest incarnation.

Rio is also famous of course for its carnival. Carnival is embraced by people of all cultures, and the fact it takes place just before the start of Lent shows its importance to Catholics. But its most distinctive features are all imported from African culture: the costumes, the masks, the street parties, the bodyshaking and the drumming. Carnival music is poles apart from refined music made in recording studios: big drumming ensembles bring life and noise to the streets. Since the first samba schools were started in Rio in the 1920s, Rio's samba schools have been the beating heart of carnival, organising communities all year round to create the spectacular parades. The early samba schools would have felt very different from the big professionally organised operations that exist today. Cartola, Nelson Cavaquinho and Paulo da Portela were all black samba singers who'd grown up in Rio's slums and who took on leading roles in the samba schools back then, alongside other singers and composers. What they'd have been playing was what's known today as samba de morro, or samba de raiz. Morro is a reference to the hills where Rio's favelas sprawl, while 'raiz' just means 'roots'.

Elza Soares was born in 1937, and by the time that she began her career samba had become this great national music, played everywhere on the radio, and spinning off into all kinds of sub-genres. What Elza brought to the music was her own experience. Born and raised in a Rio favela, she was raped at the age of 12 and because she was pregnant, forced by her father to marry the rapist. Her husband continued to beat her and rape her, and her first three children died in childbirth. She learned how to fight for herself. Her first radio appearance as a teenager left a lasting impression: the show's host, celebrated samba composer Ary Barroso, seeing this scruffy girl who'd obviously come from the favelas walking on set, asked her what planet she'd come from. "From the same planet as you, sir – planet hunger," she memorably replied.

By 1962, as a rising star, Elza got herself an invite to go to Chile, where the Brazilian football team were playing in the World Cup. Here she began an affair with Garrincha. Elza's husband had died a few years earlier of tuberculosis but Garrincha was still married. Garrincha was the star of the tournament: his inspired performances carried Brazil though to the final. In the semi-final against the hosts, Chile, the Chilean defender Eladio Rojas did a number on Garrincha, kicking him and poking him in the eye, all to no effect. Finally, with the match already lost, Rojas kicked Garrincha once too often and Garrincha appeared to retaliate. Rojas went down, acting hurt, and the Peruvian referee sent Garrincha off. As he walked off the pitch, his eyes on Elza, he was struck in the head by a stone thrown from the stands. Elza ran to the front of the crowd screaming. As it turned out he was OK, but it took a controversial hearing to get him clearance to play in the final, where he kept his promise to Elza to win the cup.

By now the affair was all over the press. It was a national scandal and Elza Soares was depicted as the villain. It would have been easy for her to walk away, especially after she began to learn about Garrincha's chaotic lifestyle, his carelessness with money, his alcoholism and a dozen other faults. But she stayed with him for 14 years. She recognised in him a kindred soul: one who'd endured hardship and agony, who'd had to fight to overcome many setbacks and who was ruled by passion.

On **EU QUERO É SORONGAR** the heavy percussion and the horns lend the song a flavour of street carnival. But what really stands out for me is the flow of Elza's voice. Her control seems effortless and her natural singing style means that, when she sings, we believe every word that she utters.

Half a century on, she's still alive and still fighting. In 2003 she broke three ribs after falling on stage; in 2007 she caught a digestive disease and required three surgeries. But she couldn't bring herself to stop performing: "Without music I am nothing. Without the stage, I am nobody." [2]

While Elza and Garrincha were getting to know one another in Chile, Clementina de Jesus (1901–87) was working as a domestic maid. She's never known what it meant to have money, to have opportunity. For her, singing was everything: it expressed her roots, her identity. Her family had moved to Rio when she was aged eight. She used to listen to her mother sing as she washed clothes – old songs from her youth, remembered fragments of Brazil's African heritage. She learned hymns when singing in her church choir and became a student of samba through involvement in the Portela Samba School. And she continued to sing through those long years when she was working for a meagre living.

Then one day Herminio Bello de Carvalho saw Clementina perform. He was a producer, a composer, a promoter and a champion of old school samba. He knew he'd found something unique. With his help Clementina appeared in musicals, and on record. Public and critics alike gave her a rapturous welcome. Such a voice! So deep and husky – no one had ever heard its like before. Fortunately, in Herminio, she was in good hands, and she got to record some of the old Afro-Brazilian jongos that she knew, and songs by old samba composers. In January, 1968, she recorded an album with two living legends from the very early days of samba music, Pixinguinha and João da Baiana, backed by a few other old musicians. They didn't rehearse; they just sat down and played, so there's quite a bit of improvisation. Gente da Antiga is a magnificent album, a window to Brazil's African heritage. On the featured track **ROXÁ**, Clementina de Jesus takes the lead while Pixinguinha's saxophone, the percussive beat and the backing choir all contribute to the joyous sound.

In the 1960s and '70s samba became something of a cultural battleground. Herminio was just one of a number of revivalists who wanted to reclaim what he saw as its true soul. It was noticeable that most of the artists who showed an interest in old composers and early samba were themselves people of colour: Clara Nunes, Dona Ivone Lara, Alcione and Nelson Sargento to name just a few. Though all were based in Rio, unlike Elza Soares, most hadn't experienced the brutality of the slums when growing up. But sociology professor, Dmitri Cerboncini Fernandes, claims that they included a black intelligentsia who in the 1970s tried to reclaim samba's Afro-Brazilian roots and even to redefine samba itself. This was in the period when Brazil was ruled by a military dictatorship. Prominent musicians including Paulinho da Viola, Nei Lopes, Candeia and Martinho da Vila, though not acting as an organised group, formed "a strongly aware, politically active Negro intellectuality, which was against the military dictatorship, and which began to view the samba as one of the main Negro legacies to be protected and valued." [3]

At the centre of these cultural battles was a white singer whose father was a lawyer. As a kid, Beth Carvalho was exposed to many kinds of music, even flirting with the idea of becoming a ballerina, but growing up in Rio she was entranced by the passion and spectacle of carnival. The 1964 military coup took place just before her 18th birthday: at the time she was singing bossa nova. In 1966 she saw a show that changed her life: it was the Rosa de Ouro concert produced by Hermínio Bello de Carvalho. The show itself was an act of cultural resistance that brought together black musicians like Paulinho da Viola, Jair do Cavaquinho and Nelson Sargento, but it was the performance of the hitherto unknown

Clementina de Jesus that left Beth Carvalho in total awe. Before long Beth had become a leading samba singer. She didn't have to look far to find traditional samba music: it was there in the samba schools, and in the circle of musicians who worked with Hermínio. Over time Beth got to know some of the older black samba players who were still alive, men like Cartola and Nelson Cavaquinho, and to familiarise herself with their work. Again and again she would pay homage to these samba pioneers, recording many of their songs and even making whole albums in tribute.

AGONIZA MAIS NÃO MORRE was written by Nelson Sargento. Nelson had grown up in a poor family in Rio's Salgueiro favela, and the song's implicit message is that samba music belongs to us. Beth Carvalho sings it as a song of resistance. Beth says that she gets her politics from her liberal father, but it's clear that she was also inspired by the radicalism of the time, the struggle for democracy, the Cuban revolution. She identifies with the culture of the favelas because she sees in it a means by which the poor can take back control over their own lives. "The CIA wants to end the samba," she says. "It's a struggle against the Brazilian culture. The United States wants to dominate the world through culture... Samba is resistance. My record's an act of resistance..." [4] And, from another interview: "samba is more than a musical genre; it's a religion, a philosophy of life. It's democratic: when you sit round the mesa de pagode (pagode table) the whole world is equal." [5]

Beth also became known for sponsoring musicians she admired and helping them to launch their careers; among the more notable being Zeca Pagodinho, Grupo Fundo de Quintal and the ex-Fundo de Quintal members Almir Guineto, Arlindo Cruz and Jorge Aragão. They in turn affectionately referred to her as their godmother.

One of her first protégés was a man 20 years her senior, Bezerra da Silva (1927–2005). Born in Recife, as a youth he served in the Merchant Marine but left after an officer sexually abused him. So at the age of 15, carrying little more than the clothes on his back, he stowed away on board a ship carrying

sugar and travelled the thousand miles down the coast to Rio de
Janeiro in the hope of starting a new life and of reconciling with
his father. Things didn't work out with his father, and he became
just one more penniless migrant living in a shack and trying to
find construction work. At one point he met Jackson do Pandeiro,
from whom he learned to play coca de roda, a traditional dance
from the north-east of Brazil, thought to have origins in both
African and indigenous Brazilian culture. But in 1954 his mental
health deteriorated, his life fell apart and he spent seven years
on the streets, surviving by scavenging and begging. He cured
himself after converting to the Umbanda religion and gradually
got himself back on track, returning to his music.

In 1975, Bezerra da Silva released his first album, Bezerra da
Silva, O Rei do Coco. It's a fine example of coca de roda music,
but his real legacy rests on later albums on which he sings songs
penned by himself or some of Rio's other ghetto poets. He
becomes a spokesman of the favelas. "In Copacabana," he says,
"the police need an authorization to enter someone's house, but
on the morro, they enter without one, and rob and kill. Everyone
thinks that those who live on the morro are all bandits. So these
songwriters live there, and they write about the day-to-day reality
of the morro." [6] In Se não fosse o samba he sings about the
experience of getting arrested and locked up just for living in the
wrong place, while in Vítimas da Sociedade (Corporate Victims)
he warns us that the real thieves are those hiding behind their
well-tailored suits. There is much more in similar vein. The
featured song SÓ VIA FACA VOAR is a colourful, amusing account of
what happened late one night down at the forró dance. A lively
dance number, it has a memorable chorus line.

Brazil's music today is noted for its diversity, but what's less
widely appreciated is the richness and diversity of its traditional
styles. Samba de morro is far from being the only genre deserving
of protection. Choro, which was popular in the 1930s and '40s, is a
European-influenced form of instrumental music. The traditional

choro ensemble was flute, guitar and another stringed instrument called the cavaquinho, but brass instruments were also used. A current choro group are Quarteto Roda de Choro from São Paulo who play Brazilian seven-stringed guitar, cavaquinho, clarinet and the pandeiro drum. Capoeira is a martial art, which can also be played as a game, it involves music, dance and ritual. For a long time it was popular among Brazil's slaves. The lead instrument, the berimbau, is a wooden bow with a wire strung across played using a small stick. The addition of various drums and percussion instruments makes an exciting primal sound, somewhat harsh on the ear! The Nzinga Institute of Capoeira Angola has operations in São Paulo, Salvador and other cities, and as Grupo Nzinga they released an album in 2003. Afoxé is a music with chanting and drumming associated with the Candomblé religion. It enjoyed a brief revival in the 1970s when the musician Gilberto Gil (later Brazil's minister of culture) recorded a song. More recently, Afoxé Oya Alaxé, a cultural and educational project from Recife, have released an album of Afoxé music.

Samba chula is more endangered than any of these. Two men who've helped keep it alive are the brothers Joao and Antonio Saturno, better known as John of the Ox and Aluminio, who are the core of the band, Samba Chula de São Braz. A few years ago the drummer, Aluminio, contracted prostate cancer, so to help him out cultural activist Sparrow Roberts released their album on bandcamp for $9 as a fundraising venture. The album's a delight: the fast, southern African-style guitar rhythms are unexpected, but the strings, drums and chanted vocals blend very naturally, and the eight minutes of MEU AMOR JÁ ME CHAMOU seem to pass very quickly. Sparrow tells us that: "João can't read or write and he lives in a fishing village founded as a quilombo, a refuge of runaway slaves. But he is one of Brazil's most important musicians, the Charlie Patton of Brazil, if you will." [7] It's the music of former Bahian slaves who never made it as far as Rio, and the music and dance would once have played a part in Candomblé ceremonies.

Dona Onete is a one-woman endangered species: there's no copies been made. She was born in the Amazon delta, in the musically fertile north-east of the country. She remembers from her childhood that she'd often go to events where people danced the sensual dances of the region: the carimbó, siriá and banguê. By the age of 15, bars were booking her to sing regional songs: "They used to give me beer as payment, but I didn't even drink it. I was just singing for my own enjoyment." [8] The idea of a singing career, though, didn't seem like a serious option. She got married, continued her academic work and became a professor of history and Amazonian studies in her hometown. This opened up many doors for her: "I researched a lot into black and indigenous culture. I discovered rhythms, dances and customs of our people." [9] She became an ardent champion of traditional music and culture, and formed several music and dance groups.

After retirement Dona began singing again for her own enjoyment. But she wasn't a teenager any more: she'd grown as a woman and as an artist. People loved her larger-than-life character. And she had the benefit of those years of research, and years in which she'd been composing music herself, even creating her own hybrid genre, carimbó chamegado. So it came to pass that at the age of 73 she recorded her first album, Feitiço Caboclo. The album fizzles with spirit: it's true to her roots as you'd expect, capturing the north-eastern dance rhythms, with some salsa and samba and maybe a few other genres thrown in the mix. The album was an international hit and Dona's hardly stopped touring since.

My final song from Brazil is **NO MEIO DO PITIU**, from Dona's second album Banzeiro. Pitiu is a slang word for the smells coming out of Belem's fish market, a place where herons stalk the dockside while vultures fly overhead. The song is a light-hearted, upbeat carimbo. In the video the stockily built 77-year-old dances among the herons and the fish stalls, bedecked in floral headgear, coloured beads, red shoes and a carefree smile.

NOTES

1. http://www.socialstereotype.com/_/Features/Entries/2006/2/9_AFROREGGAE.html, retrieved June, 2015
2. http://blackwomenofbrazil.co/2012/12/02/elza-soares-brazils-tina-turner-and-celia-cruz-the-bbcs-singer-of-the-millenium
3. http://revistapesquisa.fapesp.br/en/2012/02/27/a-pol%C3%ADtica-que-acaba-em-samba
4. http://blogdotarso.com/2013/12/30/beth-carvalho-socialismo-pode-salvar-a-humanidade-a-midia-censura-no-brasil-e-cia-quer-acabar-com-o-samba
5. http://www.revistaemdia.com.br/net/index.php/beth-carvalho-o-samba-faz-bem-ele-salva-ele-cura
6. Chris McGowan and Ricardo Pessanha – The Brazilian Sound: Samba, Bossa Nova, and the Popular Music of Brazil (Temple University Press, 2009), p52.
7. http://www.salvadorcentral.com/samba_chula_de_sao_braz.htm
8. http://womad.co.uk/lineup/dona-onete
9. http://marajonamidia.blogspot.co.uk/2012/03/o-carimbo-chamegado-de-dona-onete.html

CHILE

Never had such a thing happened before. In October 2017, La Moneda, the presidential palace, was to stage a concert the like of which Chile had never seen, with the balconies of the palace being used for the first time as a stage. And what was it that was of such great national importance that nowhere else but the president of Chile's official residence would do? The answer is that they were commemorating the centenary of a folk singer and one-time Communist Party member. Every Chilean will know who I mean: her name was Violeta Parra.

The 1960s is often remembered as the heyday of protest song in the United States. But during the same period in Chile a musical movement was taking shape that in its own way was even more radical. And, as events were to prove, it posed a more direct challenge to the established order.

The two most inspirational figures of the nueva canción Chilena both came from humble backgrounds. Violeta Parra (whose life was recently dramatised in the film Violeta Went to Heaven) was born on 4th October, 1917, in a small town in southern Chile to a father who was a music teacher and a seamstress mother. Victor Jara (1932–73) grew up in a peasant family and from the age of six or seven he would accompany his father to work in the fields.

GRACIAS A LA VIDA   Violeta Parra

PLEGARIA A UN LABRADOR   Victor Jara

MALGENIOSA   Chico Trujillo

MAS VAN PASANDO LOS ANOS   Evelyn Cornejo

By the early 1950s, Violeta was into her second marriage and was travelling into the central valleys armed with guitar, notebooks and a recorder, where she recorded and memorised great numbers of folk songs and poems. All the time her ideas were developing and deepening. She felt a bond with the poor and the dispossessed. Folk music mattered because it gave a voice to the voiceless. She dressed very simply, sang in an unadorned style and shunned commercialism.

Violeta enjoyed writing poetry, so why not write songs too? Her songs drew on folklore but the lyrics burned with the passion of one who was politically engaged. In Hace Falta un Guerrillero, the singer expresses her desire for a son who's a guerrilla fighter like Chilean hero Manuel Rodríguez. In 1957, when she met the young Victor Jara who'd also been studying rural folk songs, she persuaded him to think of himself more seriously as a writer and as a performer. Around this time Victor joined the folk group Cuncumén. The group were also involved in theatre, and over the next few years Victor built up something of a reputation as a theatre director.

Then one day these small beginnings gave rise to a movement. The day it really began was the day in 1965 when Violeta's children, Isabel and Angel Parra, opened the Peña de los Parra at the address Carmen 340 in central Santiago. It was a hub, a place where folk musicians and like-minded people could hang out and perform or listen to music. It brought together the Parras, Rolando Alarcón, Patricio Manns and Victor Jara and many others. Rolando Alarcón had been a founding member of Cuncumén, but by 1965 both he and Victor Jara had left the band to focus on their own development as political singer-songwriters. Patricio Manns is another whose songs were to become part of the movement. Joan Jara remembers the Parras with special affection: "Angel was a masterly guitarist. When he sang he tied himself into knots around his guitar, and his deep, rather harsh voice seemed to struggle against his own strength. He seemed too small and frail for such explosions of emotion. But when brother and sister sang together in duet, they were all vitality, their voices mingling in perfect coordination, complementing each other exuberantly." [1]

GRACIAS A LA VIDA is far and away Violeta's most celebrated song, covered on numerous occasions. The song offers thanks to life, which has awakened her senses and given her gifts such as love and language and song. And yet for all its beauty, it's a tragic song. In the chapter on Bolivia I described Violeta's love affair with Gilbert Favre: for her this had been all-consuming, and now he'd left her; he was in Bolivia. She was desolate. Her final album, Las Últimas Composiciones, bears many signs of her depression, and Gracias a la Vida is usually interpreted as the song of a woman who knew she was going to die. Within months she'd put a gun to her head and killed herself.

Meanwhile, the movement was still growing. The peña at Carmen 340 became fuller and fuller as artists and singers flocked there. Walls were knocked down to enlarge the original space while the remaining walls were covered with art and graffiti. By now other peñas had sprung up in towns and universities all across Chile. Victor Jara found himself travelling around to perform at as many of these as he could. In Valparaiso he met three men who'd just formed a group they called Quilapayún. The band's name, meaning 'three beards' in the Mapuche language, signalled their musical and political intent. They performed using Andean instruments, they identified with indigenous people, and in Chilean folk circles at the time beards were fairly much a badge of radicalism. There were various changes and additions to the line-up in future years, but Joan Jara remembers that: "while the numbers multiplied, generally the three beards remained constant, although they moved from chin to chin." [2] Victor agreed to become the group's musical director.

Inti-Illimani was formed in 1967 by a group of engineering students in Santiago. Musically they shared an interest in Andean instruments and a desire to explore Latin American indigenous music, but they too were swept away in the febrile political atmosphere of the time, and became famous in Chile for their song Venceremos, consciously written as a political anthem.

In July 1969, the first Festival de la Nueva Canción was held in Santiago. The organisers were anxious that this should not be seen as a leftist event, and controversially decided not to invite the band Quilapayún because they were too political. Undeterred, Victor Jara composed for the event one of his greatest political songs PLEGARIA A UN LABRADOR (Worker's Prayer), in which he calls to peasants to join hands with their brothers in the fight for a just society. To the dismay of the organisers, he invited Quilapayún as his backing group for the event (held in the Estadio Chile where Victor would later meet his death). The song received a rapturous reception and was awarded joint first prize by the festival jury.

The movement now had its own name – nueva canción. Internationally it was championed by the likes of Atahualpa Yupanqui and Mercedes Sosa in Argentina and Daniel Viglietti in Uruguay. But it was Chileans above all who took the troubadour singers to their hearts. Perhaps they felt a connection to the traditional culture that Violeta Parra and Victor Jara had sought to revive. Or perhaps the folk singers had given people a new sense of hope and of their own national identity, and touched a nerve in their descriptions of the rural poor. In 1970, as the presidential election loomed, Chileans were enervated politically like never before. Every barrio (neighbourhood), every factory was alive with politics. Though numerically folk singers were few in number their role was very important, their songs were part of the message at pro-Allende political rallies. The campaign also witnessed a flowering of street art. Wall painting teams sprang up everywhere. They weren't just painting slogans: artists who supported Allende created striking murals with colourful images of people and nature.

Victor Jara and the singers he worked with didn't see themselves as protest singers: they saw themselves as revolutionaries and made no secret of it. And for a time following the election of Salvador Allende as president, social revolution seemed possible. Despite howls of rage from the opposition, Allende was able to introduce a number of policies aimed at redistributing wealth and educating the poor. Joan Jara says, "we felt optimistic and confident that anything could be achieved." [3] Allende embraced this optimism. Mitchell DeMazza describes how he co-opted the new cultural movement: "In response to the propaganda flooding the Chilean media, artists of La Nueva Canción Chilean movement were asked to be representatives of Allende's Chile as Cultural Ambassadors of their country. These artists included Quilapayún and Isabel Parra who campaigned in an extensive tour in Europe; Inti-Illimani who toured in Ecuador and debunked the rumors that Chileans had fled there after the election of Allende; and Victor Jara who travelled around Latin America." [4]

And then on 11th September, 1973, Pinochet made his move. The deaths of Allende and Victor Jara reverberated through Chile. As the horror stories multiplied, many prominent supporters of Allende, who were able to do so, went into exile. The groups Inti-

Illimani and Quilapayún had been touring abroad at the time of the coup, and they made new homes in Rome and Paris. Victor's wife, Joan, returned to her native UK. Angel Parra (who was imprisoned by the regime), Isabel Parra and Patricio Manns each had to fight their own battles to leave the country, all eventually ending up in Paris.

The exiled musicians for the most part stayed true to nueva canción Chilena, continuing to make acoustic folk music that often came with a message. In the decades since 1973, though, the Chilean musical landscape has transformed. It's very cosmopolitan: hip hop, electronic music, global beats and Latin rhythms. For me, one of the more interesting trends has been the growth of Chilean cumbia. This Colombian music has been adopted and popularised in Chile and given a genuinely Chilean flavour. But it's morphing all the time as young bands keep pushing the boundaries, fusing the traditional rhythm with rock, hip hop or electronic music, and creating new sub-genres. Chico Trujillo are one of the standard bearers of Chilean cumbia, boldly claiming on their website to be "the soundtrack to every party from Arica to Punta Arenas". It's hard to argue: MALGENIOSA is good-time party music, an intoxicating cocktail of fast-paced cumbia beats, horns, and an unpretentious sense of fun.

Chilean folk music has also transformed. With few exceptions Chilean folk singers today write their own songs and tap into other musical genres, other cultures. To Pascuala Ilabaca this makes perfect sense: musical experimentation, she says, is necessary "because our Chilean identity is genetically nurtured in many cultures and we carry this in our genes". [5] The sense that Violeta had, of belonging to an indigenous culture rooted in the soil, seems to have been lost.

Violeta would have been pleased, though, to see so many female songwriters making their mark today. And a great many of these folky songstresses say that Violeta's work was an inspiration to them. Pascuala Ilabaca has recorded an album of Violeta Parra songs. Magdalena Matthey and Elizabeth Morris, with the actress Francisca Gavilán, put together a stage show of Violeta Parra songs, El Cantar de Violeta, and this wasn't just a one-off: they were still giving performances six years later. Evelyn Cornejo is another long-time admirer who's often paid tribute to Violeta in concerts and songs. What was it about Violeta's legacy that made them all connect so strongly? It's no accident that the artists I've just mentioned are all very socially conscious. It's about more than this, though. Pascuala Ilabaca again: "Her figure is still like that of a mother, a presence to whom we can go back to and feel safe and who can inspire our music. She was a really strong and complex character and I think of her as a patron saint." [6]

Born in 1981, in the small village of Caliboro, Evelyn Cornejo was exposed to folklore songs from an early age, and the influence runs deep in her songwriting. Her debut album, simply entitled Evelyn Cornejo, brought a remarkable new voice to Chilean music, a strong voice denouncing capitalism, injustice and environmental destruction. In powerful protest songs such as La Huelga (The Strike) and Alerta, with its incitement to 'resist', she spoke up for the marginalised, the dispossessed and workers in struggle. She named her band Chusma Inconsciente – unconscious rabble – and this became the title of her second album, which came out in 2017. La Golondrina is dedicated to the Mapuche people, whom she sees not simply as victims of injustice but as a people with a great deal to teach us about respect for life and for the planet. **MAS VAN PASANDO LOS AÑOS** is written by Violeta Parra – but she only wrote the words, which she recited like a poem. The musical arrangement is entirely Evelyn's, and it adds hugely to the song without detracting from its meaning. What a song it is, though: she's tortured by what she sees in the world, it burns her up inside, but at the same time she's compelled to sing about it.

Violeta's two musician children, Isabel and Angel, have devoted a great part of their lives to honouring her legacy. In

1991, they set up the Violeta Parra Foundation to coordinate these efforts. The Foundation's proudest achievement was the architect-designed Violeta Parra Museum in Santiago, which was opened by President Michelle Bachelet on 4th October, 2015. On display here are many artworks by Violeta never before exhibited. Angel Parra died in March 2017 in Paris, his adopted home. His discography lists 38 studio albums, nine live albums and a variety of other projects and collaborations. But, according to the French newspaper Libération, what meant most to him was the work that he'd done with the Foundation. In their obituary they quoted him saying that: "with the book and the film, the museum, the publication of the full works of my mother in thirteen CDs, I will judge my mission completed." [7]

That, though, was from 2012, before the centenary celebrations. The year 2017 was to see countless events and concerts throughout Chile celebrating the life and songs of Violeta Parra. The artists performing at La Moneda were to include Violeta's only surviving child Isabel, Isabel's daughter, Tita Parra, rapper Ana Tijoux, and Evelyn Cornejo. Owing to stormy weather the concert did not go ahead on 4th October as planned, but was rescheduled for 13th October.

Victor Jara's widow, the English-born Joan Jara, had also, since 1973, been pursuing a long quest not just to preserve Victor's legacy but to obtain justice. The Victor Jara Foundation was formed in 1993. In 2003, the Estadio Chile – the national stadium where Victor was murdered – was renamed the Estadio Víctor Jara. On 28th December 2012 a Chilean judge, Judge Miguel Vásquez, charged eight retired army officers with Victor's murder. Four of the eight had reportedly been trained at the School of the Americas in Panama. Hugo Sánchez, a lieutenant colonel, was second in command at the stadium at the time, and Pedro Barrientos is believed to have fired the fatal shot. After the USA failed to extradite any of the men, a civil suit was issued on Joan's behalf against Barrientos in a Florida court. On 27th June 2016 the American court found Barrientos guilty of the torture and extrajudicial killing of Victor Jara. The court ordered Barrientos to pay $28 million in damages to the Jara family.

I leave the final word to Victor's first band, Cuncumén, who are also still active:

"Sabemos que nada ha sido gratis a través de la historia de la humanidad, y en esta oportunidad, gracias a la existencia de hombres y mujeres con conciencia en el territorio nacional e internacional, hemos ganado una batalla para obtener el castigo a los culpables. Queremos toda la verdad.

No descansaremos en nuestro intento por encontrar la justicia, que es lo que se merece quien fuera integrante y director de nuestro conjunto, y uno de los pilares del canto de raíz chileno y latinoamericano." [8]

NOTES

1. Joan Jara – Victor: An Unfinished Song (1998 edition), p82.
2. Ibid., p104.
3. Ibid., p152.
4. http://www.hormantruth.org/ht/ncsamd
5. http://www.lahoramujeres.cl/sin-categoria/entrevista-pascuala-ilabaca
6. http://www.rhythmpassport.com/articles-and-reviews/interview/interview-pascuala-ilabaca-fauna-november-2014
7. http://next.liberation.fr/musique/2017/03/15/angel-parra-une-voix-du-chili-s-eteint_1555868
8. http://www.cuncumen.scd.cl

COLOMBIA

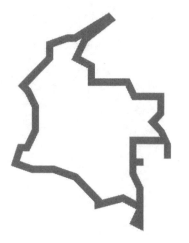

I have an interest to declare: my Colombian music collection dwarfs that of any other South American country. And I'm not sated yet – I want more. Colombian cumbia music is roots music for the rock generation (Joe Strummer was a fan), and in a better-ordered world no self-respecting music lover would be without a cumbia CD in their collection.

If you have yet to get started, you can do no better than to check out one of these compilation albums, all on Soundway Records:

- *Colombia! the Golden Age of Discos Fuentes – The Powerhouse of Colombian Music 1960–76 (2007)*
- *Palenque Palenque: Champeta Criolla & Afro Roots in Colombia 1975–91 (2009)*
- *The Original Sound of Cumbia: The History Of Colombian Cumbia & Porro as Told by the Phonograph 1948–79 (2011)*
- *Cartagena! Curro Fuentes & The Big Band Cumbia and Descarga Sound of Colombia 1962–72 (2011)*

A far cry from the kind of compilations that recycle hits to generate income, these are all genuine labours of love. The Original Sound

PRENDE LA VELA	Lucho Bermúdez
CANTO NEGRO	Andrés Landero Y Su Conjunto
LA CANAGUATERA	Isaac Carrillo
RECORDANDO AL GRANDE	Sixto Silgado "Paito" & Los Gaiteros de Punta Brava
ESTO ES CANDELA	Sexteto Tabala de Palenque
FIESTA VIEJA	Totó La Momposina

of Cumbia was compiled by Quantic (aka English musician and producer Will Holland). A modern-day musical troubadour, he arrived in Colombia with little more than a "12-channel portable mixing console, four boxes of records, and some clothes". [1] He planned to stay six months: six years later, he was still there.

> "'There's got to be a woman involved, right?'
> 'Yeah! [Laughs] When is there not? But I've spent a lot of time on this. I've driven round Colombia a lot by car, on my own and with friends, looking for music, and checking things out. It's not like I just met a record collector in Bogota whilst on a trip there, and compiled it from his knowledge. It has all been avidly researched. I've spent more time and money probably than I should've. It is a big passion of mine.'" [2]

There are 55 tracks (count them) on the album. These are recordings made often on a shoestring, without the kind of support that big labels such as Discos Fuentes were able to give: recordings that needed preserving but recordings that also deserved to be remastered. It's a fantastic collection, raw, immediate and very danceable. And though cumbia is played in many countries nobody, says Quantic, can dance the cumbia like the Colombians.

> "In Colombia, it's still a respected folk dance. If you put it on, people will immediately pretend to hold a candle… For Colombians, it's within the DNA. They could be into anything in music – heavy metal or whatever – but if you put on a cumbia, they'll go absolutely crazy… Even people who I didn't think could dance, and I've never seen dancing, they'll be at a wedding, and there'll be a cumbia playing suddenly, and they have to dance." [3]

This brings me neatly to my first track, **PRENDE LA VELA** (light the candle). The significance of the candle is that in years gone Colombians would dance the cumbia after dark under candlelight, so 'prende la vela' is also like a call to dance. It's a very famous song, often performed today, but when Lucho Bermudez first recorded it in 1939 some didn't like it at all. It sounded too black with its tropical percussion and exuberant horns, and, what was worse, with the music came a more sexualised style of dancing.

Colombia is a country of great geographical contrasts, and this is reflected in its people. The peoples of the Pacific and Caribbean coasts are largely of African origin and are more likely to be economically deprived than the population of inland cities like Bogotá and Medellín. Nor are the Pacific and Caribbean coasts the same: their histories are different, and so also is their culture and their music. Lucho Bermudez grew up in El Carmen de Bolivar, less than 50 miles from the Caribbean port of Cartagena, once a centre of the slave trade. At the age of 23 he moved to live in Cartagena, which along with the nearby city of Barranquilla (host to one of the great Caribbean carnivals) was then, as now, a melting pot where musical genres are forever shifting and new musical styles emerging. Lucho, we're told, studied the folklore and learned to play all the cumbia, porro and vallenato rhythms. Along the way, he combined this with a jazzy, big band sound, which wasn't so unusual in Colombia, but it was unusual in the context of costeño music. This was to be the catalyst that would transform the rustic costeño styles into a national music that could overcome Colombia's geographical and ethnic divides.

After a decade in Cartagena, Lucho moved to Bogotá.

"He began to recruit a new orchestra that was mainly made up of whiter-skinned people, who are all trained musicians, whose background was not in Caribbean coastal music, but was in other kinds of music associated with the interior of the country. And then, Lucho Bermudez met and very soon later married the woman called Matilde Diaz, who was a white woman from the interior of the country, who became the main singer in his orchestra." [4]

He wanted to be the best he could, and this was his main motivation. And Matilde was a great singer and a strong character (the first woman from the country, it's claimed, to sing in a professional orchestra). The marriage lasted 18 years and they were a highly productive working partnership. During this time he travelled to Mexico and to Cuba, where he performed with many of the leading Latin musicians of the day. Lucho was always creating, experimenting, adding new rhythms to his repertoire. In this, too, he was ahead of his time. As costeño music continues to change and diversify in the 21st century, the music of Lucho Bermudez feels as relevant as ever.

Close by El Carmen de Bolivar is another small town called San Jacinto, known today as a centre of handicrafts, its flagship product the hammock. Back in the 1940s, when Andrés Landero was trying on his first sombrero there, and getting his first kiss, hammock making was just one way for families to try and scrape a living – the weavers were likely to be women, wives and mothers of campesinos (peasant farmers). The son of a gaitero (flautist), Andrés took to music from an early age, and his first love was to be the instrument with which he would later become synonymous, the accordion. Tales still circulate of how, when still very young, he did his first live performance in front of an audience of slaughtermen.

Throughout his career Andrés stood up for the campesinos, the rural poor, and the region that he knew and loved. In his music as in his lyrics he took pride in championing traditional costeño rhythms. Wherever he went he wore the sombrero vueltiao, a symbol of his rural origins, a hat made from the tall grasses called caña flecha. Again and again he drew attention to what he claimed were the African origins of cumbia: whether or not people in Bogotá wanted to listen to overtly black music didn't bother him; it was a matter of pride. As a dance track, **CANTO NEGRO** can hardly be improved, its combination of accordion melodies and hypnotic beat are proof that great music doesn't need to be ornate or complex. But Canto Negro is also a statement song. The singer is telling us that cumbia is a black music, making passing references to historical antecedents.

Andrés was a gaitero who played the accordion in a rustic style that incorporated elements of gaita playing. He fell out with the accordion community because he refused to play in the more homogenised vallenato style that was coming into vogue. Also he played many cumbias, which was part of the fabric of San Jacinto culture, while on the Pacific coast accordionists would normally play vallenatos. To the casual ear these variations may not sound so great, but the consequence of it all was that Andrés found himself shut out from the big competition prizes, never receiving the fame and recognition in his own country that his talent deserved.

Ironically, for someone whose music was so rooted in his home region, Andrés Landero's greatest successes were achieved outside his home country. In Mexico he was crowned Rey de la Cumbia and for decades afterwards Mexicans regarded him as this archetypal cumbia musician. He was also idolised in Argentina. They loved his authentic style, his songs, which brought to life the simple rugged lifestyle of the campesinos, his durability (he wrote over 400 songs) and his refusal to bow to commercial pressures.

Andrés died in 2000, but his story has a neat postscript. Los Gaiteros de San Jacinto had been part of the San Jacinto musical community even longer than he had: the group was formed back in 1940. In 2006, a newly recorded album of their music was released in America on the Folkways label. It was just traditional peasant music with gaitas, maracas and drums, but to everyone's surprise it walked away with a Latin Grammy for best folk album.

A couple of years later, Folkways were back in Colombia again, this time to record ¡Ayombe! The Heart of Colombia's Música Vallenata. Colombian music had never been more popular in the USA: thousands of Colombian immigrants were arriving every year to escape the seemingly endless violence, and in 2006 the Colombian singer Shakira topped the Billboard chart with Hips Don't Lie. Vallenato music embodied the character and spirit of the Colombian people. Since 1968 the Vallenato Legend Festival has been the focal point for lovers of vallenato music, turning the city of Valledupar into a Latin Nashville. Thanks in no small part to the festival, vallenato has a large and growing base of loyal fans, while still retaining its integrity.

The traditional conjunto has three instruments, drawn from three cultures: the European accordion, the guacharaca (scraper) from the indigenous peoples, and the caja (hand-played African drum). In modern times a fourth instrument, the electric bass, has been added. The album has 25 musicians including major figures from the past and present, so it's a good introduction to vallenato. And LA CANAGUATERA is a lovely track. The singer, Isaac 'Tijito' Carrillo, originally wrote the song some 50 years earlier. He'd packed in his job as a bus driver and was in Valledupar trying to make it as a musician when, one day, passing through the Cañaguate district his eyes were caught by a woman on the terrace of her house. He talked himself in, they got chatting and in no time they were seeing each other. He wanted to marry her but she put him off, and after less than a year she left without warning to go and live in Venezuela.

So, La Cañaguatera, for all its jaunty rhythm, is really an expression of pain, a lament for lost love. He was to see her just once more, about five years later. She thanked him for the song, though her name doesn't actually appear in it, and so they parted. Meeting women would never be a problem for Carrillo – though short in stature (hence his nickname, Tijito), he made up for it in other ways. He's had 10 children with six different women, but the memory of La Cañaguatera still has a place in his heart, and to this day the song that he wrote in her memory is the one that all his audiences want to hear.

Another Colombian gaita group was beginning to build an international profile. Paito and Los Gaiteros de Punta Brava used similar instrumentation to Los Gaiteros de San Jacinto – gaitas accompanied by alegre, llamador, tambora drums and maracas – but their sound had an added swagger to it. The ageing figure of Sixto Silgado Paíto in full flow is a sight to see: the gaita's not like any flute that I'm used to seeing; it's a huge, long instrument made from natural materials, and the wind sails out from deep in Paito's lungs as he tries to imitate the accordion sound. Add to this his age-encrusted vocals and RECORDANDO AL GRANDE has a real primal energy to it that makes you wonder why cumbia musicians ever felt the need to use keyboards, but more on that later.

Gaita, by the way, is the Spanish term, and it's a bit of a misnomer. The original word that is still used is kuisi, and every gaita group uses two types of kuisi, the female kuisi bunsi (gaita hembra) for the melody, and the male kuisi sigi (gaita macho), which keeps a constant rhythm.

Paito was born in 1939 in an Afro-Colombian village not

far from Cartagena and the Caribbean coast, and his father was a gaitero before him. A veteran of many gaita competitions, he's acclaimed as a tradition-bearer, a master of gaita negra, an Africanised style of gaita playing specific to the region. But as he's shown on his recordings he recognises that tradition is never static: he's open to different options, ways of enriching the music.

Sexteto Tabala, from San Basilio de Palenque, represent another strand of Afro-Colombian culture. In the early part of the 20th century plantation managers were shipping in Cuban workers to work in Colombia's sugar mills. The Cubans brought with them box drums that they called cajons and a new African-based musical style that they called son. Black Colombian workers were sufficiently impressed to go away and create their own version of Cuban son, which was the sexteto. Palenque's first sexteto, Sexteto Habanero, came together in 1930 when a group of men decided to make their own instruments. Palenque de San Basilio is a town with a remarkable history: it was established in 1603 by escaped slaves. Protected by the hills and swamps that surrounded them, they were never recaptured. Finally, in 1691 the Spanish issued a decree granting their freedom, making Palenque de San Basilio the first free African community in the Americas.

Rafael Cassianni, born in San Basilio de Palenque in 1934, spent a lot of time around the Sexteto when he was growing up: decades later it fell to him to lead the group and steer it through some difficult years. One day they were playing in Cartagena and when they came off stage someone asked: why do you call yourselves Sexteto Habanero when you're not from Havana? Rafael didn't have a good answer, so it was decided there and then that they would take on a new name, Sexteto Tabala.

ESTO ES CANDELA could easily be mistaken for an African song with its call-and-response vocals and percussive beat. Listen carefully, though, and you'll notice there's quite a lot going on – different types of drum, guacharacas, claves, maracas and very importantly the marimbula, a wooden box with metal keys on one side that acts as a bass. For me this is part of what makes the song funky and interesting despite its repeated refrain. For Palenquians, though, the song signifies more than this: carried within the music are the voices and the spritual beliefs of their ancestors, those who worked the plantations, and before them, those who came from Africa and who fought for their right to be free. Rafael wrote some of the group's songs, but this has the feel of an older track, one that their fathers and grandfathers might have sung before them.

As I write, Colombia is feeling its way to a formula that can bring about lasting peace after decades of savagery and fighting. The numbers are shocking: from 1985, to July 2013, 166,069 civilians were killed, alongside 27,023 kidnapping victims and over six million internally displaced by the violence. Those most affected have been the blacks, the indigenous peoples, the rural poor: these are the people crying out for a settlement. If the cycle of violence is broken, what changes can we expect for Colombia's music?

The answers are already out there. Colombia is open for business, its music scene is thriving and international producers are knocking on the door. In the 2010s, Madonna, Beyonce and the Rolling Stones have all performed in Colombia for the first time. There are still issues of course. With or without the violence, Colombia is a risky investment. Musical events are heavily taxed and many people are too poor to attend big shows and festivals. For Colombian artists, though, it's never been easier to get their music heard, whether through festivals at home, opportunities to tour overseas, or the use of social media and digital platforms to help build up a fan base and to put their music out in the global marketplace.

What we find is that younger generations of musicians are again and again trying to position themselves within a global market which in turn is influencing their musical choices in all manner of ways. So among the exciting names to emerge in the last few years are Orquesta La 33, who describe their genre as 'Urban Salsa', while La Mambanegra have invented their own term, "Break Salsa". Sidestepper are an example of an electro-cumbia band: cumbia is seldom heard except in combination with other genres. In the 21st century, nu cumbia has become a huge cult musical genre in many countries, and some of it I enjoy, but most of it is only very distantly related to the organic sound of classic Colombian cumbia. Finally, there are several important electronic artists who often incorporate elements of roots music in their beats and are in demand at world music festivals: Bomba Estéreo, Systema Solar and Palenke Soultribe.

Totó La Momposina has her own perspective on all of this:

"As for these youngsters, mixing traditional sounds with genres like pop, rock or hip hop; I'm not against it, but time will tell if their music will stand the test of time! If you really want to find out about the traditional music of Colombia… you'll have to look in the small villages, where people still remember their heritage, not in the big cities. There you will find the so-called 'cantadoras de alabaos' who sing at funerals and other ceremonies and whose songs reinforce a sense of solidarity, bring the community together, and maintain the traditions of the Afro-Colombian communities." [5]

I saw Totó days before her 75th birthday, singing at Womad 2015. As well as knocking the spots off most younger singers, she's also a very articulate champion of Colombian roots music, which she insists is very much alive: "While I respect the word 'folklore', to me it means something that's dead – in a museum. Traditional music, or the music from the old days, is still alive: many people are working with it and it's always evolving. The people of the pueblo don't know about 'folklore'. They say música antigua or música de antes (from before)." [6]

La Momposina means 'from Mompox'. Mompox is an island

in the mighty Magdalena river. Once it was a great trading post, a jewel in the colonial crown, but those days are long gone. In the 19th century the river began silting up, large boats were forced to seek other routes and Mompox was slowly turned into an island. If you want to get there today you have to take a long journey by road and river. Totó's sense of what it meant to be a Momposian began to form in the late '40s when her family were living in Bogota and had to endure a lot of racism. Luckily her mother was made of strong stuff and she organised a family band, using music as a way of showing the children the positive side of their Afro-Indian culture.

Over the years she listened, she studied and grew to know and love the rhythms of the Caribbean coast. Her career though was destined to follow an unconventional path. In 1982, the Colombian writer Gabriel García Márquez won the Nobel Prize for Literature and Totó was invited to come and sing at the ceremony in Oslo. This was a departure from the Nobel custom of having a piece of chamber music, but for Márquez, who was intimately acquainted with the Magdalena river, it made perfect sense. The next year, having fallen in love with French cinema, she decided to move to Paris. Now she was busking for passers-by who had no knowledge of Colombian music – "I sang in the street, in the Metro, in flea markets, in bars, in universities, outside the Pompidou…" [7] She stayed for four years, during which time she made her first Womad appearances, in 1984 and 1985.

When Real World released La Candela Viva, Totó was already in her 50s. The album made her an international star, but more importantly from her point of view it brought música antigua to thousands of people around the world. This – and all the albums that followed it – reflected all the ethnic and musical variety of her own heritage and the music of the Caribbean coast, and radiated with the warmth of her personality. FIESTA VIEJA, a song by the composer Pablo Flórez, is from La Bodega (2010). Totó is equally at home in different traditional genres, and she demonstrates that here, bringing in brass and strings for a richer orchestral sound, which is all flawlessly arranged. The song canters through its six and a half minutes, coming to an end far too soon.

Several times in her interviews Totó touches on her role as a cantadora, and I was curious: there didn't seem to be an exact translation. It turns out that the cantadora is many things: a traditional bearer, a giver of knowledge and of healing, a leader of festivities and an honoured representative of her community.

> "The village cantadora does everything from healing with herbs and giving marital advice to running celebrations and leading songs. 'Imagine the backyard of a thatched poor homestead. Chickens have been moved out of the way,' explains John Hollis, Totó's manager and son-in-law. 'There's lots of dust and it's really hot, and in the middle is a group of drummers. And around them are the cantadoras, leading the songs, and around them people stand clapping and singing the chorus.'" [8]

There's something very cool about this: Totó could have made a life for herself as a pampered diva. Instead, she is still a Momposian village cantadora, doing what she feels that she was brought on this earth to do.

NOTES

1. https://www.theguardian.com/music/2014/apr/24/quantic-all-music-is-authentic-hispanic-colombia
2. http://djmafondo.weebly.com/mafondos-music-blog/2cd-compilation-of-the-original-sound-of-cumbia-the-history-of-colombian-porro-as-told-by-the-phonograph-1948-1979
3. Ibid.
4. http://www.afropop.org/9794/interview-with-peter-wade
5. http://www.rebelbase.be/interviews/detail/toto-la-momposina---sfinks-072010

6. https://realworldrecords.com/news/article/2896/toto-la-momposina-tambolero-out-29-june

7. http://www.eltiempo.com/bocas/entrevista-con-toto-la-momposina-en-bocas/16683662

8. http://archive.rockpaperscissors.biz/index.cfm/fuseaction/current.press_release/project_id/443.cfm

ECUADOR

"Julio Jaramillo es mi más grande inspiración. Me hubiera encantado nacer cuando él aún se encontraba vivo. Desde que tenía 11 años de edad, yo me escapaba de la casa y corría al mercado a comprar sus discos. Realmente me encanta su música. Considero que en el mundo, aún no nace un artista como él… La versatilidad de la voz de JJ, fue su mejor arma. Interpretó exitosamente temas en ritmos tan variados como bolero, tropical, tango, vals, pasillo, joropo, balada e incluso rock and roll. Mi conclusión es, que a Julio Jaramillo lo podrán imitar, pero nadie lo podrá igualar."

Fernando Vargas [1]

It's as if young American singers were coming out and saying their favourite artist is Hank Williams. Fernando Vargas was born in 1990, just when Nelson Mandela was being released from prison, while the honey-voiced Julio Jaramillo had risen to fame in the 1950s with gentle songs of love and heartbreak. What could this long-dead singer have to say to young artists like Fernando Vargas who were starting their singing careers in the 21st century?

INTERROGACION	*Julio Jaramillo*
SARINA	*Papa Roncon*
MUSANKA	*Mishqui Chullumbu*

As highlighted in the above quote, Jaramillo's music covers a number of different genres, but the one on which he left the greatest imprint was pasillo. To many people to this day, pasillo is Ecuadorian music: it's the main and most essential element of what's referred to as musica nacional – music of the nation – which transcends the regional difference between costa and sierra, transcends age and social class.

Julio Jaramillo (1935–78) was born in Guayaquil: his parents had moved there to the city to find jobs and escape poverty. He had an older brother, Pepe, and a younger sister, who died when still an infant. His father was in his workshop making a cross for the girl's graveside when the heavy cross slipped and fell on him, and he died later in hospital from the injuries. The mother was left to raise the family by herself, but her wages were poor, and Julio was constantly ill: he suffered from bronchopneumonia and asthma, had early infantile paralysis, and contracted diphtheria, amoebic dysentery and even typhoid fever. When a few years later Pepe and Julio became interested in singing, the mother's reaction can easily be imagined: she implored them to get honest jobs that would feed their future families. Eventually Pepe went to university in Colombia, but Julio continued to mix with bohemian types.

What rescued him, what marked him out from all those other singers working odd jobs while hoping to get themselves noticed, was his voice. He didn't seek fame: Fresia Saavedra, who sang with him in 1954, remembers him at the time as "un chico muy tranquilo" (a quiet boy). [2] But in 1955 he recorded a song, Fatalidad, that was to change his life forever. The song, a romantic waltz, had been a hit the previous year for Olimpo Cardenas, but Julio's version somehow captured people's hearts. The record sold out within a week, and radio stations across the continent picked it up.

In the space of a few years Jaramillo put the music of Ecuador on the map in a way that it has seldom been before or since. Pepe was having some success in Colombia; for Julio new horizons were opening up as he came into contact with musicians and promoters from far and wide, and all this must have played on his mind. The international tours started: he went to Colombia and Peru. In 1958, at the height of his popularity, 16,000 people crammed into the Palacio de los Deportes in Montevideo to see him and the army was required to maintain order among the thousands stood outside who couldn't get in to see the show. At another concert in Uruguay people threw coins and bills onto the stage.

Jaramillo was no saint. In his short life he was married five times, had sex with many more women, and no one knows exactly how many children he sired (though all are agreed that it was well over 20). He wasn't the best of fathers, but neither was he an unfeeling monster. According to Pepe, "it's not true that he died in poverty. It's a fact that he didn't end up stinking rich, because he was very generous to his friends and to women." [3]

INTERROGACION is a beautiful but desperately sad song: while the guitar picks out the bolero rhythm the lyrics speak of burning jealousy. Was Jaramillo happy? There was a recklessness in his pursuit of women that came back to bite him from time to time, and he seems to have found it difficult to lay down roots. He lived in several Latin American countries, including Mexico a couple of times, and a lengthy spell in Venezuela. Wherever he went people took him to their hearts, and there were more than a few who went to their graves still believing him to be a great Mexican or Venezuelan singer. What were his feelings through all this about his home city? Were there associations and memories that he preferred to forget, or was he concerned that malicious rumours were circulating about him?

In 1976 he returned to Ecuador and to Guayaquil. Thousands lined the streets to greet him. But now his past was catching up with him: his voice had altered and his health was deteriorating, and though he tried to shrug off doctors' advice it became clear that he'd have to curtail his live performances. Finally, on 9th February, 1978, his death was announced on the radio.

> "No one could have foreseen what would happen then. People began to arrive from everywhere. On foot, by bus, by car. Alone or accompanied, families or groups of people from the city's districts. Some wept... The crowd filled the streets for several blocks around (the clinic) and completely disrupted traffic. The cops called for reinforcements, but to no avail. People kept coming, and here and there some lit candles. Spontaneously, many groups began to sing Fatalidad and Nuestro Juramento." [4]

And this was just the first day. The next day, authorisation was obtained to escort the coffin to the Palacio Municipal. A simple ceremony was held there. But so great were the crowds of people coming to see and touch the casket that there were fears for the safety of the great building. And so the decision was made to transport the coffin again, to the Coliseo Voltaire Paladines Polo, the city's sports stadium. The third day was a Saturday: the street processions were even more massive, while countless more people across the country followed events on the radio. TV star Lucho

Gálvez delivered a brief eulogy in which he asked in a cracking voice, "Why did we not see a tribute too when Julio Jaramillo was alive?"

There have been many tributes since. Argentina celebrates its national music with a National Tango Day, which takes place every year on 11th December, the birthday in 1890 of the singer Carlos Gardel. So Ecuador decided to follow suit with el Día del Pasillo Ecuatoriano – National Pasillo Day – which falls on 1st October, Julio's birthday. Like Gardel, Jaramillo is of course an emblem of a golden age in which great talent thrived, and anyone inclined to buy Jaramillo's music is also urged to check out some of his contemporaries, such as Carlota Jaramillo (no relation) and the duo Benítez-Valencia.

Pasillo is a hybrid music, an amalgam of the European waltz and Andean rhythms. Ecuadorian music reflects the varied ancestry of the country's people. There's a white minority with European roots; a black minority most concentrated in the north-west that calls itself Afro-Ecuadorian; and indigenous communities, some living in the high sierra, others in the Amazonian rainforest. Most Ecuadorians, though, are mestizos, with complex racial histories. Historically, many mestizos have aspired to become more white, as this was seen as a route to higher social and economic status. But attitudes are beginning to change as disadvantaged ethnic minorities have made themselves heard and asserted their rights and their identity. In 1996, changes were made to the country's constitution declaring Ecuador to be a pluricultural, multiethnic state. In 1998 it was further amended: Article 82 gave official recognition to the Indian and Black presence, and Articles 83 and 84 provided both groups with a set of rights relating to territorial and cultural issues. [5]

In the construction of Afro-Ecuadorian identity in particular, music played a large part. An African import, the marimba (from the xylophone family) became a symbol of Afro-Ecuadorian music. Here's American musicologist Jonathan Ritter:

"When I started working in Esmeraldas, in 1996, the symbolic stature of the marimba was still embryonic; today, its presence is ubiquitous: it is in murals painted on the streets and important buildings and monuments built by the administration of Estupiñán mayor since 2001. And, of course, it is the main instrument of festivals..." [6]

Traditional Ecuadorian music comes in various forms and is alive and well in many small communities. There's an issue with which I'm becoming familiar: because it's deemed to be non-commercial, it doesn't often get recorded, which limits its reach. This is why the recent project by the producer Ivis Flies and his partner Mariana Pizarro is so valuable. After spending several years travelling round Ecuador, researching musical culture and seeking out artists who lived and breathed roots music, they released not one but six CDs by six different artists.

De Taitas y de Mamas is named after the Quechua words for grandfathers and grandmothers. With the help of funding from the Ministry of Culture and Heritage, Flies and Pizarro were aiming to preserve the music of the elders. They chose musicians who had musical knowledge in their bones, and who could still turn in a powerful performance. And they chose well. The six CDs are consistently good, and each one of them brings to wider attention an artist who would otherwise be little known outside of their own community.

Las Tres Marias are three sisters from the Chota Valley. Since the 16th century, when the sugar plantations were first established, the Chota Valley has been synonymous with the presence of black people in Ecuador. In recent decades it's been associated with Afro-Ecuadorian bomba music, thanks in no small part to the commitment and passion of the Congo family, whose members have researched and promoted the music over several decades, participating in groups such as Los Hermanos Congo and Oro Negro. Las Tres Marias are essentially a vocal group with an unusual ability to reproduce the sounds of certain instruments using only their vocal chords.

Of the six artists, Papa Roncon, born in 1930 in a small fishing village in Esmeraldes, was perhaps the most established name. His deep, gravelly voice could have been made for singing, it carries such rich tones, and it compels you to listen. **SARINA** is a folk song whose meaning eludes me, and yet I can't listen enough to that voice and that melody. I have a small confession: this is a guitar song, but it's as a marimba player that Papa Roncon is known. He's devoted to the instrument, which he says helped black people free themselves from the bonds of slavery. He's been married for 60 years, and the marimba has been a part of his life even longer than that. He enjoys a good read, yet most of his knowledge doesn't come from books: "The rivers, the mountains, the voices of the ancients, the knowledge of elders, were his teachers. And that wisdom, those memories of the fields where he was born and raised, is what Papa Roncón prizes so much now, because young people mustn't forget." [7]

Papa Roncon came late to performing: one day a friend suggested to him that he form a group and earn some extra money, so he did, teaming up with his wife and some of his kids. Years ago he retired from his job so he could devote himself more fully to music. Renowned for his storytelling as well as his singing, he earns good money now when he performs; he's taught dozens of local kids how to play and to construct marimbas; and as an ambassador of Afro-Ecuadorian culture he's received several awards. He seems very grounded, though: he lives simply, and nothing gives him more happiness than seeing the marimba's revival and his own children taking up his legacy.

Also among the six: Don Naza, from the town of San Lorenzo on the northern coast, weak in body now but still on the evidence of the CD able to make exciting marimba-driven roots music into his 90s. Mariano Palacios sings amorfino, a poetic song style from the Pacific coast. And from his Andean home, multi-instrumentalist Julian Tucumbi pursues his dream of raising consciousness of Quechua tradition through music and performance. Indigenous music, he says, can't be written down as a series of notes. Each new generation must interpret the music in its own way, and it's a creative process: it has to come from within. This is why it's important for musicians to craft with their own hands their own instruments. "Instruments are made of materials that come from plants that grow in the paramo. The horn, for example, comes from the huaramo plant; the flute and the pingullo from sticks of tunda; the huancara, bombo and caja drums from the maguey (agave) plant." [8]

Just as the music of the Andean Quechua is bound up with their ways of living among the paramo ecosystem that covers this mountainous region, so also the indigenous tribes that inhabit the Amazonian rainforest in the south of the country have a vital relationship with the land that sustains them – a relationship that is at risk because in many places multinational oil companies covet the land that they call home.

Mishqui Chullumbu's music is the yumba: the ancestral music and dance of the Quechua who live near the Napo river, traditionally performed with pingullo (flute) and drums. MUSANKA is a superb example of the yumba rhythm: the full band give the music an added energy and drive, and the Flies/Pizarro production can't be faulted. Elsewhere on the album sounds of the rainforest have been sampled and worked into the music.

Mishqui formed his group, Yumbos Chaguamangos, in the late 1960s and ever since then has been a great ambassador for Quechua music and culture. He writes songs about village life, the care of nature, and rituals; he writes books about indigenous culture; he illustrates children's books. He's performed in several countries, but although he comes from the poorest of communities it's never been about the money. His one desire is to do more: "I am encouraging a group of families in the community to build an ancestral village and show people how our elders lived thousands of years ago." [9] Thanks to De Taitas y de Mamas, this vision is now close to becoming a reality. Which will no doubt delight Flies and Pizarro, who had set out with the aim of supporting traditional musicians and their communities. De Taitas y de Mamas was a non-profit initiative, with 30% of the royalties from the CDs going to the musicians who are also guaranteed future access to state services including health care.

NOTES

1. http://www.ppelverdadero.com.ec/component/zoo/item/fernando-vargas-julio-jaramillo-es-mi-inspiracion.html, retrieved January, 2016
2. https://www.eluniverso.com/2010/02/09/1/1379/julio-jaramillo-conoci.html
3. http://paiscanela.org/indexrpt.php?accion=entrevistas&id=1475, retrieved January, 2016
4. http://ecuadormusica.homestead.com/files/juliojaramillo/JulioJaramillo.htm
5. Harry Goulbourne – Race and Ethnicity: Critical Concepts in Sociology. Volume III, Racism: Exclusion and Privilege (Routledge, 2001), p347.
6. Jonathan Ritter – Hibridez, Raza y la Marimba Esmeraldeña: Repensando las Fusiones Musicales en el Pacífico Negro Ecuatoriano (2010).
7. http://www.eluniverso.com/2004/08/29/0001/1065/060C96B67865467AA3533D4221DA2527.html
8. https://ethnomusicologie.revues.org/1566
9. http://www.revistamundodiners.com/?p=4550

GUYANA

The UK parliament abolished the slave trade in 1807; however, not until the Slavery Abolition Act 1833 was slavery itself abolished in the British Empire. In the meantime, Britain had acquired a new colony – British Guiana. The colonial economy was dependent on sugar cane, and the sugar cane plantations were dependent on African slave labour. After abolition the plantation owners had a problem. Former slaves were quitting in large numbers. They called on the British for help, and the British came up with a remarkable solution: one which would involve transporting men across the full breadth of the British Empire.

Between 1838 and 1917, 238,909 people survived the months-long sea voyage from British India to British Guiana. These were 'indentured labourers' – workers who'd signed a contract binding them to their employer for a fixed number of years. Critics of the indenture system operated by the British have compared it to slavery. [1] Labourers were paid 25 cents a day, from which rations were deducted, and were completely without protection against employers who exploited them, abused them and made their lives a misery.

BASA BONGO   *Yoruba Singers*
MORWA BOLEE   *Joyce Harris*

Most, however, stayed in South America when their contract ended, rather than risk their lives a second time by taking a ship back to India. The result of all this is a country with a diverse ethnic mix and a plurality of religious faiths. A majority of the population are of either Indian or African origin, some consider themselves multiracial, and there's about 10% who are indigenous.

If you live outside Guyana, the two Guyanese musicians you're most likely to have heard are Eddy Grant and Mad Professor. Both moved to London during childhood and began their musical careers there. Eddy Grant found success through pop, while Mad Professor is a dub artist in the tradition of Jamaican MCs. Guyana itself has struggled to establish its own musical traditions reflecting the country's unique history and racial make-up. In the view of Eze Rockcliffe, founder member of the Yoruba Singers, the blame for this lies in lack of support for the music industry post-independence:

> *"In the '60s, Guyana was on par with Trinidad and Jamaica when it comes to music and musicians used to come here for us to give them leadership... Several Calypsonians such as the Mighty Panther used to go to Calypso tents in TT*

and perform and that is no more. Johnny Braff used to fill theatres in Barbados and right through the Caribbean, Ivor Lynch and others did the same and that is no more... I think we have a problem when it comes to marketing and investing in our people and the industry has failed us." [2]

In the years leading up to independence in 1966, the Guyanese music industry had never looked healthier. Georgetown's studios were 'vibrant' and musicians would come over from Trinidad to record there. [3] Steel bands were springing up everywhere. Big band music was in its heyday, with fabulous bands like Al Seales and His Washboard Orchestra and Tom Charles and the Syncopators.

Guyana's early years were a time of optimism, of nationalism and of returning to one's roots. The various ethnic groups began looking at what they could do to promote their own music and culture. New organisations were set up, music festivals founded. Mashramani, held for the first time in 1970, became Guyana's annual carnival. In the midst of all this a few politically minded musicians found a place that let them play their kind of music: a meeting hall run by a new African cultural organisation called ASCRIA. It wasn't very long before they were travelling round Guyana, performing everywhere. After being jokingly compared to the travelling Yoruba tribes of Africa, they decided that the name fitted, so they became the Yoruba Singers.

"We started off as a folk group; a culturally oriented group from an African standpoint," says Eze Rockcliffe. "Our writings of those days were based on struggle and redemption." [4] The description hardly does them justice. **BASA BONGO** is proof that even back in their younger days the band knew how to scorch the dancefloor. It's a light-hearted number with no serious intent but the most infectious rhythm anywhere west of the Congo. There's a lot happening in it – little shifts and variations on the theme every time that a different instrument is introduced. When it was first released in 1975 as the B-side of Black Pepper, the single broke Guyanese sales records.

Eze Rockcliffe is the one constant in the band's 45-year history. When members began to leave and look for other projects he was always the one to keep faith. From the 1980s we find him going out and recruiting the best musicians he could find. Today, Eze remembers the many musicians and singers who played a part in the band's success just as fondly as all the concerts that they played around the world. "The goal of our music," he once claimed, "is to spread our Guyanese sound… so that Guyana could get the recognition it deserves." [5]

More accurately, what people were buying into wasn't so much Guyana but rather the ever-evolving package that was the Yoruba Singers. Unlike Trinidad & Tobago, famous around the world for the carnival music that it's pioneered over many decades, Guyanese music still lacked a strong brand identity or recognition factor. According to one leading critic,

> "Guyana was never able to produce the necessary volume of native music to drive a popular festival as large and vibrant as Mashramani in the way Trinidadian music drives carnival. There has always been a dependence on imported numbers from Trinidad, Jamaica and Barbados. While a Road March is declared each year in Mashramani, the road march tradition is not deep and the winning song usually cannot compete with many of the imported ones. Few Guyanese songs can actually claim to have been the true popular road march the way Mahendra Ramkellawan's Dem A Watch Me was in 2010." [6]

The one original music form to emerge in Guyana post-independence is chutney music. Chutney sprang up in the 1960s and '70s when Trinidadian and Guyanese artists of Indian origin returned to their ethnic roots. It used folk acoustic instruments:

dholak, harmonium and dhantal; it was sung in Indian languages as well as Caribbean English. Guyanese chutney was no imported music: its roots lay in the folk singing of British Guiana's Indian agricultural workers, and a number of chutney classics such as Dis Time Nah Lang Time used old folk songs as their basis. Within a few years much of its charm and distinctiveness had been destroyed by the addition of electronic instruments and commercialisation. It morphed into 'chutney soca', an unremarkable variant of soca music.

MORWA BOLEE is a taste of early chutney. It's got quite a fast tempo, it's music to dance to, but it's also music that's proud to let us know its roots. It's like a little piece of South Asia, transported to the South American continent and performed by local musicians. And it has a bit of zest, a bit of swagger to it.

The singer, Joyce Harris, left school with little in the way of qualifications but with a love of singing. Her parents were singers too, and with their encouragement and support she managed to get a foot in the door as people hired her to sing at community events. Her first single was a light-hearted song that she'd written about her own marriage, called Taxi Driver. Half a century later, it's still the first song of hers that audiences want to hear whenever she's in Guyana. After working as a police officer for a few years, she moved to New York City, where she's lived for a long time now. She loves her country still and returns there every year for Mashramani, usually managing to play a few concerts while she's there. Her repertoire now includes chutney, soca, calypso, gospel (Christian songs), bhajans (Hindu songs) and qaseedas (Islamic songs). Looking back on her long career, she says, "singing gave me everything that I own in my life; I got everything through my voice… I feel when I sing, I make people happy; and when I make them happy, I am so happy. Even if I'm sick, I sing. Singing makes me happy." [7]

There was only one moment when she questioned her desire to sing, and that was when her son, the only one of her children to show an interest in singing, died in an accident at the age of 22. In 2015, though, now with 11 grandchildren, she was still declaring her intention to keep singing "until I can sing no more". [8]

NOTES

1. https://guyanachronicle.com/2014/05/05/east-indian-immigration-1838-1917
2. http://www.kaieteurnewsonline.com/2016/06/13/arts-and-culture-cornerthe-yoruba-singers-part-two
3. http://www.stabroeknews.com/2010/features/02/14/pre-independence-guyana-had-a-vibrant-music-industry
4. http://www.guyanatimesinternational.com/?p=2023
5. http://www.kaieteurnewsonline.com/2016/06/06/culture-and-artsthe-yoruba-band-a-legendary-pioneer-of-the-true-guyanese-sound
6. http://www.stabroeknews.com/2015/features/02/01/carnival-mashramani-evolution-calypso-soca-chutney
7. https://guyanachronicle.com/2012/06/30/the-legendary-joyce-harris
8. http://www.kaieteurnewsonline.com/2015/03/01/joyce-ormela-harris-over-50-years-of-sweet-singing

PARAGUAY

araguay's national instrument, the harp, is of course of European origin. Jesuit missionaries – who apparently took musical education of the indigenous population very seriously – first introduced it to the Indians. After the Spanish expelled the Jesuits in 1767 the harp stayed in use as a folk instrument, but we don't know a lot about the people who played it or the music that they played. It's only in the 20th century that the story of the harp really starts to get interesting.

The Paraguayan harp hadn't followed any of the evolutionary developments that had been taking place in Europe. It had no pedals and it was diatonic rather than chromatic, so the range of notes was more limited. The custom in Paraguay was to pluck with the fingernails rather than the fingertips – guitarists will be familiar with just how much this affects the tone of an instrument.

The year 1912 saw the formation of Banda de Músicos y la Escuela de Aprendices de la Policía de la Capital. I've not been able to establish quite why it was set up under the auspices of the Asunción police, but it was to be the leading institution for professional musicians in the country's capital and, although it employed many foreign musicians, from the start it played a key

MALAGUENA SALEROSA

Luis Alberto Del Paraná & Trio Los Paraguayos

AHATA CHE NENDIVE

Quemil Yambay y los Alfonsinos

----

role in developing Paraguayan artists. In those early years some of Paraguay's greatest composers and musicians passed through the police band: José Asunción Flores (1904–72), creator of guarania music; the composers Herminio Giménez (1905–91) and Felix Fernandez (1898?–1984); Mauricio Cardozo Ocampo (1907–82), who did so much to define Parauguayan music after 1945 through his music, his teaching and his writing; and many more.

Félix Pérez Cardozo (1908–52) was never in the police band, but for a short while he was part of the Asunción scene before in 1931 he and his band moved to Buenos Aires, setting a trend that many other Paraguayan musicians would follow in later years. He is celebrated for adding four strings to the Paraguayan harp: since his day, most Paraguayan harps have had 36 strings.

The inter-war period was a vital time in the construction of Paraguayan national identity. In the 1920s, nationalist politicians pushed the cause of the campesinos and promotion of the Guarani language, then in the early 1930s, credit for successes on the battlefield in the war with Bolivia was attributed to a sense of national solidarity and the influence of paraguayidad. The term 'paraguayiadad' encapsulated the idea that Paraguayans were a people united by language, land and cultural traditions. Thanks to the police band, and to Pérez Cardozo, harpists were no longer seen as penniless folk musicians; they carried some prestige. After 1945, Luis Bordón would champion the idea of the harp as a solo instrument, thus raising its status still further. Under the military dictators who ruled Paraguay from the 1930s onwards, Guarani language and harp music were to become pillars of state culture. Behind this lay a political calculation: that they could entrench their power by appealing to people's sense of national pride.

While the diatonic harp remains very popular in Paraguay, on the great majority of harp albums being made it's used as a solo instrument, with no vocals and minimal accompaniment. I have an issue here, and I may as well be honest about it. I confess to finding this to be rather dull: for me the vocals added a great deal. If I had to choose an instrumentalist to listen to, Martin Portillo would be high on my list. Besides his album on Bluecaps (Martin Portillo, Arpa Paraguaya), he appears on several tracks on the Folkways compilation Maiteí América: Harps of Paraguay. A harpist since the age of 12, he takes pride in composing his own songs, but for form and content he keeps mainly to traditional format: "I'm working with Paraguayan rhythms, guaranias and polcas, but I also have some Latin American rhythms." [1]

Luis Alberto del Paraná (1926–74) had a golden voice. A large part of his career was spent living abroad and promoting Paraguayan music across the Spanish-speaking world, and his repertoire would always include songs from across Latin America, which he delivered in his own style. One of his Mexican songs, MALAGUEÑA SALEROSA, is achingly romantic: the singer is telling a woman how beautiful she is, and how he longs for them to be together but that he understands her rejecting him for being too poor. In Trio Los Paraguayos's version it's the moments that we hear the solo voice, when Luis Alberto shows off his ability to hold a note, that the band extract the maximum emotional intensity.

The young Luis Alberto seemed to have an insatiable urge to see the world. With a harpist and guitarist by his side he travelled round Argentina and spent time in Mexico and Peru. He wasn't yet a big star, but his work was getting appreciated in high places. In 1953 he was back in Paraguay and forming a new trio, Los Paraguayos, with his long-term companion, Digno Garcia, and another legend-to-be, Agustin Barboza. That year a government decree was issued, signed by the president and the minister of finance, giving each of the three band members US$3,200 (a significant sum in those days) to go on a 'Cultural Mission' to promote Paraguayan music across Europe. They didn't let the president down.

Many more adventures were to follow. When the end came it was sudden and unexpected: he dropped dead in a London hotel at the age of 48. Rumours that this was somehow drugs-related are, as far as I can tell, unfounded. What appears to have happened is that Luis Alberto believed that he could carry on living the way he'd done in his youth, always on the road. He didn't take too much heed of the medical advice that he was given. On 11th September, 1974, after a long tour of Russia he flew to London, where he was due to perform at the Royal Albert Hall. He'd been complaining of headaches and he suffered from high blood pressure but his family weren't around to get him to take the medication that he'd been prescribed and to encourage him to get his health checked. He died just four days later. [2]

Quemil Yambay (born 1938) has his very own superpower: he can imitate with great precision the sounds of up to 100 different species of animal and bird. It's something he taught himself by ear from a very young age. Inevitably perhaps he's been called the walking zoo. I prefer, though, to think of him more as a people's poet.

Quemil Yambay gets his unusual name from his father, a Lebanese Syrian who came to Paraguay in hope of a better future. In a career that's lasted over half a century Quemil has performed on countless stages, but he's never forgotten his roots – which would be rather difficult anyway, since he named his band, Los

Alfonsinos, after his home town of Alfonso Tranquera. One of 10 children, he knew poverty when he was growing up, and the hardships and the joys of farm life were in his blood. As an artist and an entertainer, "Mi mayor satisfacción es el cariño de la gente" (my greatest satisfaction is people's affection), [3] and he earned this affection through the warmth of his character, his humour and his tear-jerking songs.

Although Quemil did write many of his own songs, **AHATA CHE NENDIVE** was written by Alíder Vera Guillén, a poet from San Ignacio. It's a song about loss, but there's a defiant optimism in the swinging accordion music and in the song's theme – you're leaving home? Well I'm not staying alone, I'm going with you.

Quemil suffered from degenerative eye problems and for many years he has been completely blind, but he has never let this stand in the way of him singing to the people. Interviewed in 2013 he declared "I'm feeling very well, I'm 75 years old and thanks to God I'm still good-looking, I'm going to continue singing."

NOTES

1. http://www.abc.com.py/espectaculos/martin-portillo-y-un-cd-de-temas-propios-861828.html
2. http://www.abc.com.py/articulos/luis-alberto-del-parana-la-leyenda-322670.html and http://www.musicaparaguaya.org.py/parana.html
3. http://www.ultimahora.com/quemil-yambay-me-siento-bien-soy-guapo-todavia-y-voy-seguir-cantando-n754250.html

PERU

Geographically and culturally, Peru divides into three regions.
The costa (coastal) region stretches along 1,500 miles of
Pacific coastline: much of it is dry, hot desert, but some regions
enjoy a pleasant sub-tropical climate. Most of the population live
in this region. Musica criolla is the generic name for the region's
music, which is a fusion of Spanish, Mediterranean and African
influences. Of the many dances the most famous is the marinera,
a couples' dance which involves much swishing of handkerchiefs.

To the east of the country lies the sierra, the Andean mountain
region. This region includes the altiplano – Peru's great high
plateau, once a stronghold of the Inca empire and home today to
many of Peru's Quechua and Aymara indigenous population. I've
always associated the region with panpipes, but, as we will see,
not for the first time I had to adjust my ideas.

In between these two is the selva (jungle) region. This
covers over 60% of the nation's land but contains only 11% of its
population. It's home to indigenous groups such as the Shipibo-
Conibo (known for their ceramics, textile painting and shaman
singing), and the Asháninka, whose main instruments are drums
and sōkari, a type of panpipe that requires the use of a particular
species of bamboo. This region's ethnic folk music is little known,

SON DE LOS DIABLOS	*Perú Negro*
RESBALOSAS	*Susana Baca*
QUIERO QUE AMANEZCA	*Cumbia All Stars*

and you'll have to do some exploring to find any. You may have better luck searching for la cumbia amazónica, which enjoyed a brief heyday in the 1960s and '70s with groups such as Juaneco y su Combo and Los Mirlos. Disaster struck the genre in 1977 when five members of Juaneco y su Combo were killed in a plane crash, but in recent years Bareto and the Cumbia All Stars have been rekindling the flame of Peruvian cumbia.

Beyond these boundaries, there have always been invisible divisions cutting through Peruvian society. For over half a century, music, arts and culture have been battlegrounds where people have tried to shake off the shackles of racism. That struggle is far from being over, but a corner has been turned, and today it's possible to speak of important victories.

In 1958, Victoria Santa Cruz (1922–2014) and her brother Nicomedes (1925–92) founded the black theatre company Cumanana with the aim of staging black Peruvian folklore. This was unheard of at the time. The minority black population still bore the stigma of the colonial era when the Spanish imported them from Africa and treated them as slaves. While the mestizos – people of mixed race – enjoyed some rights and freedoms, blacks and indigenous people were forced to perform the most menial jobs. Slavery was formally abolished by President Ramón Castilla in 1856 but blacks continued to experience prejudice and discrimination. Even their culture was despised and marginalised, as Cumanana's Teresa Mendoza remembers: "in this era, you didn't see Black music. You didn't hear it. Look, Ramon Castilla freed the slaves, but for the Blacks, life continued as it had before, marginalized as ever." [1]

The first Cumanana play, Zanahary, portrayed black life in Lima, where their parents had grown up, but there was more: in the final act a striking drum and dance performance with chanting aimed at eradicating an evil spell. This was Victoria's first imaginative attempt to recreate the culture that the slaves had brought over from Africa.

This was followed by a second and more ambitious production, Malato, complete with song, poetry and dance. The Santa Cruzes had been doing their research, but Victoria also worked with the group of black actors to raise their consciousness and encourage them to access their 'ancestral memory'. The concept of an ancestral memory appears far-fetched, even whimsical. Yet for Victoria Santa Cruz it was a vital element in the creative process. She created new versions of long-lost Afro-Peruvian dances, and has written that: "one of my most important choreographic works was the creation of the 'disappeared' lando dance, which had disappeared as a form, but was alive in my ancestral memory." [2]

In 1964, Nicomedes released a landmark double album appropriately called Cumanana. The result of extensive research, it featured the first recordings of several rescued genres, and was accompanied by a booklet of over a hundred pages that attempted to map out the music's African origins. The festejo, for example, had long been a part of black culture, but few now remembered how it used to be performed. Porfirio Vásquez (another key figure, who spent several years mentoring Nicomedes) devised a choreography for the dance by combining aspects of other black dances including the resbalosa, zapateo, son de los diablos, agua'e nieve and alcatraz, and then Nicomedes and the Cumanana musicians took up the baton. Their song, No Me Cumben, helped to inspire a revival of festejo and the energetic festive dance is now a staple of Afro-Peruvian culture.

Meanwhile, Victoria was in Paris, studying theatre and choreography. When she returned it was with a renewed sense of commitment. She created a new company, Teatro y Danzas Negras del Peru, which over the next few years would be her main vehicle for reviving Afro-Peruvian culture and consciousness.

Already the seeds sown were starting to bear new life. In 1969 two former Cumanana musicians, Ronaldo Campos and Jesus 'el Niño' Nicasio, founded what was to become by far the most influential of all Afro-Peruvian groups, Peru Negro. The heartbeat of the music was the cajon: a humble wooden box. The origins of the cajon go back a long way: it's believed that the early slaves, deprived of drums, had to improvise. Thanks to the Santa Cruzes and Ronaldo Campos the instrument has been restored to its place of importance in Afro-Peruvian culture.

Peru Negro had a single aim: to raise interest and awareness in black Peruvian music, and they carried this off superbly wherever they travelled. Their 1974 album, Son de los Diablos, is made up of six festejos, three landos and a waltz, and casting an eye over the track listing I see that Mi Compadre Nicolás was written by Afro-Peruvian pioneer Porfirio Vasquez, Congorito by criollo composer Eduardo Márquez Talledo, then Juan de Mata is credited to Ronaldo Campos, and Alcatraz Quema Tu to his cousin and fellow band member Caitro Soto. Of special interest is the title track:

"SON DE LOS DIABLOS *is an Afro-Peruvian street masquerade dance that originated in colonial Lima. In the 1500s, Spanish colonialists prohibited Africans generally from dancing, but also forced them to perform traditional African dances in morality plays and Corpus Christi pageants, dressed as devils in straw and goatskins. By the time slavery was abolished in 1854, Afro-Peruvians had appropriated this dance as a symbol of cultural resistance... Dancers painted their faces with flags of African countries, performed stunts and tricks in masks, and burlesqued and parodied devils, with marching cuadrillas (teams of dancers and musicians) of little devils kept in line with the Diablo Mayor's (Head Devil's) whip. These performances evolved into fierce zapateo competitions, lengthy theatrical pieces, and religious parodies, such as one in which the Diablo Mayor forced the little devils to form a choreographic cross." [3]*

Described in the song are a few of the colourful masquerade characters.

After Ronaldo Campos died in 2001, leadership of the group passed to his son, Rony Campos. Decades later, their sound has changed remarkably little. On Zamba Malato they're once again collecting Afro-Peruvian dance tunes – the festejo, the lando, the zamacueca – and knocking them back with the same passion and vibrancy as before. Included here is a version of another famous dance inherited from the days of slavery, the Toro Mata:

"The dance Toro Mata mocks the minuets and waltzes that slaves observed while serving the parties of slave masters who danced pompously dressed in colonial ruffles. The stiff, almost military alignment of the dance imitates the opening of the minuet, but the dancers mock the rigidity and absence of natural grace required for this dance." [4]

Back in 1969, at the start of their career, Peru Negro had been fortunate to get an invite to play at a big festival in Argentina thanks to the recommendation of Chabuca Granda. Chabuca was a white criolla singer who'd known Ronaldo Campos since the mid-1950s. In the band's early years they toured and performed together with Chabuca quite frequently. In the last decade of her life (she died in 1983) she started performing some of the Afro-Peruvian songs herself.

This in itself was quite a landmark: as well as being white, Chabuca was something of a legend in Peruvian music. "I was born," she says, "in the Andes, 4,800 metres (15,750 feet) above sea level, in the Cotabambas Aurarias mountains… I am, then, a proud and sober sister of the condor; I was born so high up that I used to wash my face with the stars." [5] The region where they lived is called Apurímac, a Quechua word meaning 'where the Gods speak', a reference to the towering mountains that overlook the land. It's a predominantly Quechua-speaking area to this day. Chabuca didn't remain there long. When she was still young her brother died suddenly and her father decided to give up his job in the copper mine and move back to Lima. Growing up in Lima she forgot how to speak Quechua, something she later regretted as she found she wasn't able to fully appreciate the beauty of Quechua poetry. Instead she developed a new bond of love with the city of Lima – a love affair consummated in her most famous song La Flor de la Canela. This waltz, the first hit song that she wrote herself, was an ode both to the city and to the woman who inspired the song, a black woman called Victoria Angulo. It's been translated into over 30 languages and is an unofficial anthem of the city of Lima.

There've been several compilations of Afro-Peruvian music, but by common consensus the most important and influential was The Soul of Black Peru (El Alma del Peru Negro), released by David Byrne on the Luaka Bop label in the mid-1990s. Pioneers of the music were represented on the album by Nicomedes Santa Cruz, Abelardo Vásquez & Cumanana, Peru Negro and Chabuca Granda. Then there were artists such as Eva Ayllón, identified on the sleeve notes as having made the music popular with modern audiences, and Susana Baca, "who truly was the inspiration for this album. Her soulful rendition of Maria Lando captivated us and convinced us to explore more of this music. We found, surprisingly, that though her voice is stunning and she is a very respected singer, she has never had a record released on a commercial label in Peru." [6]

For both Eva Ayllón and Susana Baca, the music of Chabuca Granda was a seminal influence. Both have recorded tribute albums: Eva's is called Eva Ayllón Canta a Chabuca Granda, and Susana's is Seis Poemas. Susana's debt to Chabuca is a personal as well as a musical one. When they met, Susana was just a young aspiring singer from a poor neighbourhood of Lima, but Chabuca took her under her wing, they became close friends and Susana worked as Chabuca's personal assistant. When she was dying Chabuca wrote to her friend, "Don't forget me, sing me." Susana took these words to heart: the song that appears on The Soul of Black Peru is also a Chabuca Granda composition. Not all of the Seis Poemas, however, were actually written by Chabuca. **RESBALOSAS** is a deeply emotional traditional folk song about a woman whose heart hurts so deeply that she can't go on.

Susana Baca achieved recognition and fame quite late in life. For years she studied the history of Peru's black heritage, carried out fieldwork and made recordings. In 1992, she and her husband founded the Instituto Negrocontinuo in their home neighbourhood of Lima to preserve and promote Afro-Peruvian culture. She followed this by building a black cultural centre in her mother's home town of Santa Barbara. On her first album with Luaka Bop, several of the songs that she recorded had roots that were centuries old. She was now in her 50s, but her career was just beginning.

At the age of 67 her story took another unexpected twist when new president, Ollanta Humala, offered her the job of minister for culture. She accepted the post in a spirit of guarded optimism: she, more than anyone, knew that the battle against racism was far from over. Just two years earlier, outgoing president, Alan Garcia, had made a formal apology to the country's black citizens for centuries of abuse, exclusion and discrimination, but

Susana wanted to see more than words: racism against blacks and indigenous people was no means as bad as it had been in the 1960s when she was growing up, but it was still real. Thus, when the New York Times asked, "When you were a girl, was it even possible for a black woman to dream of becoming a minister?", she didn't try to paint a rose-tinted picture: "Not just when I was a girl. It was only a short time ago that we managed to become respected, to have status." [7]

After just 133 days she was dismissed by Humala as part of a cabinet clear-out. At the time she said that it had been a positive experience, and she was proud to have played a part in introducing the historic 'prior consultation' law, which guaranteed indigenous peoples the right to prior and informed consent to any projects affecting them and their lands. But by 2015, after witnessing a series of climbdowns by Humala over implementation of the law and a sharp rise in murders of environmental activists, her tone had changed, accusing Humala of 'una traición' – a betrayal of indigenous peoples. [8]

As mentioned at the start of this chapter, I'd been looking forward to listening to Peruvian panpipes, but what I found was rather different. Even in the Andean region, bamboo panpipes are just one of several traditional instruments, and commercial recordings by locally based artists are few and far between. Panpipe ensemble Qhantati Ururi, from a village near Lake Titicaca, have released three albums, but they're not easy to get hold of. If you're interested in hearing a more typical representation of modern Andean folk music then you should listen to some huayno. Huayno is a vigorous couples dance with roots in indigenous culture, and the music's provided by ensembles usually with a mix of traditional and modern elements. Other traditional instruments commonly used include the charango, guitar, quena (flute) and harp. The roots of the Peruvian charango are in the Andean region of Ayacucho, and the Ayacuchan charango player, Jaime Guardia, has, in a career lasting over half a century, set the standard by which other charango players judge themselves. Other notable soloists include Manuelcha Prado (guitar), Raymond Thevenot (quena) and Luciano Quispe (harp).

Andean music is changing all the time as the use of modern and electronic instruments becomes more and more pervasive, while government bodies do little to promote the use of traditional instruments. Opinions are divided as to what view we should take of this. Jaime Guardia bemoans the fact that the music of today isn't huayno as it was sung by the people, [9] while Manuelcha Prado argues that "we need to break with prejudices against everything modern" because a certain amount of opening up can enrich one's own culture. [10]

Travellers seeking experiences of indigenous culture and panpipes are encouraged by the tourist literature to go to Puno on the shores of Lake Titicaca, a music and folklore hub that every February hosts the Fiesta de la Candelaria, a festival of folklore, music and dance.

A very different kind of festival experience is offered by Selvamonos, a major new annual music and arts festival in selva country, in the jungle of Oxapampa. It was here in 2012 that the Cumbia All Stars were formed, a supergroup of eight musicians all drawn from legendary Peruvian cumbia bands of the past: Los Destellos, Los Mirlos, Los Diablos Rojos, Los Beta 5 and Compay Quinto. The original intention had been to just perform one show at Selvamonos, but after a rapturous reception they all decided to carry on. They were invited to perform at Womex in 2013, and it was a joy to witness their enthusiasm and love of the music. On the debut album (Tigres en Fuga) they're still rocking just as hard. QUIERO QUE AMANEZCA is chosen for no other reason than it's sublimely catchy and danceable. The guitars are backed by a variety of drums: bongos, congas and timbales.

These were men who would have grown up listening to Colombia cumbia in the 1950s and '60s. Peruvian cumbia took off with the introduction of the electric guitar. Each band added their own riffs and effects as they tried to create a flavour of surf rock or Cuban rhythms or any of a dozen other styles. Lucho Carrillo, one-time lead singer of Los Diablos Rojos, reckons that the mix of influences was what brought the music to life. At live concerts there was an electricity in the air, a joyful abandon, and a sense that something very special was happening. Lucho recalls:

"Years ago... I was invited to Bucaramanga in Colombia, and when I arrived they had closed several streets of the city. It was a tremendous party in the whole city. They had put together a huge sound system. More than three blocks of people dancing in the street and they were dancing Peruvian cumbia! The DJs put Los Destellos, then my group Los Diablos Rojos... Everything!" [11]

NOTES

1. Heidi Feidman – Black Rhythms of Peru: Reviving African Musical Heritage in the Black Pacific (Wesleyan, 2007), p65.
2. Quoted by Heidi Feidman, Ibid., p73.
3. http://worldartswest.org/main/edf_performer.asp?i=23
4. http://archive.rockpaperscissors.biz/index.cfm/fuseaction/current.press_release/project_id/126.cfm
5. http://issuu.com/embassyofperuintheusa/docs/chasqui_november_2008/11
6. Sleeve notes by Gregorio Martinez and Fietta Jarque, http://www.luakabop.com/directory/album_pages/?id=afro_peruvian_classics_the_soul_of_black_peru
7. http://www.nytimes.com/2011/08/20/arts/music/susana-baca-peruvian-musician-and-culture-minister.html
8. http://www.larepublica.pe/08-02-2015/humala-traiciono-a-los-pueblos-indigenas
9. http://diariocorreo.pe/perfiles/arguedas-venia-a-mi-casa-y-haciamos-un-duo-575009
10. http://puquioencanta.8m.com/riqchari.html
11. http://vinylhead66.blogspot.co.uk/2013/11/cumbia-all-stars-tour-europeo-2013_24.html

SURINAME

"Before Lieve Hugo a Surinamese band was a bunch of old men on deckchairs who played one song and waited until someone came to give them a portion of rice with beans. After Lieve Hugo they were all musicians. He brought life into the brewery... As a musician, I learned from him that you should never work towards a climax. No, once people arrive: grab them right away!"

Edgar Burgos [1]

He was adored for his good looks, his charisma, his beautiful voice. A one-time resident of a home for maladjusted children, he still had something of the devil within him and a reputation as a womaniser. He was known as Lieve Hugo (1934–75) and he was also the greatest artist that Suriname has ever produced: a creative genius who came up with startling, exciting new rhythms and wrote songs that struck a chord with ordinary people.

Suriname took a big step towards independence in 1954 when it became a fully autonomous part of the Netherlands. Political parties sprang up that were based largely on ethnicity, and they developed a model of cooperation and power-sharing of which

NA FOE SANG ÉDÉ   *Lieve Hugo*

the political elites were very proud. They saw Suriname as a place where diverse populations could co-exist, though the reality was that ethnic tensions simmered under the surface that would play a part in the armed conflict that broke out in the 1980s. In the 1960s and '70s, though, while politicians paid lip service to accepting diversity, musicians put this into practice.

A popular style was bigi pokoe, a lively, danceable fusion of kawina (a Surinamese street music of African origin that involves drumming and chanting) and Dixieland jazz. When Lieve Hugo joined Orchestra Washboard they were essentially a bigi pokoe band. Hugo had been recruited as a drummer, but before long he was singing more and more and coming up with his own ideas about the musical direction the band should take. Using as his inspiration the black, Creole and Asian cultures of Paramaribo, he became a musical adventurer, sifting from many styles, rearranging songs. It helped that he was working with some superb musicians and they had a real chemistry together.

In 1970, Orchestra Washboard toured the Netherlands. Their performance at Amsterdam's Royal Concertgebouw is the stuff of legends: in the concert hall's glittering interior dancing wasn't exactly encouraged, but on that night the Dutch audience not only left their seats but some were wriggling along the floor. On their return to Paramaribo, Hugo fell seriously ill. Doctors told him that he had a heart condition and advised him to go back to the Netherlands for medical treatment.

And so Hugo settled in Amsterdam, forming a new band, The Happy Boys, and signing a record contract with EMI. He was now at his artistic peak. His debut album, released in 1974, sparkles with life and beautiful melodies. Now at last Suriname was about to become independent. Hugo returned to the studio to record a second album to mark the occasion. He was booked to perform at the official ceremony; he was the singer most Surinamese wanted to see. Few of them, though, had any idea how much his health had been deteriorating. Tragically, his flight home was in a coffin. Ten days before independence, his heart gave up. In the same plane as the coffin was the Dutch prime minister Joop den Uyl, on his way to put the seal on Suriname's independence. So, on the eve of independence, a very special funeral took place, people from all walks of life lining the streets of Paramaribo with tears in their eyes for the singer struck down in his prime at the age of 40. Some whispered about possible conspiracies – was poison or black magic at work? – but the truth was far more mundane.

After Hugo's death The Happy Boys asked Edgar Burgos to lead the band in his place. They made a few more albums before Burgos left to form Trafassi and the band split up. The joy and optimism of Suriname's music scene in the 1970s was not to last, and kaseko music was never to recapture the heights of those years. The music's been kept alive just as much by the Surinamese community in the Netherlands as in Suriname itself, and that's where some of the best albums have been made. It also owes much to those veterans of the '70s who were still around in the 21st century to introduce a new generation to kaseko: musicians such as trumpet player Stan Lokhin (who died in 2010) and Edgar Burgos.

NA FOE SANG ÉDÉ is Lieve Hugo's most famous song, and a fitting epitaph. When he wrote the song he knew that his days were numbered, so he laments the fact that he has to die when there's so much more to do and see. Yet it's also a joyful song, pulsating with life. You can hear the calypso influence, the carnival dance rhythms. And you know even without understanding the Sranan language words that Hugo still has his eye on the women.

NOTES

1. https://www.vn.nl/trafassi-edgar-burgos-als-ik-puur-surinaamse-muziek-zou-maken-denk-ik-niet-dat-ik-een-living-had

URUGUAY

Uruguayans have never been ones to let mere facts get in the way of a good argument.

On 24th June, 2014, the Uruguayan footballer Luis Suarez sank his teeth into an opponent, Giorgio Chiellini, during a match at the World Cup in Brazil. It was the third time in his professional career that Suarez had bitten a player, and his punishment was the longest ban in World Cup history. Instead of condemning the player for actions that may well have damaged the country's sporting reputation, Uruguayan public figures rushed to his defence. Uruguay's president José Mujica, a man of considerable integrity, declared that "I did not see him bite anyone", and after Suarez was banned by FIFA he dismissed the governing body of world football as "a bunch of old sons of bitches". While by no means all Uruguayans would have agreed with these sentiments, there's no doubt that they were reflective of the public mood.

Uruguayans are equally passionate – and equally obstinate – on the subject of tango music. The two nations, Argentina and Uruguay, which are separated by the Río de la Plata, share tango music as part of their DNA. And both can be possessive about what they regard as their own heritage. Carlos Gardel was the golden boy of tango music, and although he died in a plane

PASIONAL
Francis Andreu

LA EMBRUJADA

(THE BEWITCHED POLKA)
Los Gauchos de Roldán

crash in 1935, he is still regarded today as a national icon in both Uruguay and Argentina. In recent decades a minor industry has grown up dedicated to proving that the singer was born in the Uruguayan town of Tacuarembó. While there's some basis for this claim, the balance of the evidence strongly points to his having been born in France. Although he did himself claim later in life to be Uruguayan-born, this may have been motivated by a desire to avoid being drafted into the French military during the Great War. If he had been Uruguayan-born, what difference would this have made? He never lived in the country. It was in Buenos Aires that he grew up, started his career, learned his trade and won the hearts of thousands of women, and was embraced by Argentinians as one of their own.

Another tango-related controversy concerns the famous tango La Cumparsita. In the 2000 Sydney Olympics, the Uruguayan Olympic Committee submitted an official protest over the fact that Argentinian athletes had marched out to the tune during the opening ceremonies. The song, they felt, was Uruguayan, because the tune had been written by a Uruguayan, Gerardo Hernan Matos Rodriquez. The problem with this (the pointlessness of the actual protest aside) was that the lyrics had been composed at a later date by a couple of Argentinians, and lyrics are very important in tango music. While this may not make the tango Argentine, it does make the claim of exclusivity seem rather silly.

If any Uruguayan readers are feeling offended by all of this, let it be said that they have many reasons to feel proud. For over a century the contribution of Uruguayan musicians has been essential to the story of tango music. And on the football field the achievements of the Uruguayan team can't be bettered by any other country when reckoned by head of population. Uruguay has long had a reputation for being a stable democracy, but in recent years its politics have become rather interesting, and not in a bad way. The aforementioned José Mujica, a former left-wing guerrilla leader, was elected president in 2010 for a five-year term. In 2012, his government enacted a groundbreaking law to legalise state-controlled sales of marijuana. Abortion was legalised in 2012 and gay marriage in 2013: real victories for liberal values in a predominately Catholic country. The president also inspired people through his personal lifestyle: "the man who most Uruguayans call El Pepe drives a 25-year-old Volkswagen Beetle, lives in a tiny house on a rural smallholding, and gives away 90% of his salary." [1]

The tango took root in the barrios of Buenos Aires and Montevideo in the latter half of the 19th century. At the time, immigrants were arriving from Europe in large numbers, and the working-class slums of the two cities were teeming with different nationalities. The earliest tango musicians would have included many of these immigrants, and of their many contributions to the music none was to be more important than the importing of a German instrument, the bandoneon.

Francisco 'Pirincho' Canaro was the son of two Italian immigrants. When he was still a child, the family crossed the Río de la Plata to settle in Buenos Aires. There was not enough money to pay for schooling, so the young Pirincho took to the streets as a shoe shine boy and a paper boy. His first violin he made himself from wood and an empty oil can. A few years later when he started performing the only gigs he could get were in rough and disreputable cantinas and bordellos. He worked hard and before long was performing regularly in the cafés of the capital. He teamed up with the bandeonist, Vicente Greco, they became one of the best tango ensembles in town, and people would pay good money to see them. At the age of 26 Canaro began conducting his own orchestra. Canaro's orchestra helped to pave the way for the success of later artists such as Carlos Gardel. They ended the embargo on the playing of tango music in aristocratic circles, and in 1925 they settled the question of its status once and for all when they travelled to fashionable Paris and performed to great acclaim.

PASIONAL is everything that a tango should be: a grandiose expression of sexual longing, full of physical imagery, and ending with a melodramatic declaration of all-consuming love. Francis Andreu's voice – surprisingly deep for a young woman – is adeptly complemented by the guitar.

Francis Andreu got her big break at the age of 16 when she went to a concert by the Argentinian tango singer Adriana Varela. Varela's manager, Horacio Pessagno, heard the teenager humming the songs and was sufficiently impressed to invite her to record a demo. It wasn't long after this he offered her a contract – but to general amazement she turned him down. She wanted to take the time to develop her skills and become the best that she could; she didn't want the pressure of producing instant hits that goes with a recording contract. In the following years she would turn down a string of attractive offers. Finally, in 2011 – still only in her mid-20s – she released the album Francis, which confirmed her growing reputation as a torchbearer for the new generation of Uruguayan tango.

Today, Uruguayan tango can no longer be said to live on reflected past glories. Each week crowds flock to Montevideo's milongas, and not just older people but a good many under-30s who know all their dance moves and are ready to be tango'd. At a time when international interest in tango music is growing, Uruguay is well placed to cater to this market.

It would be easy to stop here, but I feel compelled to report that Uruguayan tango has at times faced stiff competition from musicians with different ideas about where the roots of Uruguayan music can be found.

The 1960s was a time of cultural ferment. A young, politically conscious generation of writers, poets and musicians was questioning everything. This decade saw the emergence of some of Uruguay's greatest folk singers: Alfredo Zitarrosa, Daniel Viglietti and the duo Los Olimareños. Dissatisfied with the music they heard around them, they sought out more 'authentic' Uruguayan sounds and styles. According to Daniel Viglietti, the Cuban revolution was an inspiration: it taught them that it was possible for Latin American countries to transform themselves without relying on imported models and ideas, staying true to their own language and culture. [2] Zitarrosa found his true voice in milonga song. Milonga has roots in gaucho (peasant) culture – Zitarrosa used to call it "Montevideo's blues". [3]

Around the same time a young Rubén Rada was starting out on a recording career that would reshape popular Uruguayan culture. He took the tradition of candombe drumming and dancing and played around with it, blending it at different times with many different styles (rock, pop, funk, tango, jazz...). There was a purpose to all this: he wanted to succeed, but he wanted to do it as a black man and bring African-influenced candombe rhythms into the national lifeblood.

The track **LA EMBRUJADA** has no highfalutin pretensions: it's a light, fun polka. But what it does do is to bring together two very important Uruguayan instruments in the accordion and the bandoneon. The result may not be entirely traditional but it has an honesty and a charm, and is representative of the creativity of Uruguay's large immigrant communities.

Los Gauchos de Roldán are a group formed in Tacuarembó

by the accordionist Walter Roldán (born 1943). According to José Curbelo's liner notes,

> *"The northern department of Tacuarembó has been a rural center of the cultural mixing of indigenous descendants, Afro-Uruguayans, Brazilians and European immigrants, and a center of the northern Uruguayan tradition of accordion and bandoneon. In the mid-19th century, the popular European dance forms of the time – polka, mazurka, waltz, and schottische – arrived in Uruguay, and… made their way into rural areas, where they were 'reshaped in the style and way of thinking of the paisanos (rural people),' says Walter Roldán. The principal example of this process is the polca, which became one of the most important social dance rhythms in rural Uruguay toward the beginning of the 20th century, developing an original playing style and unique repertoire, especially north of the Rio Negro."* [4]

It's this cultural mix, not any one unsullied ethnic cultural tradition, that gives Uruguayan music its unique character. As the popularity of instruments such as the accordion and the bandoneon spread among these diverse rural communities, the music began to change and to take on a new form.

NOTES

1. http://www.theguardian.com/world/2014/sep/18/-sp-is-this-worlds-most-radical-president-uruguay-jose-mujica
2. http://resumen.cl/index.php?option=com_content&view=article&id=512 5:daniel-viglietti-en-las-movilizaciones-de-concepcion&catid=18:cultura &Itemid=62
3. Pablo Vila (ed.) – The Militant Song Movement in Latin America: Chile, Uruguay, and Argentina (Lexington Books, 2014), p111.
4. http://media.smithsonianfolkways.org/liner_notes/smithsonian_folkways/ SFW40561.pdf

VENEZUELA

Bisecting Venezuela, the great Orinoco River wends its way down from the Sierra de Parima to a sprawling delta on the Atlantic coast. The region of lowland plains that surrounds it – Los Llanos – is geographically quite unique. During the dry season the hot sun scorches the land, water becomes scarce and only the hardiest vegetation can survive. But when it rains it really rains. Every year vast areas of Los Llanos are submerged by floods for weeks on end. It's a great time for wildlife watchers, who come to see the region's stunning bird and fish life – or, for the really intrepid, a glimpse of a giant anaconda or the endangered Orinoco crocodile.

In the Orinoco plains the cattle rancher is king. As the early Spanish settlers found, the land can't support agriculture but it can support cattle. Venezuelan cowboys (llaneros) are a hardy breed who drive their cattle great distances during the rainy season to reach higher ground. They've developed their own cowboy music and dancing, which for more years than anyone can remember have been symbols of national identity.

Joropo is a couples' dance. The pair embrace each other with one arm while holding their partner's hand out to one side. Typically they begin with graceful movements, then the music

TONADA DEL CABESTRERO	*Simón Díaz*
PAJARILLO DE MI TIERRA	*José Gregorio López*
COME CANDELA	*Gerardo Rosales*
LA CARCAJÁ	*Monsalve y Los Forajidos*

quickens and things get lively. They remain clasped together, but now their feet are flashing backwards and forwards at high speed. They keep their bodies as still as possible while letting their feet do all the work.

That the dance had some European roots was undeniable, but it became the culture of rural Venezuela, and before radio's rise to dominance in the mid-20th century this was where you had to be to hear it performed. Different forms of joropo grew up in different regions, but its character remained much the same: it was music of the soil, played using stringed instruments such as the arpa llanera (harp), cuatro and bandola by men of the soil.

The great legends of joropo music tend to have similar types of background. Ignacio 'Indio' Figueredo (1899–1995) was born on a farm in the west of the country. His father was a musician, but he says he only really tuned into music after spending an entire night watching the harpist Pedrito Herrera performing at a local dance. Afterwards he begged his mother to buy him a harp, and she traded in one of the family cows to get him his instrument. She did well: the kid gave his first public performance at the age of 11 and went on to write hundreds of songs and to inspire generations of musicians.

Among his students was one Juan Vicente Torrealba. He too grew up in a farming community where the main form of entertainment was the joropo dances. He moved to Caracas without any intention of becoming a full-time musician, but he formed his own band, and one thing led to another. The success he achieved back then has followed him in later life. Part of the key to this is that he's an innovator, someone who's always tried to be ahead of the game. Even now, at the age of 101, he needs no lessons from anyone in his social media skills. On his 100th birthday in February, 2017, he was at the Miraflores Palace to meet the country's president, Nicolás Maduro, who presented him with Venezuela's highest honour, La Orden del Libertador, and a replica of the sword of Simón Bolívar. This followed many other tributes, including a performance the previous year of a selection of his songs to an audience of 2,500 people by the National Philharmonic Orchestra. It was all quite an achievement for a cowboy who'd never had much of a formal education: "My music is original. I didn't go to any school, I had no teacher, or cuatro, or arpa, all my music I learned on the plain. And those feelings present in my music were learned herding cattle..." [1]

Simon Diaz (1928–2014) was born in Barbacoas, a small town where everything revolved around cattle breeding. With his father's encouragement, he learned to play the four-stringed cuatro. Then, when he was 12 his father died. The eldest of eight children, he became the head of the family. While struggling to earn a few bolívares he discovered that he had an aptitude as an entertainer, performing as a stand-up comedian and storyteller, and as a musician in the Cuban music band Orquesta Sidoney. In 1949 he moved to Caracas, just as Torrealba had done a few years before him. Within 24 hours he'd got a job, working for a bank as a debt collector. And within three months he was enrolled at the music school, where he resumed his musical education.

TONADA DEL CABESTRERO is a simple stripped-down song made extraordinary by the tenderness of Simon's vocals and his beautiful long-drawn-out high-pitched notes. It's a song that first appeared on his very first album and would have had a lot of meaning for him. Tonadas are work songs, in Venezuela mainly associated with cow milking time. Simon loved the plains and all the traditions of plains life; he wanted to capture this and preserve this through his music, so as well as the knowledge that he carried with him he wrote songs that were grounded in the rural experience. He was the perfect ambassador for llanero music with his likeable easy-going character, his warmth and his humour. In the 1960s he became a popular radio broadcaster and television presenter, and his show, Contesta por Tio Simón, which aimed to bring rural folk culture to children, earned him the nickname Uncle Simon.

Venezuelans still love their llanero music (Hugo Chavez himself was a big fan), and naturally there's a fair amount of nostalgia and romanticism attached to this. But Simon Diaz was no sentimentalist. His lyrics are honest, he sang of what he knew and he never abandoned his connections to the plains and the hard-working lifestyle of the llanero.

The arpa llanera, the plains harp, is the star of my next featured song **PAJARILLO DE MI TIERRA**. The little information that I have about the harpist, José Gregorio Lopez, comes from the sleeve notes, which tell us that he's from Barinas, he's in his 50s and his musical influences include both Indio Figueredo and Juan Vicente Torrealba. The CD is a collection of recordings made 'in natural settings' with a portable digital recorder. Most of the tracks are instrumental pieces, which seems a shame, as Carlos Alvarado's vocals on this song complement the arpa so well: there is so much of himself, so much feeling in the vocals and the rapid fingerwork of Gregorio Lopez that it gets your feet tapping and your heart pounding. The contrast with Simon Diaz's tonada is quite striking: the music is faster and the singing more dramatic – this llanero vocal style is known as canto recio (rough singing).

In the 1970s, a new phenomenon was exploding across the Latin world. Salsa music took off in the clubs of New York

City, where there was a fantastic scene with a host of red hot big bands largely made up of first- and second-generation Caribbean immigrants. Perhaps the most famous were the Fania All Stars, who sold out the 63,000-capacity Yankee Stadium; many of New York's top salsa musicians played in the orchestra at one time or another. In Caracas, six young musicians formed a band that would make Venezuelan salsa renowned around the world. The band was called Dimensión Latina and its vocalist, Oscar D'León.

Johnny Sedes claims that 'salsa' as a musical term was coined in Venezuela, not in Cuba. The first album with salsa in the title, he says, was Federico Betancourt's Llegó la Salsa: "I then recorded in 1967, the LP Vitín López, el cantante de la salsa, because I copied that of Federico." [2]

Salsa revolutionised Venezuelan music. It did so in several ways. On the one hand it was a pan-Latin music, spread by the magic of radio, a vibe that people from New York to Havana and San Juan to Caracas could relate to and claim as their own. At the same time, with its horns and drums, salsa's debt to black Caribbean music was apparent. And, as D'León well knew, "Cuban music was influenced from the roots of Africa". [3] In Venezuela it was in the barrios, the poorer urban neighbourhoods, where salsa music first caught on.

Los Dementes (Crazy Men) and Los Kenya sound like the names of rock bands. Ray Perez and his fellow musicians were living in the barrios of Caracas and certainly felt an affinity with rock music. The music they played, though, was guaracha, a type of Cuban music. "The 'high class' people, the ones they call oligarchs now, the ones who had money, they danced to Billos, what we called musica gallega," remembers Ray. "The new music was of our generation, we gave the guaracha a different feeling." [4]

Between 1969 and 1971, Ray Perez spent a couple of periods in New York, where he studied and played salsa music. "I played with Kako y sus All Stars, when I got up on the piano everyone got up to sing, Cheo Feliciano, Chivirico. Palmieri, instead of playing piano, took the timbal… this was on Second Avenue, Kako's after hours. Later we left at six for a musician's breakfast on Broadway." His close friend Perucho had joined him there, but for Perucho the American experience was to end in tragedy:

> "They went to play in Boston, and it gets cold in Boston. It was springtime, when it gets real cold sometimes. When they got back from the show, Justo told Perucho to stay in his house. But because Perucho felt pena with Justo' s wife, Perucho stayed down below. I guess there was a window open, and he felt cold, so he went into the car and closed the windows and turned on the car to run the heater. When they opened the car in the morning he was dead from monoxide inhalation. It was an accident… He was maybe thirty two, thirty three. A good singer. He danced incredibly, like El Gran Combo. He moved all over the stage – he was a real showman."

Ray and his bands went on to record many more albums of hard-hitting salsa music. And though he prefers these days to keep himself out of the spotlight I see from his blog that as he approaches his 80th birthday he still performs concerts with Teo Hernández, one of the original Dementes.

In the '70s Gerardo Rosales was just a kid, but he couldn't get enough salsa music:

> "I often listened to the radio, specially the program La hora de la salsa by Phidias Danilo Escalona. In the '70s, Radio Aeropuerto played salsa brava 24/7. When I was a child, I saw the Fania All Stars, Típica 73, Dimensión Latina, Ismael Rivera, Tito Puente, Machito, Ray Barretto and many others on (black and white) television. I learned to play music just by listening to and looking at these programs. Venezuela was the door to the success for all the Latin-American artists. Everybody went through there." [5]

Gerardo is a percussionist who's played with many leading Venezuelan bands, but salsa's what's closest to his heart. He started off playing all the pots and pans in the house before his family relented and bought him his first set of drums. Since 1993 he's been living in the Netherlands.

Gerardo tells the story of how, in 1994, he had illegal immigrant status, and the opportunity came along to record with the great Cuban pianist Bebo Valdés in Germany.

"I decided to take the risk that the police would catch me and deport me immediately and took the train to Germany. I travelled eight frightening hours, hiding myself in the toilet each time the police passed by. Thank God that when I arrived in Dusseldorf, the president of Messidor was waiting for me at the railway station. I was able to record this musical jewel and enjoyed an unforgettable week with all these legends... I returned to Holland by train and said to myself, 'What the heck, if (I'm) deported, I recorded a CD with Bebo and that will be for history.' Apparently the police came and asked for my passport. When he saw the cover with República de Venezuela, he looked at me and said: 'Aaah, Venezuela, no problem.' He didn't open the passport and left. God was with me that day."

While researching this book I've seen many cases where artists in exile drift away from their cultural roots. But it doesn't always work that way. When Gerardo started to make some salsa albums of his own he was free from the commercial pressures of the Venezuelan market. He felt a responsibility to show his European audiences what real salsa music, the music that he'd grown up with, was all about. He assembled his band with great care – the instruments had to be authentic. A couple of the releases were tribute albums, to the Fania All Stars and to the Afro-Cuban drummer, Mongo Santamaría. It's from this latter album that the track **COME CANDELA** is taken. Come Candela is Latin jazz with the flow and rhythm of salsa played in a spirit of creativity and artistic freedom. It's joyful uplifting music, and there's some lovely interplay between the instruments.

While Venezuelan music was beginning to feel blacker and more African, black and indigenous Venezuelans were just finding their voice. One consequence of this is that we now know considerably more about Afro-Venezuelan music and culture than we did 50 years ago. Besides all that's been written, a few compilation albums have appeared over the years. On Pan Records we have Tierra del Cacao – Afro-Venezuelan Music and Dance (1999), then from Merusa, Bocón – Afro-Hispanic Music from Venezuela (2007), and in 2014 Folkways brought out Venezuela: Afro-Venezuelan Music. The group, Los Tambores de San Millán, have also made recordings, but these aren't easy to get hold of.

These albums are living proof that there are still many communities in Venezuela who've inherited a culture and a music that in many ways are distinctively African. Each community has its own traditions, its own festivals, so there's quite a bit of diversity, though most of the music is based around drumming. They are Roman Catholic, but the influence of African belief systems is still present in their rituals, dances and music. This is a legacy of slave culture, when the black slaves outwardly adopted the religion imposed on them by the Spanish colonists but continued to observe their own traditions. It's no accident that the most important Afro-Venezuelan festival to this day is La Fiesta de San Juan: on 24th June every year the colonists took a day of rest and the slaves were relieved from their labour and left unsupervised.

Foremost in the struggle to preserve this culture has been the efforts of the communities themselves to promote awareness and to educate young people. In some places old festivals and celebrations have been revived. Herman Villaneuva, director of Los Tambores de San Millán, was also involved in reviving the San Juan Festival in San Millán. He well remembers the days when

Afro-Venezuelan culture was reviled. Since the '70s, however, he believes that: "music has helped their community regain their dignity and autonomy. It is through music that Sanmillaneros transmit and interpret their history. Music helps them control and promote their historical awareness." [6]

Hugo Chavez's arrival on the political scene in the 1990s was electrifying. Here was a leader of mixed race, proud to have indigenous people among his ancestors, who committed himself when campaigning for president to champion indigenous rights and then made good on this promise by giving indigenous leaders positions in government and codifying indigenous rights in the new 1999 constitution. There is no question that all this has raised awareness, given many people from ethnic minorities a sense of empowerment and opened doors for them. With all this activity as you might expect there have been plenty of debates about the pace and direction of change. But the achievements seem solid enough:

> *"Initiatives include... building 400 new community centres around the country with community radio stations, computer rooms, courses such as learning to play the Cuatro, how to record local culture and setting up community museums (In 2007, the Misión Cultura gave courses to 35,000 Venezuelans). One participant said: 'We aim to recover popular tradition, art and music that is characteristic of our country... to recover our heritage, local history, not history told by a group that imposes a version that never was.' [7]*

In addition, Venezuela's flagship musical programme, El Sistema, has provided astonishing numbers of children with training in classical music.

Afro-Venezuelan music has also received support. But one must bear in mind that many black people self-identify as Venezuelan rather than Afro-Venezuelan or some other special group, and the kind of cultures represented in the albums listed above have little or no relevance to them. So something rather interesting has been happening – the emergence of artists of diverse backgrounds who are introducing African elements into their music.

It's hard to speak in generalities here because for each artist the experience has been different. Here are the multiracial band Bituaya:

> "Chávez and Chavismo have been an inspiration... It has enabled us to experiment, to undertake processes and projects, whether they're musical, artistic or social. It has been our framework and our space. It has given us free reign to experiment, to fail, to try again, to fail again, to find the right ways of doing things. But above all, it was as if we untied the ropes that bound us." [8]

And here's Raúl Monsalve of Monsalve y Los Forajidos:

> "I started to study the music of a region in Venezuela whose community has very strong links with Africa. Its an Afro-Venezuelan community. I got really involved in the music and became friends with lots of community members. I started to mix and make connections between afrobeat, funk and our Venezuelan music. For me there was a really clear link, they have the same roots and it was easy to do. I used to invite people from the villages and we mixed with electronic instruments and drums. They started to dance and it was so fluid. It was a really big moment for me because I had an idea in mind, and now I was seeing it work. Now I work with that as my inspiration. I wanted to mix these genres and I really love to see that all Afro-American music goes well with Afro-Venezuelan music." [9]

Raúl is a prime example of a musician who's benefited from the thriving musical culture that's existed in the country the last couple of decades. He studied at the Lino Gallardo music school and at Caracas Jazz Workshop before graduating from the School of Arts at Venezuela's Universidad Central. If that wasn't enough, he later went to London to study ethnomusicology. He now teaches music in Paris.

Los Forajidos means 'outlaws', and the term is fitting. **LA CARCAJÁ** is renegade music, a heady mixture of Afro-Venezuelan drumming, Afrobeat, free jazz and funk. It's a fabulous track; there's so many things going on in it. Apparently it's a collaboration with Afro-Venezuelan musicians from Curiepe, which immediately rang bells for me: some of the tracks on the previously mentioned album Tierra del Cacao are credited to Villagers of Curiepe.

NOTES

1. http://www.radiomundial.com.ve/article/la-filarm%C3%B3nica-nacional-rinde-tributo-juan-vicente-torrealba-en-el-teresa-carre%C3%B1o

2. http://elsonerodebarrio.com/wp/entrevista-johnny-sedes/

3. https://progressivepupil.wordpress.com/2013/09/10/chavez-salsa-and-afrovenezolanos

4. http://www.descarga.com/cgi-bin/db/archives/Interview48, retrieved May, 2016

5. http://www.herencialatina.com/Geardo_Rosales_Eric/Gerardo_Gonzalez_Marzo2011.htm

6. Daniel Nunez – Music, Identity, and Afrovenezuelan Culture: The Dynamics of a Contemporary Tradition in the Central Coastal Region (graduate thesis, 2004), http://scholar.colorado.edu/cgi/viewcontent.cgi?article=1003&context=muco_gradetds

7. http://latinolife.co.uk/node/217

8. http://www.huffingtonpost.com/dan-kovalik/music-revolution-an-inter_b_7010878.html

9. http://soundsandcolours.com/articles/venezuela/interview-raul-monsalve-from-monsalve-y-los-forajidos-on-afro-venezuela-29103

ACKNOWLEDGEMENTS

This book was inspired by a love of world music, and while writing it there has rarely been a week gone by in which I've not found new inspiration. Some of the music I've listened to and the stories that I've read will stay with me all of my life. So to all the artists featured here, a very heartfelt thank you: you're an amazing group of people.

Particular thanks are due to the many who've given me their time – your wisdom, your support and the faith that you've shown in this project are greatly appreciated. I've tried to include you all in the lists below: if I've left anyone out I do apologise; please consider yourself thanked as well.

Those who gave me interviews (with special love to those who aren't native English speakers and those who helped with translations): Aaron Bebe Sukura, Alhousseini Anivolla, Andrea Konstankiewicz, Andrew Alamango, Andrey Vinogradov, Andy Patterson, April Verch, Attila Buzás, Boima Tucker, Conor Lamb, Damily, Daryana Antipova, Etsuko Takezawa, gamin, Gusztáv Balogh, Hanna Flock, Kimi Djabate, King Ayisoba, Kristi Stassinopoulou, Lakha Khan, Lisa Lestander, Louise Mulcahy, Marcus Gora, Mari Kalkun, Mariam Handani, Mariem Hassan, Marita Kruijswijk, Mark Humphrey, Msafiri Zawose, Nuru Kane,

Pål Hægland, Pete Doolan, Petra Käppi, Raymond Ammann, Saeid Shanbehzadeh, Sergei Starostin, Sibongiseni Shabalala, Sona Jobarteh, Steven Sogo, Temesgen, Terry Miller, Teta, Thomas Mapfumo, Wendy Cao Romero, Xavier Fethal, Yuval Ron.

Those who gave specific permission to publish music on my website: (record labels) Akcent, Amarrass Records, Asasi Records, Aztec Musique, Cobiana Records, Contrejour, Crammed, Cumbancha, Drag City, EMI/Virgin, Felmay, Fidjomusic, Filfla Records, Fire Museum Records, FM Records, FolkClub Ethnosuoni, Frequency Glide Enterprises, Fusion Embassy, iASO, Japan Overseas, JARO Medien, KKV, Lee Thorp Entertainment, Nubenegra, Ocora, Par les chemins productions, Rattle, Riverboat Records, Routes Nomades, Sahel Sounds, tanz raum, Yantra Productions, Zamzama; (other projects and organisations) The Amalgamation Project, Awesome Tapes from Africa, Bushman Music Initiative, Cambodian Living Arts, Maison Jephte (Togo), Raw Music International; (bands and artists) Annie Lou, Buttya, Di Naye Kapelye, Hudaki Village Band , Hüsch!, Marewrew, Pham Thi Hue, Sinan Celik, Suzanna Owiyo, Veja, Yuval Ron.

I'm very grateful to everyone who contributed to the crowdfunding campaign for this book; in particular, Kevin Donnellon, Harvey Duckers, David James, Richard Shield, Etsuko Takezawa, Catherine Wall and Sandra Wall.

This work has been brought to press without an agent or a publisher – yes, it can be done: it's a little bit scary, but there is support out there. So thank you to the people at Matador for their faith in the project, and for the many services that they were able to provide; to Forshaw Media for the crowdfunding video; and to my brilliant designer Makak Studios.

Finally, thank you to my parents Sandra and Terry for never stopping believing in me.